Handy Harbor Guide

Handy Harbor Guide

The Bays and Waterways of the Great Lakes

by Bruce Jenvey
and the Staff of *Great Lakes Cruiser*

Momentum Books, Ltd.
Troy, Michigan

Cover photograph by Bruce Preston
Illustrations by Ken Miller

Momentum Books, Ltd.
6964 Crooks Road, Suite 1
Troy, Michigan 48098

ISBN: 1-879094-58-4

This book is dedicated to the memory of Jon Kaplan. Jon's first cruising experience was a simple overnight trip in a sixteen-foot Sandpiper. Provisions were primarily a pair of peanut butter sandwiches and some apples. He went from the northern reaches of Lake St. Clair all the way to the Ambassador Bridge on the Detroit River. He then stayed over at the Detroit Police docks as there were no transient facilities yet in the area. On the next day he came home, fighting wild winds and rough seas.

Jon would later admit that this was not much of a trip, but it was his first and he was darned proud of it. It was followed by many more, both farther and longer. The boat grew as did his cruising range. Over time, he gained confidence and skill. Before his cruising days were over, there wasn't anyplace he wouldn't go and he was ready anytime. He embodied the phrase we have so often invoked in our magazine, "Just pack up and go!" That was Jon Kaplan.

While he had put many miles under the hull, he never became overconfident in his abilities, he never forgot the basics, and he never forgot that others would try to follow his stories. In fact he would often belittle his own capabilities. Just before we lost Jon in a tragic automobile accident he submitted what was to be his last cruising story to me for publication in the magazine. We had been talking about that very first cruise of his and comparing it to how far he'd traveled since. He said, "Bruce, if I can do this, anyone can!"

It is with that spirit that I dedicate this book to Jon, and with the same words, give it to you.

Contents

Lake Superior

Lake Huron

Preface

I hope you find this to be a unique and especially helpful book. What it is, is a summary of every cruising and destination story ever published by *Great Lakes Cruiser* magazine (for more detailed information refer to back issues of the magazine at http://www.concentiric.net/~Glcruise). We present it to you in an easy-to-use, one-harbor-per-page format, listing the most important information you'll need. We've included the latitudes and longitudes of relevant navigational aids, transient dockage and favorite restaurants. For those of you who prefer to travel by "land yacht" we have even included the local inns and bed & breakfasts with their phone numbers. If you're new to our culture, "land yacht cruising" is where you throw the same luggage you used last summer into the trunk of that land yacht thing you keep parked next to the house and travel that way. At considerable savings of time and gas, you can visit even more harbors than you can by boat. And better yet, you can do it year 'round, too!

For every harbor, you will also find a descriptive section where we have done our best to condense several pages of magazine story into several paragraphs here. It tells you the most important things to do and sights to see in that harbor including museums, lighthouses, and of course shopping districts. Condensing this information proved to be the hardest part of bringing you this book. As those of you familiar with the magazine know, we have always prided ourselves on giving you more detail than you can find anywhere else. It is our hope that these insights will help you plan your trip without a mountain of material beside you, that it will help you choose a last minute or impromptu port on your cruise or land yacht excursion, or maybe it will entice you enough to do what we have always encouraged you to do: "Just pack up and go!"

For flavor we have also included a number of human interest stories from around the lakes. These are unique and colorful pieces of history we have uncovered in our travels that are little known outside of their local communities. They are stories of determination, glory, perseverance, humor, generosity and even tremendous luck that make life in these Great Lakes what it is today. I hope you enjoy them as much as I have.

Finally, while my name may be on the cover as author, what is within these pages represents the hard work, research and exploration of a very select number of people I am pleased to call my friends. You'll read the work of our senior editor Ken Miller who spends several weeks each summer in the northern reaches of the lakes. Dennis Boese and his wife Dyan continue to explore both new and familiar harbors in the western end of the region. Don Stockton goes anywhere we have ever asked him to, and then he goes farther. Sandra and Bob Swanson have explored as many harbors as they have ways of getting there—from trailer to canal, and even by tug boat! Bruce Preston has perhaps more years experience than all of us combined in his own detailed exploration of the lakes. He'll take you where no one else ever has. I also need to thank Marv Slocum, Andy Redies, Chuck and Sue Glisch, Kirk Merley, Terry Searfoss (*The Two Burner Gourmet*), Cynthia Johnson, John Kenneth Bruce, Marlon Samuel Pike, Barbara Wilson, Jack Edwards and of course Jon Kaplan. Without their contributions the magazine wouldn't be what it is, and without the magazine there would be no book.

Navigator's Note

Throughout this book positions may be referenced by latitude and longitude or navigational bearing. These references are given for your convenience to help you locate a position on your chart. They are not intended to replace nor be used instead of your own plotting or navigational computations. We encourage you to chart your own course and follow your own headings because mathematical and typographical errors can occur. Remember, any time you venture more than an arm's reach from shore you are out of your natural element and do so at your own risk.

ken miller

Lake Michigan

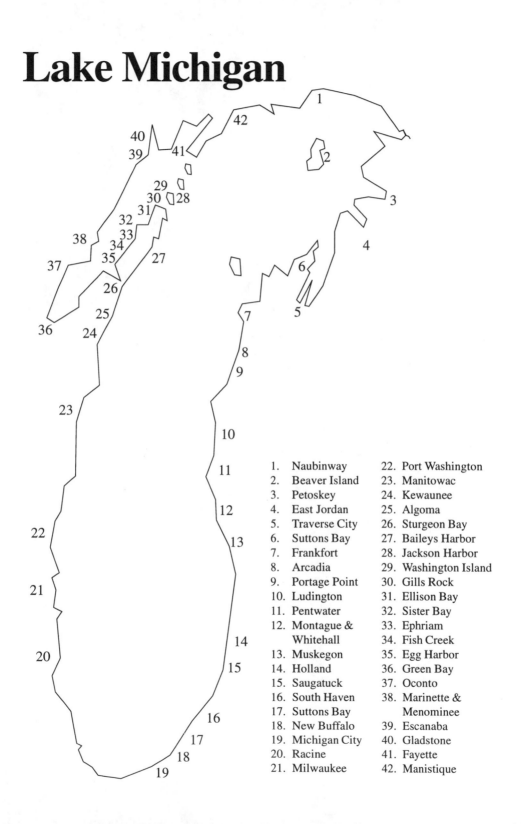

1. Naubinway
2. Beaver Island
3. Petoskey
4. East Jordan
5. Traverse City
6. Suttons Bay
7. Frankfort
8. Arcadia
9. Portage Point
10. Ludington
11. Pentwater
12. Montague & Whitehall
13. Muskegon
14. Holland
15. Saugatuck
16. South Haven
17. Suttons Bay
18. New Buffalo
19. Michigan City
20. Racine
21. Milwaukee
22. Port Washington
23. Manitowac
24. Kewaunee
25. Algoma
26. Sturgeon Bay
27. Baileys Harbor
28. Jackson Harbor
29. Washington Island
30. Gills Rock
31. Ellison Bay
32. Sister Bay
33. Ephriam
34. Fish Creek
35. Egg Harbor
36. Green Bay
37. Oconto
38. Marinette & Menominee
39. Escanaba
40. Gladstone
41. Fayette
42. Manistique

Harbor Algoma, Wisconsin
Location Algoma Pier Light: L44°36.4'N, Lo87°25.8'W
Dockage Algoma Marina, Pier 42 Marina, Captain K's Landing

Places to Stay Contact: Algoma Area Chamber of Commerce 1-800-489-4888

Places to Eat Captain's Table, Penguin City Restaurant,
Hudson's Bar & Grill, Pier 42 Marina Bar & Restuarant,
The Chocolate Chicken Confectionery & Espresso Bar

Algoma is located at the base of Wisconsin's Door Peninsula on the Lake Michigan shore. It's just twelve miles south of the entrance to the Sturgeon Bay Ship Canal and because of it's proximity to the entrance of this area's prime cruising grounds, it is often passed by.

However, Algoma has a lot for the cruiser to see. The harbor is guarded by a most historic lighthouse dating back to the mid 1890s. Before that, the oversized steeple of the St. Agnes-by-the-Lake church provided the same service.

In the marina, a boardwalk leads you along the shore to the city's award-winning visitor's center where you can find all sorts of things to do and explore. At the top of your list, put the Von Stiehl Winery just one block from the harbor. This is Wisconsin's oldest winery and is on the National Registry of Historic Places. They started brewing beer here in 1867 and eventually developed a taste for wine. Tours are available as is free wine tasting in the European-style salon.

While here, also visit Dettman's Shanty. This is a small park-like museum that tells the history of this community's commercial fishing industry through pictures and retired fishing equipment.

Algoma is a Native American word meaning "park of flowers." I'm certain you'll find it has lived up to its name.

Harbor Arcadia, Michigan
Location Red & White Buoy ½ mile offshore: L44°29.1'N, Lo86°15.5'W
Dockage Veteran's Memorial Municipal Marina, Arcadia Marine

Places to Stay The Eber Haus 616-889-3738,
The Pleasant Valley Resort Motel 616-889-4194,
Sunset Valley Resort Motel 616-889-5987

Places to Eat The Big Apple Bar, Arcadian Cafe

Arcadia, Michigan, is a very quiet harbor on the state's western shore. Like many harbors in this area, it's really an inland lake that eventually carved itself a channel to Lake Michigan. During lumbering days this harbor was a very busy commercial port. It continued its prosperity into furniture manufacturing, but as the century came to a close, so did many of the businesses in Arcadia. It became a forgotten town.

But today we value towns on a different scale. The very seclusion that spelled the end to the town's commercial viability has made it an undiscovered tourist haven. Here you will find a very sleepy village with a quiet but recently remodeled marina. There are only a handful of streets here but they are tree-lined and very picturesque. Old homes from the lumbering days have been lovingly restored to their original grandeur, and the Trinity Lutheran Church towers over the village as it has since 1888. There's a small grocery store in town and that's about it. There are a few other businesses a good stroll away up on the highway, but for the most part the village is a quiet, antique, residential community.

Two things not to miss while here: The Arcadia Area Historical Society operates a wonderful museum. They are in the process of restoring a Victorian mini-mansion that once belonged to one of the lumber barons, to serve as their museum. Right now they are housed in an old storefront next to the grocery store.

The next thing not to miss—the sunset. Sunsets over Lake Michigan are spectacular. The local Lions Club has built The Sunset Station in Veteran's Park not far from the marina. From high up on these sand dunes you have an unobstructed view of these natural fireworks. The rest of the community will join you here for this most important event.

Harbor Baileys Harbor, Wisconsin
Location Baileys Harbor Directional Light: L45°04.2'N, Lo87°07.1'W
Dockage Baileys Harbor Yacht Club & Resort, Silver Gull Marina

Places to Stay Baileys Harbor Yacht Club & Resort 920-839-2336,
The Blacksmith Inn 920-839-9222,
The Log Home at The Scofield House North 920-743-7727

Places to Eat Harborside Grill, Voights Sandpiper Restaurant,
Coyote Roadhouse, Weisgerber's Cornerstone Pub &
Restaurant, The Florian II Restaurant

Baileys Harbor is located on the Lake Michigan side of Wisconsin's Door Peninsula. This is a small village with an interesting past. The harbor was discovered by a Captain Bailey, the skipper of a steamer carrying passengers and lumber along the coast. A very frightening storm caused him to take refuge in an uncharted cove along the shore. When the storm cleared he realized the abundance of fine quality stone and timber around him. He took samples back to his employer who commissioned the building of a dock—and so began a village. Like so many other harbors named for their founders, the apostrophe denoting possession, as in Bailey's Harbor, was eventually lost by some map maker leaving Bailey's, Sackett's and Kelley's, among many others, in the plural rather than the singular possessive.

The town is much more interesting than the grammar lesson. Once settlement began, people from all over ethnically-diverse Wisconsin settled here, especially those of Scandinavian descent. You will find all kinds of shops, churches and historical buildings that reflect this ancestry. Of special note is the Boynton Chapel, a replica of an ancient Norwegian Stavkirke. This structure is adorned with magnificent wooden carvings of both Christian and pagan significance.

One more place not to miss is the Ridges Sanctuary. This is an area of preserved coastline serving as a haven for wildlife and wildlife watchers. You will also find the historic Baileys Harbor range lights here. These two lighthouses date back to 1869 and formed a navigational range (now dark) for the heavy steamer traffic that once used the harbor. The lights and the two-hole privy are all on the National Registry of Historic Places.

Harbor Beaver Island, Michigan
Location St. James Light: L45°44.3'N, Lo85°30.3'W
Dockage Beaver Island Municipal Yacht Dock 616-448-2252,
Beaver Island Marine 616-448-2300

Places to Stay Contact: Beaver Island Chamber 616-448-2505

Places to Eat Bailey's, The Shamrock Restaurant & Bar, The Wild Rose Cafe,
The Stoney Acres Grill, The Circle M Supper Club

Beaver Island is one of the most fascinating destinations you can visit. This is due in part to its notorious reputation. Besides two wonderful lighthouses, several tightly focused museums and a seemingly unlimited choice of trails and backroads, Beaver Island has lots of history.

Prior to the Civil War this was once the home of a cult-like splinter group of Mormons. Their leader, James Jesse Strang, ruled the group with an iron fist. There was great competition at the time for fishing rights and cordwood contracts with the steamers in northern Lake Michigan. There is evidence that Strang gave orders for Mormon fishing crews to capture and confiscate the catches and equipment of non-Mormon fishermen from nearby St. Helena Island. This escalated to rumors that Mormon lighthouse keepers in the area would douse their beacons as gentile ships entered the dangerous waters around the island. Allegedly, the ships were wrecked, looted and the survivors killed. Conflicts with the federal government eventually led Strang to declare Beaver Island an independent nation and himself king.

It all came to an end when two disgruntled followers shot King Strang in the back of the head on the main street of St. James Harbor and then immediately sought refuge on the battleship *Michigan*—which just happen to be right there with her gangplank down.

The captain refused to surrender the assassins to the Mormon constable but took them to Mackinac Island, the center of Strang's opposition. Local society members took turns treating the assassins to dinner, and their trial lasted less than an hour—charges were dismissed for lack of evidence.

The morning after the assassination a flotilla of gentile ships arrived in the harbor and escorted each and every Mormon off the island.

Harbor East Jordan, Michigan
Location Southern Breakwater Light for Round Lake Entry: L45°19'12"N,
Lo85°15'53"W
Dockage Irish Boat Shop, The Municipal Harbor, Swan Valley Marina,
East Jordan Tourist Park

Places to Stay Contact: East Jordan Chamber of Commerce (616-536-7351)

Places to Eat The Round Table Restaurant, Lumber Jack's Saloon,
Chick-a Dee's, Nancy's Restaurant, Sam's On The South Arm,
B.C.'s Pizza, Main Street Pizza

 East Jordan is a quiet community with a long history. Technically it's not on a Great Lake (Michigan) but a ways inland via a navigable channel and the natural harbor of Round Lake.

It has a very nice business district with modern shops in old storefronts along the main drag. You can find all the basics plus antiques, pet supplies and dried flowers and gifts. Like I said, it's a quiet town with a nice business district.

But this is also a town that has preserved its past very well. Right across from the marina is a large steam locomotive under a protective roof. This is Engine No. 6 and its presence and restoration is a memorial to the East Jordan & Southern Railroad. It was this transportation company that really built this northwest Michigan town as a lumber capital. The restoration was completed by the East Jordan Portside Art and Historical Society. If you're impressed with their efforts here, wait until you see the work they have done at nearby Elm Point. This was the site of the farms of the first two families to settle here. The Society has restored and preserved the buildings on this 11-acre site using some as a museum and others as a haven for the arts including sculpture, ballet and music appreciation. This is a sure, "Don't miss!"

Also see the famed East Jordan Iron Works. You have undoubtedly seen their products covering manholes all over the Great Lakes!

One other attraction is really a place to stay. The Easterly B&B on Easterly Street was originally built in 1906 for Walter French, a well-known lumber merchant. The home is decorated in high-Victorian style and filled with many antiques. The master bedroom is in the turret of the home and features a hand-carved walnut bed and curved-glass windows.

Harbor Egg Harbor, Wisconsin
Location Harbor's center, approximate: L45°02′85″N,Lo 87°17′00″W
Dockage Municipal Dock, Alpine Resort

Places to Stay Alpine Resort 920-868-3000, Ashbrooke Suites 920-868-3113,
Landmark Resort 920-868-3205, Egg Harbor Lodge 920-868-3115

Places to Eat Sgt. Pepperoni's Pizza, Old Stage Station Tavern & Grill,
The Village Cafe, The Dough Exchange Bakery,
The Horshoe Bay Pub, 19th Hole Pub & Grill, Casey's Inn,
The Trip Restaurant

Egg Harbor is a snug little port in Wisconsin's famed Door County. This particular harbor faces the Green Bay side of the peninsula rather than the Lake Michigan side.

This is rustic Door County at it's best. The village is filled with quaint shops to explore and each is uniquely landscaped with colorful flowers and ferns. There are also a number of wonderfully preserved historic buildings in town too. The Cupola House is perhaps the most photographed structure in town, and St. John the Baptist Catholic Church is undoubtedly the most beautiful.

There's a park, Harbor View Park, high above the water that can take you all day to climb to if you're in less than average shape. There are meticulously maintained gardens up there as well as a pretty impressive view too. On Thursday nights in the summer time you can also enjoy musicians, magicians and storytellers plying their craft here.

There are two stories as to how the village came by this unusual name. One cites the many bright, smooth egg-shaped stones to be found along the shore in this area. The other is probably more true. It involves a fleet of fur trading ships in the early 1800s and a race for the best spot in the anchorage. When the finish was near, one crew began to "shell" the other crew with eggs. The other crew responded. The battle carried on and off into the evening until by the next morning the shore was littered with egg shells. After that day the crews began to refer to this anchorage along their regular route as "Egg Harbor." And like a good omelet, the name stuck.

Harbor Ellison Bay, Wisconsin
Location Center of town, very approximate: L45°15.3′N, Lo87°04.4′W
Dockage Ellison Bay Town Dock, Cedar Grove Resort Marina

Places to Stay Cedar Grove Resort 920-854-2006,
Grandview Motel 920-854-5150, Hillside Inn 920-854-2928,
Norrland Resort 920-854-4873, The Griffin Inn 920-854-4306,
The Hotel Disgarden 920-854-9888

Places to Eat Voight's Super Club, The Hillside Inn Restaurant, The Viking
Restaurant

 Ellison Bay is yet another of those picturesque villages that make Wisconsin's Door County the wonderfully popular cruising grounds it is. However, this is one of the peninsula's smallest communities with a permanent population of only 125. Because of its size it is also one of the area's least commercialized harbors. There isn't even a navigational aid here to reference. Out of frustration, Dennis Boese picked the latitude and longitude of the shoreline in the middle of the village for his reference!

What will you find here? A couple of quaint rental cottages, a handful of sleepy bed & breakfasts, and a general store that will cover all your general needs. This is a quiet community that has distanced itself as far as possible from the rush of the outside world. Leave your cell phone at home and don't ask to use the fax machine at the front desk. They don't have one. But if you adapt to their lifestyle for just a weekend, you may just discover why they keep it this way.

In all honesty there are a small number of other shops to explore, all located in older restored homes. There's pottery and stoneware to see and handicrafts to compare. There's also the ever famous Door County Fish Boil to enjoy. The fish boil is an art, and a meal, usually shared in the community on Friday evenings. You'll find fish boils all over eastern Wisconsin as it is an ethnic favorite brought here by the Scandinavian cultures. But somehow, the ones here seem to be the best.

Harbor Ephriam, Wisconsin
Location Horseshoe Island Light: L45°10.8'N, Lo87°12.8'W
Dockage Ephraim Yacht Harbor, Ephraim Municipal Dock,
The Firehouse Docks, Anderson Dock

Places to Stay The Ephraim Inn 920-854-4515, Edgewater Resort 920-854-2734,
Eagle Harbor Inn & Cottages 920-854-2121,
Evergreen Beach Waterfront Resort 920-854-2831

Places to Eat The Neighborhood Cafe, The Edgewater Dining Room, The
Second Story At Ephraim Shores, Paulson's Old Orchard Inn

Ephriam, Wisconsin, is a small settlement on the Green Bay side of the Door Peninsula. *GLC*'s Dennis Boese described this harbor as "simple, elegant and reminiscent of coastal New England." Judging by the photos he brought back, who's to argue?

There are several picturesque inns anchored into the bluffs above the harbor. Nearby, many older homes have been converted into shops and eateries. While there are two very historic churches in town, perhaps the most interesting structure is Anderson Dock.

This barn-like structure on the pier in the harbor was a warehouse for fish and lumber, and the loading dock for the schooners. It simply was the economic cornerstone of the community. But trucks and trains eventually spelled the end of the steamers and schooners, and Anderson dock eventually became the property of the city.

In the early 1960s it was converted into an art gallery and has served to further the station of the local artists ever since. It's an unusual tradition, but for as many years as this has been an art gallery, visiting sailors have spray-painted the names of their vessels on the building's exterior. This not only makes it personal, it makes it hard to miss!

Harbor Escanaba, Michigan
Location Off-Shore Sand Point Light: L45°44.8'N, Lo87°02.3'W
Dockage The Escanaba Municipal Marina

Places to Stay The House of Ludington 906-786-6300,
Best Western Pioneer Inn 906-786-0602, Days Inn 906-789-1200

Places to Eat The House of Ludington, Hereford & Hops Restaurant and
Brewpub, The Swedish Pantry, The Schooner, Crispigna's,
Tory's Restaurant, Ferdinand's Mexican Restaurant & Cantina,
The Stonehouse Restaurant and Car Port Lounge

 Escanaba is one of the U.P.'s oldest communities and also one of its fastest growing destinations. Just up Ludington Street from the marina is the downtown sector with a growing number of trendy eateries and boutiques. The famed House of Ludington, one of the grandest luxury hotels in the north, is once again open, providing shelter to travelers and fine meals to the public in the newly defined casual dining room. Both the famous and notorious have stayed here, from entertainers like Fred Astaire and Johnny Cash to gangland's highest kingpin, Al Capone.

When in Escanaba you must visit the facilities of the Delta County Historical Society at the foot of Ludington across from the marina. Yes, they have a fine museum with all aspects of U.P. life being preserved. It should be on your "Don't miss" list. But right next door is the perfectly restored Sand Point Lighthouse. This is a wonderful old beacon with the Fresnel lens still in operation. You will also learn about Mary Terry, one of the first women lighthouse keepers in the Great Lakes who died in a suspicious fire in the lighthouse in1886.

Also notice, the lighthouse is unique in the fact that it is built backwards! The light tower should face the lake not the street. The way these things were done, the government would send the blueprints for a new lighthouse to a local contractor to construct but the plans never mentioned orientation to the water. The people of Escanaba built theirs like a church, facing the street!

11

Lake Michigan

Harbor Fayette, Michigan
Location Red Bell Buoy at Entrance: L45°43.2'N, Lo86°40.2'W
Dockage Michigan State Park Dock

Places to Stay State Park campground (Bring your own tent!)

Places to Eat On your boat

Fayette State Park is a genuine ghost town. Located in northern Lake Michigan near the end of the Garden Peninsula, Fayette offers well-maintained transient docks and a campground. But that's about the extent of the facilities here. There is no water or electricity at the dock. A tanker wagon is hauled in daily filled with fresh drinking water. Bring your own jug. There are no showers in the marina but there are restrooms within walking distance.

Then what is this place? It's an absolutely perfect, natural snail-shell harbor surrounded by high limestone cliffs. The scenery is beautiful and the hiking trails fantastic. But it's what it used to be that draws the crowds. In the 1870s and 1880s this was one of the busiest industrial sites in the region. Iron ore was smelted here using the old charcoal-fired system. At the time, iron ore was being hauled from the mines of the U.P., but shipping all the slag that is a part of the ore was less profitable. Fayette was founded as a company town complete with a company store and company housing for those who worked the furnaces. Raw iron ore was hauled here by rail, smelted down in this relatively inefficient process, poured into pig iron bars and shipped out to the industrial cities in the southern lakes. The docks where pleasure boats tie up today is where the ore boats docked over a hundred years ago.

When coke-fired smelting was perfected, the bottom dropped out of the Fayette economy and the town was abandoned virtually overnight. Eventually the land reverted back to the State of Michigan and someone decided to make it into a state park. Wonderful idea! Restoration of the buildings is ongoing, but visiting here gives you a unique insight into the lives of those "who owed their souls to the company store."

Harbor Fish Creek, Wisconsin
Location Harbor Entrance: L45°08.0'N, Lo87°14.8'W
Dockage Alibi Dock Marina, The Fish Creek Municipal Dock

Places to Stay Harbor Guest House 920-868-2284, Thorp House Inn & Cottages 920-868-2444, The Whistling Swan 920-868-3442, The White Gull Inn 920-868-3517

Places to Eat C&C Supper Club, The White Gull Inn, Summertime Restaurant, Bayside Tavern

Fish Creek is perhaps Door County's busiest port. Even before 1900, as the lumber and commercial fishing industry began to fade as the economic cornerstone, Fish Creek became a natural destination for tourists.

Everyone with a spare room or an small cottage on the property began renting to tourists. One local resident completely made-over his entire home into a full-service hotel. Steamers would bring city folks right to the docks on package excursions that would include passage and a week's room and board. It was a busy place even then. And it still is today.

But despite all its tourist traffic, modern Fish Creek has not forgotten what has made it so appealing for all these years: You can still find quaint solitude in a most elegant setting. Nothing reflects this more than the famous White Gull Inn. Do you come here for the world renowned food, or the wonderful accommodations with the view of the water? There are those who would argue that point!

Downtown is filled with historic storefronts now presenting eateries and gift shops. The flavor is resort-like; the architecture, strictly pre-1900 boom town. The appeal is universal.

Lake Michigan

Harbor Frankfort, Michigan
Location Frankfort Lighthouse: L44°37.9'N, Lo86°15.2'W
Dockage The Frankfort City Marina, The Jacobson Marina, The East Shore Marina, The Betsie Marina, The Dudley Penfold Municipal Marina

Places to Stay The Hotel Frankfort 616-352-4303, The Morningside B&B 616-352-4008, Haugen's Haven B&B 616-352-7850, The Pierside Lodgings 616-352-4778

Places to Eat The Wharfside Restaurant, Main Sail Restaurant, The Car Frary

Frankfort, Michigan, has always existed under a cloud of misconception. First of all it was not settled by a band of German immigrants naming the place after the city in their homeland. Instead, the first permanent settlers were two men of English descent named Frank Martin and Joe Robar who arrived in 1855. During that first winter Frank Martin stayed in an abandoned cabin on the lakefront along the northern shore of the channel into Lake Betsie. The snow and sand piled up so high in the high winds, the cabin was nearly buried. Together the two built a log wall between the lake and the cabin to serve as a wind break and snow fence. From the lake it looked much like a fort that they jokingly referred to it as "Frank's Fort."

By 1859 "Frank's Fort on the Lake" was actually put on an area plot map, but when the map was sent to Lansing for registration, some well-meaning cartographer corrected the "obvious spelling error" to "Frankfort," and proceeded to put it on every other map and registration book. The rest is history.

At one time Frankfort was the hub of the car ferry business on Lake Michigan. Large lake boats carrying rail cars and automobiles would come and go from this busy harbor. But the rail business faded with the modern highways and the truck.

Today you'll find a quaint village of little shops, historic homes and a proud history. You'll find one of the most photographed lighthouses on the Lakes guarding the harbor entrance. You'll also find a community that shows up at that beach each summer evening to watch spectacular sunsets because this is an important thing to do. You will not find a German festival nor passage to the far shore.

14

Harbor   Gills Rock, Wisconsin
Location   Approximate harbor location: L45°17.2'N, Lo87°01.4'W
Dockage   The Dockside at Gills Rock, The Shoreline Resort,
Weborg's Dock

Places to Stay   Dockside at Gills Rock 920-854-9400, The Harbor House Inn
920-854-5196, The Maplegrove Motel 920-854-2587,
The Shoreline Resort 920-854-2606,
Teskie's Cottages 920-854-4063

Places to Eat   The Shoreline Resort, Charlie's Smokehouse

Gills Rock is located at the farthest end of Wisconsin's Door Peninsula. It's from here that the ferries leave for Washington Island carrying day-trippers and vacationers alike. Many people have passed right through town on the way to the ferry docks without realizing all they've been missing. This place may be small, but stop and look around.

The town was founded back in 1860 by Elias Gill who came here to quarry marble. As the marble was depleted, the agricultural and commercial fishing industries took off. While not a hub of nineteenth century commerce, there was enough business here to keep the village from becoming a ghost town. Today there are only 75 permanent residents, but the small fishing fleet is still in operation and of course the ferries are a constant source of commerce. But this is rustic countryside, as far as you can go on the Door Peninsula without a boat. Wouldn't that be a great place for a resort?

Actually you have a choice. The premier place to stay is the Shoreline Resort, which is the center of activity here. There's a very good restaurant on the grounds but you can also charter your fun here. They have everything from fishing to diving charters to book right on the premises. You can charter a sunset cruise or even a shipwreck coastline cruise.

There are a very few shops in town so you don't have to rush through just to see everything. The Top O' the Thumb Gift Shop has a wide collection of nautical gifts and Norwegian sweaters. "Don't miss!"

Harbor Gladstone, Michigan
Location Gladstone Yacht Harbor Entrance: L45°50.3'N, Lo87°01.0'W
Dockage Gladstone Municipal Yacht Harbor, Gladstone Yacht Club

Places to Stay Cartwright's Birdseye Inn B&B 906-428-3997, Kipling House
B&B, Gladstone Motel 906-428-1100, Bombay Motel 906-786-
6241, Bayshore Resort 906-428-9687, Lindberg's Cove Resort
906-428-4313

Places to Eat Four-J's, Dew Drop Inn, Delona Restaurant, Reflections, The
Saloon, Main Street Pizza, Log Cabin Supper Club

Gladstone, Michigan, is located on the Garden Peninsula of Michigan's U.P. This is a typical small northern town that will meet your basic needs as a cruising boater or roaming land yachter. But there are actually several points of interest.

All around the marina and the yacht club is Van Cleve Park. This is a beautifully landscaped naturalist's getaway that includes an arched footbridge over the pond where hundreds of water lilies bloom. There is also a lovely gazebo. But the small ones may tire of this tranquillity stuff. Good thing the Gladstone city fathers also included a fully equipped playground including a fantasy castle called Kid's Kingdom and its associated Tot Lot. This is a place of great family fun.

Also of local interest, this is the home of the Hoegh Pet Casket Company. Yes, a company that for over 30 years has built coffins and urns in which to intern the remains of a beloved pet.

Along more mainstream interests, this is also the home of the Marble Arms Company. True outdoorsmen will recognize the name of Webster Lansing Marble who invented and manufactured the ideal hunting knife, the pocket safety axe and the waterproof match safe among many other such products. By the 1920s Mr. Lansing could honestly claim that "there is no place so remote that our products are not there." There is a museum of Marble products open to the public at Back Stage Antiques right here in Gladstone.

16

Harbor	Green Bay, Wisconsin
Location	Channel Buoy "17" L44°35.2'N, Lo87°57.8'W
Dockage	The Green Bay Yachting Club, City Centre Marina, Shipyard Marina, Zeller's Marine Mart, Lakeside Marina
Places to Stay	Holiday Inn 920-437-5900, Best Western Downtowner 920-437-8771, Days Inn Downtown 920-435-4484
Places to Eat	The Beaumont Grille, Eve's Supper Club, Los Banditos, Prime Quarter Steak House, The River's Bend Supper Club, The Rock Garden Supper Club, The Sportsman Supper Club

Green Bay, Wisconsin, is a well-known port in the southern end of the bay by the same name. The heart of the waterfront is located where the Fox River meets the bay. Now while this may be a well-known destination, it's well-known because of its long standing association with America's dairy industry. It's well-known as a shipping port with a major railroad hub that brought the products to the docks. Today there is even one of the best railroad museums in the country, right on the banks of the river.

They are also famous for a group of green and gold gladiators of the gridiron better known as the Green Bay Packers. Actually there are two groups of these Packers that are famous: The ones that have recently dominated the NFL, and those who did so over thirty years ago under the direction of a man no one had ever heard of before—Vince Lombardi.

Green Bay is a well-known place, but it's not well-known as a destination for pleasure boaters. But an increase in modern docking facilities and a beautiful river walk along the banks of the Fox are changing people's minds. Also the Bay Beach Wildlife Sanctuary is earning its reputation as one of the nicest places in the Lakes to catch Mother Nature in the act of being herself.

How about some other things you didn't know were here? How about the Oneida Nation Museum in nearby Oneida. This is a wonderful display of Native American culture, specifically that of "the people of the standing stone." Don't miss the pageantry of their annual Pow Wow.

Also visit Heritage Hill, a forty-acre living museum re-creating several eras of early American Life.

Harbor Holland, Michigan
Location North Breakwater Light: L43°46.4'N, Lo86°12.9'W
Dockage Anchorage Marina, Eldean Shipyard, Lakewood Marina, Macatawa Bay Yacht Club, Parkside Marina, The Yacht Basin

Places to Stay The Centenial Inn (616-355-0998), The Holland Area Lodging Hot Line (1-800-757-7552)

Places to Eat The Ottawa Inn, The Piper, 84 East Pasta Etc., Queen's Inn Restaurant

Holland is a well-known port on the western Michigan shoreline. Like many other harbors along this coast, this is really a sizable inland lake that has "broken through" to connect itself with Lake Michigan. This lake is Lake Macatawa.

At the entrance to Lake Macatawa you will find one of the most photographed lighthouses on the Lakes: Big Red. This bright red schoolhouse-style lighthouse and keeper's quarters have guarded the entrance to this harbor for well over a century. Access to this site is limited at best and parking close to the lighthouse is virtually non-existent. Your best chance to get a close-up view is by boat. But if you just want to sit and enjoy its presence, find a spot of warm beach sand on Ottawa Beach on the opposite side of the channel from the lighthouse and bask in the sun as you enjoy this unique beacon.

Holland was settled by people from Holland, the Netherlands. Surprised? Here you will find many people hard at work preserving the old culture here in the new world. You really can buy wooden shoes at many places around this wonderfully maintained downtown district. You can also see an operating windmill on Windmill Island which is not only the historical focus of the community, but the garden spot of western Michigan as well. You see, every year Holland hosts the Tulip Festival and the entire town, especially Windmill Island, becomes the brightest colored spectacle this side of the Rose Parade. No exaggeration. This is one of the great events in the Great Lakes you have to see to believe.

Contact the Holland area Chamber of Commerce at 800-506-1299 for the annual schedule.

Harbor Jackson Harbor, Wisconsin
Location Harbor Entrance: L45°24.2′N, Lo86°51.0′W
Dockage Jackson Harbor Town Dock

Places to Stay Jackson Harbor Inn (920-847-2454)

Places to Eat Harbor Lunch Wagon

Jackson Harbor is a small bay on the northeast side of Wisconsin's Washington Island. Most tourists ride the ferry from Gill's Rock on Door County's mainland into Detroit Harbor on the Island's south shore and start their exploration from there. The only way into Jackson Harbor from the outside is by private boat.

Right there in the harbor is the Jackson Harbor Maritime Museum, open most days during the summer months. Here you will find a nice selection of artifacts and models representing the ferry boats and commercial fishing fleet that have been the island's way of life for generations. Right next door is the only bed & breakfast on this end of the island; the Jackson Harbor Inn is literally just steps from the docks.

There are still a number of commercial fishing tugs that call this harbor home, and one other commercial vessel is also a regular sight here. The *Karfi* is a small pedestrian ferry that takes day trippers and picnickers to picturesque Rock Island and back several times each day. Rock Island is a state park located just across the harbor. Along the shore between the high limestone cliffs is the massive Great Hall and Boathouse built by Icelandic-born millionaire Chester Thordason. Modeled after the great Viking halls of Scandinavia, it's now a museum and open to the public. There is also a very historic water tower on the island as well as wonderful beaches and isolated hiking trails.

Jackson Harbor will be used in coming seasons as a base of operations by the U.S. Naval Sea Cadets and the training and research vessel the *Pride of Michigan* as they go in search of the *Griffin,* the first sailing vessel on the Great Lakes which disappeared without a trace in 1679.

Harbor Kewaunee, Wisconsin
Location Pierhead Light: L44°27.4'N, Lo87°29.6'W
Dockage The Kewaunee Marina, The Kewaunee Inner Harbor

Places to Stay Marina Karsten Hotel 920-388-3003, The Chelsea Rose B&B
920-388-2012, Duvall House B&B 920-388-0501,
The Gables B&B 920-388-0220

Places to Eat Larry & Mona's Restaurant, The Bucket, The Lighthouse Cafe,
The Karsten Hotel, Gib's on the Lake

Kewaunee is set into the carved bluffs of the Wisconsin shore of Lake Michigan halfway between Manitowoc and Sturgeon Bay. The name comes from an ancient Potowatomi Indian word meaning "We are lost." Allegedly, when Natives in their canoes were caught out on the lake in sudden fogs, they would shout this word towards the shore. Someone shouting back from the natural funnel of the high bluffs would guide them in.

Bring your walking shoes here, you'll need them. The Kewaunee information center is on the north side of town just across the highway bridge. There, besides all kinds of helpful information on local attractions and the fishing charter business, you can get a map for the Marquette Historical District Walking Tour. This historical district now has 44 homes on the National Registry of Historic Places, and in a brief period of time you can get a detailed look at Kewaunee's past.

While there was settlement here of some kind 600 years ago, the area blossomed under the Gold Rush of the early 1800s. But like most rushes, they soon went bust and Kewaunee resorted to more traditional business ventures. At one time, a great dock stretched out into Lake Michigan where steamers and schooners would bring cargo and passengers alike. Even into the early twentieth century this town was a hub for the booming car-ferry business across the lakes. But as highways became more prevalent and car ferries disappeared, so did the commerce in Kewaunee. There are a number of museums in the area that tell this story, including the old Jail House and Sheriff's House that date back to 1876. It has a very complete display of Kewaunee history. What is here today is a well preserved relic of the past—just waiting to tell you its story on a quiet afternoon.

Harbor Ludington, Michigan
Location Ludington Lighthouse: L43°57.2'N, Lo86°28.2'W
Dockage Ludington Municipal Marina 616-643-9611, Thompson Marina 616-843-7000, The Star Port Marina 616-845-7692

Places to Stay Contact: Ludington Area Chamber Of Commerce 1-800-542-4600

Places to Eat P.M. Steamers, Pot West, The Ludington Townehouse, The House of Flavors, El Jardin

Ludington is located along the sandy shores of Lake Michigan between Big and Little Sable Points just a short distance north of Muskegon. While the local lighthouse greets you at the end of the entrance breakwall, this is nothing compared to other lighthouses close at hand.

Big Sable Point is one of the most prominent beacons on the Lakes, and while not open to the public, it makes a wonderful photo opportunity. It is equaled only by the Little Sable Point Lighthouse to the south. While there is no keeper's quarters at Little Sable, it is the tallest light tower on Lake Michigan. Personally, this is also the very first lighthouse I ever saw as a child, and I have revisited it at every opportunity since.

If lighthouses aren't for you, try the beach. The western coast of the state of Michigan is famous for its sugar-sand beaches, and Ludington has one of the biggest and the best. It's just a short walk into town to enjoy the old storefronts and antique shops.

If you really want to get back to nature, the Ludington State Park is close at hand and offers hiking and walking trails to fit any skill level. They also have one of the most unusual trails you will ever find. One trail is comprised of wooden walkways that extend out over the Pere Marquette River gorge and takes you literally into the tree tops to witness nature normally well above your view.

One more attraction to look for is the *Badger*. This *Badger* is a ship—a car ferry that provides regular service between Ludington and Manitowoc, Wisconsin. Go as a passenger, take your car along or not. Either way it's great fun and a rare experience!

Lake Michigan

Harbor Manistique, Michigan
Location The Manistique Light: L45°56.7'N, Lo86°14.0'W
Dockage Manistique Marina, Nest Egg Marina

Places to Stay Contact: Manistique Chamber of Commerce 906-341-5010

Places to Eat Strasler's Sunny Shores Restaurant, Jax Restaurant, Marley's Bar & Grill, Harbor Bar & Inn, Teddy's Pub, Main Street Pizza, Nifty 50s Ice Cream Shoppe

Manistique, Michigan, is located on the northern shores of Lake Michigan just east of the barrier islands that form Green Bay. Settled in 1860, the town was in its heyday around the turn of the century. From here ships came and went bearing lumber, paper, iron ore, limestone, leather and even wood alcohol. Car ferries to other Great Lakes ports were regular visitors too. Even the community's first experience with tourism came here by steamer bringing vacationers and summer residents alike.

But eventually the highways began to carry the bulk of the commerce and the industries the harbor supported began to fade from view. Today the harbor is still guarded by their very historic lighthouse at the end of the east breakwall but the vessels in the harbor are strictly pleasure craft.

In town you'll find a very typical northern Michigan village with a mixture of storefronts and services. However, there are a few very interesting sights to see. Be sure to visit Pioneer Park. It's a short walk through town and over the river. Here you will find the Manistique Historical Museum which is a collection of historic buildings in the park. There's a log cabin from 1895 and the locally famous Putnam House. Also in the park is the Water Tower. While not a water tower today, it was quite a facility in its day. This brick encased structure is anything but utilitarian and is on the National Registry of Historic Places.

One more site of interest, right next to the water tower, is the Siphon Bridge. This bridge was featured in Ripley's Believe It or Not many years ago. This bridge is supported by the water that is atmospherically forced underneath it. The roadway is about four feet below water level. It's an interesting piece of engineering!

Harbor Manitowoc, Wisconsin
Location Breakwater Light: L44°05.6'N, Lo87°38.6'N
Dockage Manitowoc Marina 920-682-5117

Places to Stay The Inn on Maritime Bay 920-682-7000, Arbor Manor B&B 920-684-6095, The Holmestead B&B 920-682-0434, The Jarvis House 920-682-2103, Mahloch's Cozy B&B 920-775-4404

Places to Eat The Inn on Maritime Bay, The Galley, Colonial Inn, Desert Jack's Bar & Grill, Luigi's Pizza Palace

Manitowoc is located on the Wisconsin shore of Lake Michigan halfway between Sheboygan and Kewaunee. This is also the "other port" visited by the *Badger*, the only Lake Michigan car ferry now in service, running between here and Ludington, Michigan.

Right in the harbor is one of the most fascinating museums you'll find along this shore. The Wisconsin Maritime Museum is a two-story structure housing over 100 years of Great Lakes shipping history. You'll see engines, wheels, old hard-hat diving suits and much more. And just outside, they keep their boat. Actually, it's the *U.S.S. Cobia*, a WWII submarine that was built right here in Manitowoc. The sub is completely restored, open for tours and is considered a national historic landmark. The museum is open year 'round.

In town you have to visit Schuette's Department Store. This is supposedly the oldest department store in the United States dating back to 1849. The current building is on the original site and was opened in 1901. Inside, this is a modern department store but it is actually an historic landmark. By the way, the Schuette family still owns and operates the store today.

Another "Don't miss" attraction is the Zunker Antique Car Museum. You'll find perfectly restored antique cars here ranging from a Studebaker pickup truck to a 1920 Essex. It's great fun and quite a car collection.

One more thing to do while you're here is sport fishing. A good number of charter captains are available right here in the harbor, ready to take you out to where the big ones swim. Record-breaking fish are caught in these waters with surprising regularity.

Harbor   Marinette, Wisconsin and Menominee, Michigan
Location   Menominee Pierhead Light: L45°05.8'N, Lo87°05.1'W
Dockage   Harbortown Marine, Nest Egg Marine, Mystery Ship Marina,
Menominee Memorial Marina

Places to Stay   Contact: Marinette Chamber 1-800-236-6681,
Menominee Chamber 906-863-2679

Places to Eat   The Avenue Grill & Bar, Best Western Riverfront Inn, Memories
Restaurant, The Brothers Three, Kathy's on the Square, The
Ogden Club, Regent Chinese & Thai Restaurant

Marinette and Menominee are the proverbial twin sons of different mothers. These twin cities have grown up together on opposite banks of the Menominee River in their respective states of Wisconsin and Michigan. Located along the relatively sheltered waters of western Green Bay, these towns have endured a lot together.

Originally this shore and river outlet was a major settlement for Native American tribes, and a trading post for the voyageurs. Marinette is named for Queen Marinette, the daughter of a Menominee chief, while the word Menominee itself means "wild rice," which once grew in abundance along the river banks.

The area grew rapidly during the early days of the lumber boom but both towns suffered greatly during the great forest fire of 1871. That was the same fire that took Chicago and was known as "the day Michigan burned." Unlike many other communities touched by that tragedy, these towns came back and helped mill the lumber that rebuilt Chicago. By the turn of the century this was a world-wide lumber port and enjoyed many years of shipping more board feet than any harbor in the world.

While they fared better than many other communities during the Great Depression, the economy diversified and the towns held stable. Today their populations (about 11,000 each) are at the same levels as they have been for the past century.

There are several excellent museums that preserve the local history including the Stephenson Island Historical Museum, The Marinette County Logging Museum and the Menominee County Historical Museum among others. You can also shop in Marinette's historic Dunlop Square where restoration is a prime example of civic pride.

Harbor Michigan City, Indiana
Location East Breakwater Light: L41°43.7'N, Lo86°55.7'W
Dockage Washington Park Municipal Marina, Goerg Marina,
B&E Marina, The Newport Marina,
Phil Sprague Municipal Marina

Places to Stay The Holiday Inn 219-879-0311, The Hutchinson Mansion Inn
219-879-1700, The Brickstone 219-878-1819,
Creekwood Inn 219-872-8357

Places to Eat The Pullman Cafe & Club Car Lounge, The 5th Street Deli

 Michigan City is a very old city along Indiana's only Great Lakes shore. It's a short drive from Chicago but what a major change in attitude!

First, Michigan City has tremendous sand dunes along the area shores, most protected in the Indiana Dunes National Lakeshore. Here you can spend time with a ranger learning about dune life. This is one of the few ecologically active dune systems in the region. It supports a multitude of unique plant and animal life.

You can also visit Washington Park, the center of the city's waterfront. Here you will find the local yacht club, the Municipal Marina, the Washington Park Zoo, fine picnic facilities and the 1858 Lighthouse, now a museum. The lighthouse at the end of the breakwall is the current navigational aid and also a museum.

The 1858 lighthouse was the first permanent lighthouse on this shore and is significant historically for two reasons. First, of all the lights ever built this is the only one to survive. The rest met their end in the never-ending battle with Lake Michigan—they were destroyed by Nature. Second, the first and longest-serving keeper in this beacon was a woman, Harriet Colfax, who tended this light from its dedication until she retired in 1904 at the age of 80. Many men tried to get her fired from this position so they could have the job for themselves. But nothing worked. The lighthouse inspector could not fire someone who turned in perfect inspection reports and was exemplary in her service.

As an historical note, Michigan City has several mansions and museums demonstrating the wealth and power the railroad brought to town. Also visiting this town were a good number of Chicago gangsters who found themselves comfortably across the Illinois state line. Among regu-

The Lights of Michigan City
by Bruce Jenvey

Of all the lighthouses in the Great Lakes, you would probably be surprised to know that one of the most interesting is in Indiana of all places. But it is! Tended lights as aids to navigation go back to the mid 1830s in Michigan City. Mostly, they were nothing more than lanterns hanging on a stick. But all that changed in 1858 when the federal government finally constructed a permanent light and keeper's quarters in what is now Washington Park.

I have found conflicting historical accounts of the light's first three years but truly, the differences are insignificant. The account I favor states that Harriet Colfax was the first keeper to take up residence in the new structure. (The other account states that a man, a Mr. Clarkston, was first, with Miss Colfax taking charge in 1861). But whatever the official date, Harriet Colfax became the most famous of all the keepers, maintaining the light until her retirement in 1904 at the age of 80.

In those days the lighthouse service was under control of the U.S. Treasury Department, and most appointments were political favors. Miss Colfax's was no exception. Her cousin Schuyler Colfax was a powerful Washington politician and later served as vice president under Ulysses S. Grant. Miss Colfax was a small woman and had just recently moved to Michigan City from New York state with her brother. Together they opened and ran the town's first newspaper. She was unmarried, and there were rumors that her move to the Great Lakes was in the wake of a failed love affair.

Whatever her past, this stranger, this newcomer, this "small of frame" woman created quite a local uproar when she won the appointment. I will assume the vast majority of that concern came from big strapping men who had grown up in the area and had hoped for the appointment themselves. In short order Harriet Colfax had not only silenced her critics but won the admiration of the locals, the schooner captains and the inspectors from the Lighthouse Service. And how did she do that? Through her exemplary performance.

Harriet Colfax was also an educated woman, having been a voice and piano teacher back in New York. She kept the light station clean, orderly and run strictly by the book. Her logs were among the most organized (and legible) in the entire service, and are today a treasure in the National

Archives. They are recognized historically as being one of the best sources to recreate daily life in the Lighthouse Service.

But neat records and clean lighthouses won't win you fame and fortune in Michigan City. The proof of her competency was in her physical ability and complete determination to tend the lights. Harriet had formed a close friendship with Miss Ann Hartwell, another New York native. Ann joined her when Harriet took up residence in the 1858 lighthouse, and the two women spent the rest of their lives together. Between them they lit the lamps and kept them going during the worst Lake Michigan could offer.

In 1871 a second light was added at Michigan City. The light in the keeper's quarters was now complemented by a beacon at the end of the east pier (not the same one that's there today). It would be the duty of the keeper to tend both lights regardless of weather. Harriet Colfax wrote many entries in her log describing the great human effort and risk to life it took to crawl out on the catwalk in hurricane-force winds and waves, a 1,500 foot gauntlet of driving winds, surf and sleet. At times the catwalk was further compromised by storm damage or collision with schooners fighting their way into the harbor.

Eventually the Pierhead beacon was moved from the east pier to the end of the west breakwater in hopes of protecting both the light and the new catwalk from the ravages of the lake, Also at this time, an assistant lightkeeper was added to the staff. Since tending the west pier light would mean crossing Trail Creek, the assistant (a man) was housed on that side of the Creek and tended that light alone while Harriet tended the main light in the 1858 lighthouse. For whatever reason, the man seemed to have more trouble keeping this new "protected" light going than Harriet had had tending it out on the east pier. However, in his defense the catwalk was completely washed away by storms on several occasions during his tenure, and once the entire pier, catwalk and light washed up on the near-by beach. It would have been hard to keep it lit under such circumstances.

Eventually, in 1904, the harbor lights at Michigan City were renovated. The west pier light was discontinued and the beacon from the 1858 lighthouse, Fresnel lens and all, was moved to a new structure (complete with a new catwalk) back at the end of the east pier. It's the same one that's there today, with it's fifth-order Fresnel lens still in use. From then on the 1858 lighthouse served as a keeper's residence only.

It was upon the dedication of these new facilities that Harriet chose to retire. After all, the keeper would now be expected to once again brave Lake Michigan storms along the catwalk in order to tend the light, and she had just turned 80!

So Harriet Colfax retired as one of the most dedicated and colorful lightkeepers in the Great Lakes. Her last log entry is dated October 12, 1904, and mentions the arrival of her replacement. Within five months she had passed away.

If you would like to read more about Harriet Colfax and the history of the lights at Michigan City, let me refer you to two books you may find at your local bookstore. *A Traveler's Guide to 116 Western Great Lakes Lighthouses* by The Penrose Family. Bill Penrose and his clan do an excellent job of documenting, locating and photographing both lighthouses and recount a fair amount of the history as well. *Women Who Kept the Lights* by Mary Louise Clifford and J. Candice Clifford covers Harriet Colfax's years at Michigan City in great detail. They even include excerpts from the station's logbook and a reproduction of a letter in Miss Colfax's own hand to the lighthouse inspector in Chicago. It's wonderful reading and by the way, the rest of the book is top drawer as well.

ken miller

Harbor Milwaukee, Wisconsin
Location Milwaukee Light: L43°01'6N, Lo87°52.9'W
Dockage The McKinley Marina, The Milwaukee Yacht Club, Duchows' Harbor Marina, Skipper Bud's Vertical Indoor Marina, Milwaukee Marine, Schlitz Park Marina

Places to Stay Milwaukee B&B Reservation Service 414-277-8066

Places to Eat John Ernst cafe, The Bavarian Wurst Haus, many more

 Milwaukee is an urban destination like none other on the lakes. I was completely surprised by what I found here and I hope I can express that same excitement to you in this limited space.

There is much to do here, but I'll skip the usual museum reviews to make room the truly unique. You can take harbor tours of the historic waterfront aboard the former Mackinac Island Ferry *Iroquois,* or explore the downtown river system aboard the much more modern *Edelweiss*, a glass-roofed observation boat.

If you love old buildings, Milwaukee has preserved their best in the historic Third Ward District and of course, along Old World Third Street. Here you will see fantastic displays of old Flemish Renaissance architecture with its ornate appointments and grand presentation. Even the old water tower on the north side of town looks like it came from some olden fairy tale.

Along the north harbor there are residential streets high on the bluff that are lined with homes in this same style. They are the true mini-mansions of the Great Lakes and are perfectly preserved. Remember, they are private residences but make wonderful photo opportunities from the street.

One more mansion you have to visit was built by Captain Frederick Pabst. It is the ultimate in this form of architecture and is open to the public as a museum. The mansion, completed in 1893, has 37 rooms, 12 baths and 14 fireplaces. If you can't imagine where this kind of money could come from to build a mansion of this magnificence, why don't you pop a cold one and think about it. It'll come to you.

Harbor Montague & Whitehall, Michigan
Location North Breakwater to White Lake: L43°22.5'N, Lo86°25.7'W
Dockage The White Lake Municipal Marina, Wesley Marina, White Bay Marina, Whitehall Landing, The Crosswinds, Ellenwood Landing Dockominiums

Places to Stay The Music Box Inn 616-894-6683,
The Timekeeper's Inn 616-894-5169

Places to Eat Beach's White Sands Restaurant & Lounge, The Crosswinds, The Lakeside Inn, The Old Channel Inn

The twin cities of Montague and Whitehall, Michigan, are located on the shores of White Lake just off Lake Michigan north of Muskegon. As you enter the channel you will encounter the White River Light Station which dates back to 1875 and the heyday of the area lumber boom. Today the light station is a museum, open to the public.

There are several unique things to see and do in these communities. First on your list, note the large wind vane on the breakwall along the Montague shore. This is the largest wind vane in the world, and the schooner depicted at the top is the locally famous *Ella Ellenwood* which was lost near Milwaukee in 1901.

There's a lot of history to discover in these towns and believe it or not, you won't find it all in dark stuffy museums. Yes, for the traditionalist, there is the usual museum experience to enjoy at the Montague City Museum where most of the displays center around the logging industry and it's contributions to the community

You can enjoy more local history over a chocolate soda. At Lipka's Drug Store in Montague you can browse through the 130-year-old business and enjoy the sweet treats that come out of their antique soda fountain. If you really like historic drug stores, be sure to visit Pitkin Drugs on the Whitehall side, but it's been there for only about 120 years.

One more history lesson can be enjoyed at the Montague Dog 'N' Suds. This is the last of the restaurant chain's outlets in Michigan and they have preserved their 60s decor faithfully. On any summer Thursday evening, the classic street rods cruise the old drive-in and stop off for burgers and admiration.

The Long Way Home
The Story of the *Ella Ellenwood*
by Bruce Jenvey

Back before the turn of the century, the 157-ton lumber schooner *Ella Ellenwood* was the pride of White Lake. On regular runs she would take the harvest of the local sawmills to the furthest corners of Lake Michigan. And then she would triumphantly return home with the bounty and profits her cargo had won. So many times the local citizenry had looked up from their labors to see this proud vessel churning her way through a morning mist as she set out for the open waters of Lake Michigan. And just as often they had seen her rigging full of sailors searching the shore for loved ones upon her return home.

But in late September 1901 the *Ella Ellenwood* set her sails and left the safety of White Lake for the very last time. On the night of October 1 she found herself struggling for her very life in a strong northeastern gale that had blown down from Canada. The crew desperately tried to hold their own in the face of the building storm but eventually found themselves hard aground on the shoals near Fox Point just eight miles northeast of the protected harbor in Milwaukee. They tried to free her, then to save her, but when it was clear that all was lost, they were forced to abandon her in the yawl. They watched helplessly as the fury of the storm pounded the pride of White Lake to pieces before the larger sections of her hull were swept from the reef and slid into the depths below.

It was a long winter that year in the twin cities of Montague and Whitehall. Perhaps it wasn't the weather as much as the loss of the *Ella Ellenwood* that made the season so cold, but whatever the reason, most of the local citizenry mourned the loss of their lumber schooner as if she were a member of their own family. Thinking of her never coming home again was difficult indeed.

In the spring of 1902 when the ice cleared the channel that connects Lake Michigan with White Lake, they made a startling discovery. A board pulled from the channel proved to be a section of the nameplate from the lost schooner's bow. She had made her way home the best she could.

Today the craft is immortalized in brass atop the giant wind vane that stands in the harbor. And depending on who you talk to, you might also get a glimpse of her through an early morning fog, churning her way through the waves towards the open waters of Lake Michigan.

Harbor Muskegon, Michigan
Location South Breakwater Light: L43°13.5′N, Lo86°20.8′W
Dockage Hartshorn Municipal Marina, Great Lakes Marina,
Lakeshore Yacht Harbor

Places to Stay Blue Country B&B 616-744-2555,
Port City Victorian Inn 616-759-0205,
Hackley Holt House 616-725-7303, plus various chain hotels

Places to Eat Many eateries in the downtown area

ouskegon is a small city on the west coast of the Michigan Peninsula. This is another of those inland lake harbors with a channel out to the big water of Lake Michigan. However, Muskegon Lake is much bigger than most of these kinds of harbors. This led to Muskegon's development in the latter 1800s as a lumber town. Indeed, she was known as queen of the lumber trade.

Muskegon came into her own just after the great Chicago fire in 1871. A large percentage of the lumber required to rebuild the great city was taken from surrounding forests and stored on huge rafts on Muskegon Lake until dragged to the mills. Lumber to rebuild Chicago is what built Muskegon.

With that history in mind, you can visit several historical sites and museums in the city. The Muskegon County Museum retells all of the area's history from the early settlements to the lumber boom. The Hackley and Hume Historical Site is actually two perfectly restored Victorian homes that were once owned by two of the area's most successful lumber barons, Charles Hackley and Thomas Hume.

If more modern history fascinates you, be sure to visit the *S.S. Silversides*. This is a WWII submarine with an impressive service record that has now been restored and put on display. You can take a tour through the entire ship including the forward torpedo rooms and the captain's quarters

If you don't like history, there are always the shops and restaurants along the renovated south shore of the lake to explore. But I'll warn you, they are located in historic buildings.

Harbor Naubinway, Michigan
Location Naubinway Island Light: L46°04.5′N, Lo85°26.5′W
Dockage The Naubinway Marina (on west shore of bay across from town)

Places to Stay Variable

Places to Eat Beaudoin's Cafe, The Ketch, Pizza Pronto, Cove Bar

This is one of the Lakes' quietest, most secluded destinations. Located along the northern shore of Lake Michigan, Naubinway is a small natural harbor that can easily accommodate pleasure boats. But they also have one of the last few active commercial fishing fleets in American waters. It's quite a sight to see these old work boats head out early in the morning, their crews looking for fish as their fathers have done generations before them.

The harbor of Naubinway is a good stroll from the rest of the village, located completely across the bay from town. It's a nice shaded walk along a heavily wooded country road.

In town there are just a handful of houses. What businesses you will find are in a strip along Highway 2, a block or two up from the water. There are places to eat and places to shop here, though it may take you longer to walk to town than to conquer it.

Of special interest is the Fisherman's Memorial on the side street just off the strip. This honors all those who lost their lives in the pursuit of commercial fishing on the lakes, but especially the three Naubinway men who drowned in a tragic collision with a freighter in recent years.

Here is one more piece of trivia: Just outside Naubinway on the highway (in case you came by land yacht) is the locally famous Naubinway Rest Area. This is the only year-round flush-toilet facility of it's kind in the U.P. They are most proud of this and I wouldn't kid about a thing like that.

Lake Michigan

Harbor New Buffalo, Michigan
Location North Breakwater Light: L41°48′06″N, Lo86°45′09″W
Dockage The Municipal Marina, Oselka's Snug Harbor, The New Buffalo Yacht Club, The Moorings

Places to Stay Bauhaus B&B 616-469-6419,
The Harbor Grand 616-469-7700

Places to Eat The Bilgewater Restaurant, Sunset Cantina, Brewster's

New Buffalo is located on Michigan's southeast coast. In fact it's the last harbor of refuge before the Indiana border. It is only in recent years that this harbor has achieved the success as a port of call that the founding father of the town had envisioned. Today there are several modern marina facilities and even more, resort condominium developments. Everything is wonderfully new and perfectly landscaped.

There are also a number of quaint eateries in town, of special note is the Bilgewater Inn. Here you'll find great food, great service and—a lighthouse! Yes, a wonderful artistic lighthouse is attached to the restaurant. While this may not be unique among the Lakes, what is different is the fact that it really is an aid to navigation. The locals said, "Gee, what a great lighthouse—right on the shore and everything!" And they put a light in it and then the Coast Guard put the light on your chart. Here's your chance to eat, drink, and ward off shipping traffic at the same time!

Historically, the town was founded in the aftermath of a ship wreck. Captain Wessel Whittaker and his crew lost the schooner *Postboy* near here in a storm in the early 1800s. They had to walk past this natural harbor of refuge on their way to Michigan City to catch a ship back to civilization. At that time the captain decided to buy the land and develop a town, named for his boyhood home of Buffalo, New York. Try as he might, he never could seem to get permanent residents to set up housekeeping here, but he did manage to get quite a few tourists.

Great resorts and grand hotels were built here but they were eventually claimed by fire. But the resort atmosphere has never faded and even today, as new condos and marinas open their doors to the public, you can sense the same magic in the air that Wessel Whittaker must have known.

Harbor Oconto, Wisconsin
Location Breakwater Entrance Light: L44°53.9'N, Lo87°49.1'W
Dockage Breakwater Park, Harbor Cove Marina, Hi Seas Marina,
Oconto Yacht Club

Places to Stay Oconto Motel 920-834-2000, Ramada Ltd. 920-834-5559

Places to Eat Main Event Sports Bar & Grill, Oconto Golf Club, The Brothers
Three, Wayne's Family Restaurant, Granny's

 Oconto is on the west shore of Green Bay about halfway between the cities of Green Bay and Marinette/Menominee. *GLC*'s Dennis Boese declares this to be the most overlooked harbor on the bay. But with new improvements and a new, deep water marina, it is one of his favorite stopovers on the way up or down the lake.

This is not a "touristy" destination. There are no T-shirt shops to greet you and no "salt water" bar and grills to charm you. In fact you may wonder where the town is. It's about a mile walk inland from the marinas. This is a very typical midwestern town established in the early 1800s. The lumber mills really built this town (there were 14 at one time), leaving behind an historic district of elegant Victorian mini-mansions. You can get a self-guided walking tour map to these homes through the local chamber. Of special note to see in the historic district is the Beyer House Museum, which is really one of these homes serving as spokesman and time traveler for the rest of the community. Also see the Christian Science Church built in 1886. This was the first church of this denomination built in the world. It predates the main church in Boston by five years. Today it appears almost as it did when first opened.

One more sight not to miss is the Copper Culture Mound State Park and Museum. Archeological digs in this area have uncovered traces of a native culture that thrived here some 4,500 years ago. That's before the Egyptians built the Pyramids. The name Copper Culture comes from the fact that these people mined and fashioned tools and jewelry from native copper. It's a fascinating display in a beautiful setting. You can see why they settled here.

Harbor Pentwater, Michigan
Location North Breakwater Light: L43°46′56″N, Lo86°26′35″W
Dockage Municipal Marina, Pentwater Yacht Club, Snug Harbor, Sail Point Marina, Charlie's Marine,

Places to Stay The Pentwater Inn 616-869-5909, The Hexagon House 616-869-4102, The Candlewyck House 616-869-5967, The Abby 616-869-4094, The Nickerson Inn 616-869-6731, The Pineric B&B 616-869-5471, The Channel Lane Inn 616-869-5766,

Places to Eat The Village Cafe, The Village Pub, Gull Landing

Pentwater is located on Michigan's western shoreline, a distance north of Muskegon. The harbor is actually a well-protected inland lake with a direct channel to Lake Michigan. This easy but protected access is what gave the community a leg up in its commercial development.

Pentwater was originally a lumber town. In fact in the center of the village you will find a small park with a very nice display commemorating the contributions the industry made to the town's development. Of special interest is a deadhead (sunken log) recovered from the harbor in recent years still bearing the brand of its owner.

Pentwater is blessed with a great number of B&Bs that were once the lavish homes of the lumber barons. Many of these homes continued in the service of the captains of local industry as the town's economy adjusted after the lumber boom into furniture making and fish canning as sources of revenue.

The downtown strip along Hancock Street is lined with historic storefronts that now house shops and boutiques of about every kind. Of special interest is the Brass Anchor, actually located in an old chandlery, and Gustafson's Gifts—a local institution here for many years. There are many more interesting stores to mention but in all honesty there are so many you could write a book!

Pentwater is also well-known for its fantastic beach. The sand is white, fine and seems to stretch on forever. If you need a place to relax with the sand between your toes, Pentwater may tempt you to stay a lot longer than you need to. But isn't that part of what cruising is all about?

The Valeria Hotel

by Bruce Jenvey

The next time you're in Pentwater, strolling along Hancock, take a few extra moments to stand by what is now called the Village Green. It's a small quiet park with a bandstand where the Civic Band gives concerts during the summer months. But at one time this, between here and 2nd street, was the site of the great Valeria Hotel.

It was 1891 and many of the communities in the Great Lakes had their equivalent of Mackinac Island's Grand Hotel. They were extravagant resort hotels built to attract city dwellers with promises of peace, quiet, and health-giving magic spring water. Of course the community would benefit too, from the jobs the hotel would create and the influx of cash the resort goers would bring.

Someone convinced the Pentwater city fathers that their community could cash in on the resort trade too, and plans were drawn for the Valeria Hotel. Construction was started that very year but the best laid plans...

The project was under-funded and the city could only afford to build one floor at a time. In fact work was stopped on more than one occasion while more money was raised. But who wanted to stay in a partially built hotel? Who wanted to vacation amongst the sawdust and the pounding?

The Valeria was never finished and never opened its doors as a hotel. It never gave shelter to a single guest. It sat empty for some time, earning the nickname "white elephant." Eventually the structure was purchased by a Mr. Gardener who at least put the building to use. At one time or another it housed a cobbler's shop, city council rooms, the local American Legion, a candy store and office space. Rooms upstairs were rented out as apartments. The large room behind the tower was used for basketball games, a roller skating rink, plays and movies.

Then like far too many of her contemporaries, the Valeria fell victim to fire. It was 1927 and the fire was complete and devastating. The remains were torn down and a new movie theater was built almost immediately.

But the sloping green lawn in the center of town still stands vacant in her memory of what was, what is, and what could have been.

Harbor Petoskey, Michigan
Location The Petoskey Light: L45°22'50"N, Lo84°57'40"W
Dockage Petoskey Municipal Marina,

Places to Stay Stafford's Bay View Inn 1-800-456-1917, The Terrace Inn 1-800-530-9898, The Florence B&B 616-348-3322, The Gingerbread House 616-347-3538,

Places to Eat The Park Garden Cafe among many others

Petoskey is located in the northwest corner of Michigan's lower peninsula at the far end of Little Traverse Bay. When you first think of Petoskey, two things come to mind: Petoskey stones, and shopping!

The stones I can explain. The unusual stone is really fossilized coral and plankton scraped from the bottom of ancient seas by glaciers and deposited in greatest numbers in this general area. In 1965 the Petoskey stone became the official stone of the State of Michigan, making this the first fossil ever to receive such an honor.

Shopping is another matter. Many of the trendiest boutiques and collectibles dealers in the nation have a Petoskey address. A trip to this city on the bay without an afternoon in the shopping district would be a travesty. Where should you go? Up the hill from the marina is the Gaslight District with it's wonderfully restored Victorian storefronts and period street lamps. There is nothing in these stores that you absolutely need, and that's the best part. Reload your credit cards, and charge!

Another required stop is the section of town known as the Bayfield Association. Established in 1875 by the Methodist Church, this became a "summer community" to advance the cause of education and religious morality. Over the next several years many gracious Victorian mini-mansions were constructed in this neighborhood. Today, many of them are bed & breakfast establishments, but far more are private residences handed down through the family by the original owners. There are 430 historic homes here. Each and every one is on the National Registry of Historic Places, making this the largest collection of historic homes in the nation.

Lake Michigan

Harbor Port Washington, Wisconsin
Location Port Washington Light: L43°32.1'N, Lo87°51.6'W
Dockage The Municipal Marina

Places to Stay The Harborside Motor Inn 414-284-9461, The Port Washington Inn 414-284-5583, The Grand Inn B&B 414-284-6719, The Inn at Old Twelve Hundred 414-268-1200

Places to Eat Bernie's, The Smith Brother's Fish Shanty, Port Hotel, The Pasta Shop, Beanie's Mexican-American Restaurant, George Wilson's House, Buchel's Colonial House

Port Washington is located along the Lake Michigan shoreline halfway between Milwaukee and Sheboygan. This is one of the most popular destinations along this coast because of its thriving business district. There is a whole collection of shops and boutiques located in historic storefronts to explore.

Almost every corner gives you a new vantage point and an added photo opportunity as you roam through these grand old buildings. Sights not to miss include St. Mary's Church, located high on the hill overlooking the harbor. This Gothic structure is well over one hundred years old and is on the National Registry of Historic Places.

Right next door is the home of the Port Washington Historical Society, which was also the community's first lighthouse, dedicated in 1860. The art deco lighthouse that's at the end of the breakwater in the harbor is the current navigational aid for the harbor and was built in 1935. While more modern, it's unusual design makes it also something to photograph.

One more historic structure to see is the Pebble House, which now serves as the Visitor Information Center. The house was hand-built in 1848 by blacksmith Edward Dodge and his wife using fist-sized pebbles from the beach.

This is also a wonderful winter cruising destination. Every December 5th, the St. Nicholas Parade kicks off the holiday season for this culturally diverse community. A European-style St. Nicholas hands out chocolate coins to the children while his assistant, Black Peter, follows along with the book that records both the good and bad deeds of local children. As the holiday approaches, you can also witness the Living Nativity in the Franklin Street Triangle.

Lake Michigan

Harbor Portage Point, Michigan
Location North Pierhead Light: L44°21.6'N, Lo86°16.1'W
Dockage Portage Point Inn 1-800-878-7248,
Onekama Marine 616-889-4218

Places to Stay Portage Point Inn 1-800-878-7248

Places to Eat Portage Point Inn

Portage Point is one of several harbors in northwest Michigan that is really an inland lake connected to the big water by a river or improved channel. This gives the inland lake excellent protection from the open water while affording the tourist the option of sheltered or open beaches. These harbors are formed by rivers flowing toward the lake and then swelling into lakes of their own as they meet the barrier of the shoreline dunes. Eventually water levels and erosion win, and the river carves a channel to the open lake.

What makes Portage Point (and Portage Lake) so special is its seclusion and its history. If you're looking for a quiet shore with nice anchorages around the shore, this is it. If you want a little excitement (and I do mean little), you can go to nearby Onekama on the far east shore of the lake. This is a small rural Michigan crossroads where little happens and even less rattles the residents. Sometimes this may be just what you're looking for.

The history of the harbor centers around that grand white structure near the channel entry. This is the Portage Point Inn and was built just after the turn of the century. In its day, it was one of the grandest resort hotels along this shore. In those days the most luxurious passenger steamers to ever ply the Great Lakes would stop at the long dock in front of the inn on a regular schedule, bringing tourists for extended vacations. Among these famous ships were none other than both the *North American* and the *South American*. The Portage Point Inn was closed for a number of years but is open again under management determined to renovate the entire resort into the grandeur it once knew.

Harbor Racine, Wisconsin
Location Southern Breakwall Light: L42°44.0'N, Lo87°46.2'W
Dockage Reefpoint Marina, Racine Yacht Club, Gaslight Pointe,
Pugh Marina

Places to Stay Radisson Harbourwalk Inn 414-632-7777,
Mansards on the Lake 414-632-1135,
Lochnaiar on the Lake 414-633-3300

Places to Eat The Chartroom, Dr. Livingstone's, The Yardarm Bar & Grill, The
Main Street Bistro, Madden's on the Main, George's

 Racine Wisconsin is one of Lake Michigan's most underrated destinations. What was once an old industrial waterfront is gone, replaced by a modern marina and a growing business district. The Lakeside Trolley will gladly take you all about town for a pittance, and on weekend evenings they modify their route to accommodate the "Pub & Grub" run. Think of this as a progressive dinner and drinking binge with a designated driver already assigned!

But there's a lot of history in old Racine. The unique architecture of the Shoop Building is something to see. Dr. Shoop was a medical doctor who made his fortune marketing pills and patent medicines in the Victorian era. The County Historical Society has a wonderful museum in a building at the corner of Main and Seventh Streets that itself is a historical landmark. Also, you can go to the police headquarters on Center Street to see more history. There's an old submachine gun on display there that was originally registered to the police in the 1930s but spent some time in the possession of John Dillinger. It seems that at the height of his career, he and his gang robbed the local bank and took the gun from a subdued guard. Years later, when Dillinger was captured in Arizona, he still had the gun, now bearing his autograph. The Racine police have kept it under glass ever since.

Also near town, visit the Wind Point Lighthouse. This is a classic old lightstation still in operation as an aid to navigation and partially open as a museum.

If you like old buildings, Racine is full of them, but one new structure not to miss is the S.C. Johnson World Headquarters in town. It was designed by a local lad named Wright—Frank Lloyd Wright.

Harbor Saugatuck, Michigan
Location South Pierhead Light: L42°39.63′N, Lo86°12.58′W
Dockage Deep Harbor Marina, Saugatuck Yacht Services,
Gleason's Marina, Singapore Yacht Club, Tower Marina,
Naughton's Marina

Places to Stay Park House 1-800-321-4535, Maplewood Hotel 616-857-1771,
4-Seasons Inn 1-800-852-1955

Places to Eat Contact: Saugatuck/Douglas Visitors Bureau 616-857-1701

Saugatuck and its twin city Douglas are located in the southwestern corner of the state on the shores of Lake Michigan. This entire coastal area is known for its natural, fine sugar-sand beaches and high dunes. There are several public beaches to enjoy but the grandest of them all is the Saugatuck Dunes State Park. Nearby you can get high-speed dune rides in a multi-passenger dune buggy.

But Saugatuck is also a place of preserved and active history. Active history? Sure. Just take a ride on the *Star of Saugatuck*, a paddlewheel excursion boat that offers one-and-a-half-hour narrated cruises of the harbor. The boat is a modern replica, similar to those found in the southern reaches of Lake Michigan 150 years ago.

You can also pull yourself through history here. The *Saugatuck Ferry* is a genuine hand-operated chain ferry that will cross you from one city to the other as the original did so very long ago. By the way, if you came to town by boat, as you enter the harbor the chain ferry has the right of way, and remember that you are responsible for your wake!

If you'd like some bigger history, take the chain ferry over to the Douglas side and visit the *S.S. Kewatin*. This is a retired Canadian National Railways steamer and today serves as a museum for all to enjoy.

One more thing, put Saugatuck on your winter cruising destination list. The business district is open year-round, and at Christmas the town takes on the flavor of a Dickens novel complete with horse drawn sleighs.

Harbor Sister Bay, Wisconsin
Location Sister Shoals Buoy: L45°12.0'N, Lo87°10.7'W
Dockage Sister Bay Municipal Marina, Sister Bay Resort & Yacht Club, The Yacht Works, Cal Marine

Places to Stay Contact: Sister Bay Information Center 920-854-2812

Places to Eat Inn At Krostofer's, Sister Bay Cafe, Al Johnson's Swedish Restaurant, Sister Bay Bowl, The Hotel Du Nord, The Door County Ice Cream Factory & Sandwich Shoppe

 Sister Bay, Wisconsin, is one of the most charming harbors in the picturesque Door Peninsula. Settled primarily by Norwegian and Swedish immigrants, much of that heritage is visible in the village today.

Many of the buildings are old storefronts offering everything from antiques and Christmas decorations to pottery, crafts and fine art—all of a Scandinavian nature. There are actually several art galleries in town presenting the works of local artists.

There are some very charming eateries in town too. The most well-known has to be Al Johnson's Swedish Restaurant. In true Scandinavian tradition, many of the buildings in town have sod and thatched roofs. The best way to maintain a live roof like this is with a goat herd. And that's just the way they do it at Johnson's! As you stand in line to get into the restaurant, a small herd of goats grazes on the roof. They know they are safe up there and actually become quite bold. They often come right down to the rain gutters just to check you out and see what you're doing there so near their turf. It's a sight to see and, by the way, the food is very good too.

If it's summertime, you may want to catch a free concert in the park on your way back to the marina. These concerts take place every Wednesday at 3 P.M. It's an odd time as these things go, but well worth the effort to be there.

Harbor South Haven, Michigan
Location South Breakwater Light: L42°40.6'N,Lo 86°12.9'W
Dockage The Municipal Marina (VHF Ch 16). There are two locations on opposite sides of the river.

Places to Stay Contact: South Haven Chamber 616-637-517

Places to Eat Huckleberry's, The Idler Riverboat, The Bayou Beach Club, The Magnolia Grille

South Haven is tucked into the southwest Michigan shoreline where the Black River meets the big water. In town there is a wonderful maritime museum (the Michigan Maritime Museum) and a selection of unique restaurants that will be enjoyed by cruisers of all ages.

The *Idler Riverboat* is perhaps the most unusual eatery on this shore. Actually it's two eateries, the Bayou Beach Club and the Magnolia Grill. But the boat is what's really fascinating. The *Idler* is over 100 years old and was originally a "party barge" on the Mississippi—elegant appointments, no engine. She was towed from port to port from New Orleans north as the summer progressed. She was at the 1904 World's Fair in St. Louis. After that she was sold to the father of Vincent Price, the famous actor, who used her for entertaining for 58 years. Then she was sold to the Nabisco people and eventually to a local family in South Haven who refurbished her for restaurant duty. You'll find her permanently moored on the south bank of the river near the Old Harbor Village.

Huckleberry's is also a fun place with big beef burgers and giant hot dogs you can "whoof down". They will also pack you a box lunch you can take out on the beach or out on the fishing charters.

Yes, I did say fishing charters! There are lots of fish still in Lake Michigan and a number of charter captains determined to help you find some. You can also go for a chartered sailboat ride on Lake Michigan. If you've never tried sailing before and have always wondered what it was like, spend an afternoon with Captain John Shaul aboard the *Wanderlust*. You'll find him in slip 41 at the Black River Yacht Club.

Lake Michigan

Harbor St. Joseph and Benton Harbor, Michigan
Location St. Joseph North Pierhead Light: L42°07.0'N, Lo86°29.7'W
Dockage St. Joseph West Basin Municipal Marina, Pier 33 Marina, Brian's Marine, Harbor Isle Marina, The Riverview 1000 Marina, Eagle Point Harbor

Places to Stay St. Joseph Holiday Inn 616-983-7341, The Boulevard Hotel 616-983-6600, The South Cliff Inn B&B 616-983-4881, The Chestnut House B&B 616-983-7413

Places to Eat Bonnie's Breakfast Nook, The Establishment, Slapstick, T.J.'s

St. Joseph and Benton harbor are located along the sandy shores of southwest Michigan. These two communities have long been harbors of refuge for the tourist trade ever since the first steamer brought the first Chicago passengers here during the Victorian era.

While there is a very interesting business district to explore which includes a hands-on kids museum and an art gallery, most of the activity in St. Joseph centers on relaxation and recreation. Even visitors from long ago realized that the pace of life was slower here and built luxurious cottages from which to enjoy it all. If you stop by St. Joseph today, above the Toy Factory in the heart of the business district, they'll give you a map for a self-guided historic walking tour of the community—but take it at your own pace.

One final word regarding Benton Harbor: If there's an electronics buff in your crew, remember, this was the home of the famed Heath Company who produced all those Heath Kits during the 50s and 60s. Much of the amateur radio equipment they produced is still on the air and the rest is considered collectible.

Harbor Sturgeon Bay, Wisconsin
Location Buoy R-2: L44°46.7′N, Lo87°17.3′W
Dockage Sturgeon Bay Yacht Harbor, Quarterdeck Marina,

Places to Stay Snug Harbor Inn 920-742-2337, Barbican/Victoria House 920-743-4854, Chadwick Inn 920-743-2771, White Lace Inn 920-743-1105, The Scofield House B&B 920-743-7727, 48 West Oak 920-743-4830

Places to Eat The Mill Super Club, Square Rigger Lodge & Galley, Dal Santo's Restaurant, Perry's Cherry Diner

Sturgeon Bay is located at the base of Wisconsin's Door Peninsula on the ship canal that connects Green Bay with Lake Michigan. This is a busy town with a well-developed industrial base. I have to tell you, this place is unique for ship-watching in the Great Lakes, not because there are so many, but because this is where many of them are built.

This has been a ship-building harbor since before World War I. They have built everything here from tugs and patrol boats to heavy naval armament and of course, 1,000-foot-long Great Lakes ore carriers. Ship-building has a deep and rich history in this community, and was the bread and butter of their economy for nearly a century.

You can find out much more about Sturgeon Bay's nautical past by visiting the Maritime Museum at the foot of Florida Street just north of the famed ship yards. Here you will find everything from rare photographs and models to the actual pilothouse from a 1907 laker. Right on the premises there are many other displays featuring boats as long as 26 feet and dating back to 1900.

Sturgeon Bay also has a highly detailed walking tour of its hundred-plus historic structures. You can start the tour just about anywhere along the route, but even in a brief visit you will see the homes of those who really "built" the Great Lakes.

..

Harbor Suttons Bay, Michigan
Location Harbor Entrance: L44°58'32"N, Lo85°38'43W"
Dockage The Municipal Dock

Places to Stay Korner Cottage 616-271-2711, Open Windows B&B 616-271-4300, The Guest House 616-271-3776

Places to Eat Judy's Suttons Bay-Kery, The Roman Wheel, The Hose House Deli, Hattie's, Cafe Bliss

Suttons Bay is a picturesque harbor village near the entrance to Grand Traverse Bay in northern Michigan. The village was founded by Harry C. Sutton in 1854 and the very first business he established was the cutting of cordwood to supply the fuel-starved steamers in this remote section of the Great Lakes.

At first the wood was balanced in canoes and paddled out to waiting ships. Eventually a large dock was built and then the ships came to the wood. As happens, one dock attracts another and before long there were several piers reaching out into the bay with warehouses and shippers conducting business out over the water. Many products were off-loaded to the steamers from here including board lumber and all kinds of agricultural produce.

But as the lumber boom ended and railways began to take over much of the agricultural commerce, the docks fell into disuse and were eventually scrapped. The only relic of this era is the Greilick Pier, better known as the "old coal dock." Fittingly, this historic dock is now home to the replica schooner *Inland Seas*, which serves as a floating classroom to students of all ages studying Great Lakes ecology and the heritage of sail in these waters.

Also in town you will discover a charming business district with shops of all kinds from antiques to crafts and even chocolate. One of the best times to visit is during the annual Jazz Festival, a true summer highlight all around the bay. Bring your bike and bring your spare time—this is a great place to spend it.

Harbor Traverse City, Michigan
Location West End of Harbor Breakwater: L44°45.1'N, Lo83°37.3'W
Dockage Duncal L. Clinch Yacht Harbor

Places to Stay Contact: Traverse City Convention & Visitors Bureau
1-800-TRAVERS

Places to Eat The Cove, Sleder's Family Tavern, Cousin Johnny's, Bower's Harbor Inn, The Bowery

Traverse City, Michigan, is a tremendous tourist mecca in the northwest section of the State. The city itself could fill a book with things to do. There are exclusive shops selling everything from fine jewelry to designer clothes. There are restaurants everywhere. Each and every establishment has something unique to offer the traveler. You can do all this with the help of the Traverse City Convention & Visitors Bureau. Call them. Here, we will take you down more unusual paths.

Right in the heart of the harbor is the Traverse Tall Ship Company. They are exactly what the name signifies. They own and maintain a feet of tall ships—windjammers, large lake schooners—that can be chartered. They have organized evening and dinner cruises as well as week-long escapes to places like the North Channel. While you sign on these ships as passengers, you are more than welcome to lend your hand as crew when the sails are hoisted and the anchor is weighed.

You are also right near Sleeping Bear Dunes National Lakeshore. These are huge, naturally occurring sand dunes that are protected by the National Park System and preserved for your enjoyment. There are paths and walkways including wooden boardwalks that extend out over the bluffs for sweeping views of the lake.

Among one of the chief local attractions is a restaurant out on Old Mission Point called the Bowers Harbor Inn. It's a very fine restaurant with excellent service, but it's also very haunted! The structure was originally built as a private residence for Chicago lumber baron J.W. Stickney and his wife, Genevieve. She hanged herself in the elevator shaft after J.W. died and left his entire estate to his personal secretary, who was also his mistress.

Harbor Washington Island, Wisconsin
Location Detroit Harbor Light: L45°19.9'N, Lo86°55.3'W
Dockage Krueger's Kap Marina, Shipyard Island Marina, Island Outpost Dock

Places to Stay Contact: Washington Island Chamber of Commerce 920-847-2179

Places to Eat The Albatross Drive Inn, Harbor Light Restaurant, The Island Country Cafe, J-B's Island Tap, KK Fiske Restaurant, Sailor's Pub, Ship's Wheel Restaurant, Cellar Restaurant at Karly's

 Washington Island is technically part of Door County, Wisconsin, though it stands several miles off the end of the peninsula. You can catch a ferry from Gill's Rock or bring your own boat to one of two harbors on the island. I will also refer you to the page on Jackson Harbor, on the north end of the island. It was covered in detail by Dennis Boese a year or so after Don Stockton visited Detroit Harbor on the south shore and wrote the story highlighted here.

Detroit Harbor is the "capital" of the island and constitutes the only business district. It's a sleepy line of storefronts spread out along the harbor road, and the road that heads north to Washington Harbor (a third harbor on the island, but with no transient facilities). There's a grocery store with a deli, a couple of bar/restaurants and some places to buy ice cream. You wouldn't do your Christmas shopping here unless you found a way to wrap up a load of quiet countryside.

Did I tell you it's impossible to get lost on the island? The roads are a basic grid pattern and the only realty company on the island uses a map of the island (including roads) as their logo. Once when I was confused while driving on the island I actually stopped, consulted a realty sign in a farmhouse yard and found my way back to the harbor!

This is a restful place with paths to explore and roads to walk. There are a good number of tourists here, but there seems to be enough island to go around. You can tour the island's several museums along the Cherry Train's sight-seeing route, or come back later to enjoy them at your own pace. There's even a farm museum!

Incidentally, it is well accepted that Detroit Harbor is where the *Griffin* last weighed anchor before disappearing with all hands in 1679.

Lake Superior

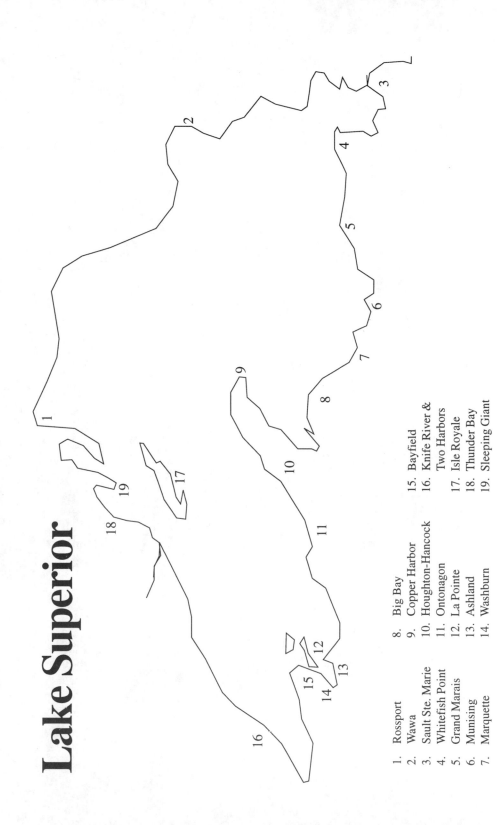

1. Rossport
2. Wawa
3. Sault Ste. Marie
4. Whitefish Point
5. Grand Marais
6. Munising
7. Marquette
8. Big Bay
9. Copper Harbor
10. Houghton-Hancock
11. Ontonagon
12. La Pointe
13. Ashland
14. Washburn
15. Bayfield
16. Knife River &
    Two Harbors
17. Isle Royale
18. Thunder Bay
19. Sleeping Giant

Harbor Ashland, Wisconsin
Location Chequamegon Point Light: L46°43.7'N, Lo90°48.5'W
Dockage Ashland Harbor & Marina

Places to Stay Hotel Chequamegon 715-682-9095, Lake Air Motor Inn 715-682-4551, Town Motel 715-682-5555, Anderson's Motel 715-682-4658, Lake Side Motel 715-682-4575, Crest Motel 715-682-6603, Best Western Holiday House 715-682-5235

Places to Eat Fifield's, Grandma Ludack's, Molly Cooper's (all within the Hotel Chequamegon), The Depot, Taco John's, Paisano's

Ashland is located on Wisconsin's Lake Superior shore on Chequamegon Bay. Originally settled by the French in the earliest days of Great Lakes traffic, Ashland did not find financial success (and its current name) until just after the Civil War.

After nearly 20 years of virtual nonexistence as a one-family settlement, the railroad came to town and linked Ashland's harbor to the shipping traffic hauling iron ore out of the Gogebic Iron Range. Prosperity grew rapidly, producing a thriving business district and Ashland's pride and joy, its centerpiece, the Hotel Chequamegon.

This is one of the last all-wooden resort hotels in the Great Lakes. There were once many, but during their heydays most of them met with fire and are gone. Of the few remaining from this era are the Grand Hotel on Mackinac Island, the House of Ludington in Escanaba, and the Hotel Chequamegon. Inside the hotel today there are shops and eateries to enjoy while taking in the architecture and history all around you.

In the rest of the town you'll find a multitude of old storefronts, houses and churches situated on quiet shady streets. There's also a civic band shell near the hotel that hosts concerts in the park on summer weekends.

The iron ore boats no longer enter this relatively shallow harbor, but the culture and history they left behind is well preserved for your enjoyment.

Harbor Bayfield, Wisconsin
Location South Pierhead Light: L46°48.6'N, Lo90°48.7'W
Dockage Apostle Islands Marina, Port Superior Marina Association

Places to Stay Contact: The Bayfield Area Chamber 1-800-447-4094

Places to Eat Granny's & Gramp's Bakery & Deli, Greunke's Restaurant, Winnie's Hungary Mariner, Maggie's, The Old Rittenhouse Inn

Bayfield, Wisconsin, is located in the western end of Lake Superior and has been referred to as the gateway to the Apostle Islands. GLC's Don Stockton enjoyed this harbor thoroughly and came to the same conclusion.

The Apostle Islands are one of the greatest cruising grounds in the world. They are rustic, beautiful, natural and for the most part uninhabited. Oh yes, there are a few pockets of civilization here and there, but when you're anchored out in the Apostles, chances are you'll have the beach to yourself. To help keep it that way, many of the islands are protected as a park and closed to further development. The headquarters of that park just happens to be here in Bayfield, and any Apostle vacation should start here.

But before you head off for the seclusion, you would miss a lot if you didn't spend some time in beautiful Bayfield. There are small specialty shops in town that offer up everything from custom jewelry to handmade crafts and fine paintings. There are no less than four galleries and fine art shops in the area!

There is a wonderful museum near the docks called the Cooperage Museum. Here you can learn about the finer points of historic barrel making, and about the commercial fishing industry that was once the principal employment in Bayfield.

But the best thing to do in Bayfield is the annual Lake Superior Big Tent Chautauqua. Held every mid-June through Labor Day, several nights a week, this has been called the Carnegie Hall of tent shows. It is based on the original concept of the Chautauqua traveling tent shows of Victorian era New York, but these people have evolved this educational/entertainment medium to a new level. Don't miss it! Call 715-373-5552 for details.

Harbor Big Bay, Michigan
Location West Breakwater Light: L46°49.72′N, Lo87°43.52′W
Dockage Big Bay Marina

Places to Stay The Big Bay Lighthouse Inn 906-345-9957, Thunder Bay Inn 906-345-9376, Big Bay Depot 906-345-9350, Picture Bay Motel 906-345-9820, TenEycks Cabins 906-345-9552

Places to Eat The Thunder Bay Inn, The Lumberjack Tavern

Today, Big Bay is a quiet resort hideaway about sixty miles west of Marquette along the Lake Superior shore. You will truly enjoy the rustic atmosphere and pristine scenery. There is also a classic old lighthouse turned bed and breakfast just outside the village. But the most fun thing to do in Big Bay is to retrace what once happened here, twice!

In the early 1950s, Big Bay was the scene of a most notorious murder case. It seems an army officer walked into the local Lumberjack Tavern and shot the owner to death over his affair with the officer's unfaithful wife. John Voelker was the defense attorney who convinced a jury of his client's innocence on the ground of temporary insanity. This was the landmark case where that defense was used for the very first time. Voelker wrote a book about the trial called *Anatomy of a Murder*. He changed a few of the names of places to protect the innocent and the guilty. The Lumberjack Tavern became the Thunder Bay Inn, which fit the description of the then Big Bay Inn down the street.

In the late 1950s the popular book was made into a movie by film great Otto Preminger, and starred Jimmy Stuart. To make the movie as much like the book as possible, Preminger changed the name on the Big Bay Inn to the Thunder Bay Inn (as it is today), and built a shell of a tavern on the side of the building to act as the attached bar where the murder took place in the book, but not in real life. Many scenes for the film were shot here.

Later, this movie prop of a bar was finished within to look like the sound stage bar used in the movie. Now you can come see the for-real bar where the murder didn't happen!

Harbor Copper Harbor, Michigan
Location Copper Harbor Light: L47°28.5'N, Lo87°51.6'W
Dockage The Municipal Marina

Places to Stay Astor House Motel-Minnetonka Resort 906-289-4449, Bella Vista Motel 906-289-4213, Brockway Inn 906-289-4588, Fanny Hooe Resort & Campgrounds 906-289-4451, Keweenaw Mountain Lodge 906-289-4403

Places to Eat Harbor Haus Restaurant, Keweenaw Mountain Lodge, Mariner North, The Pines Restaurant

Copper Harbor is located at the tip of the Keweenaw Peninsula in Michigan's U.P. There isn't any more Michigan beyond here, just water. But it's a pleasant resort town to explore.

First, they have one of the more historic lighthouses on the Lakes. Currently closed to the public and inaccessible by road, you can get a great photo of the beacon by taking the regularly scheduled cruise boat that departs from the state marina on the west end of the village.

You can also ride the local duck here. This is an amphibious vehicle that takes you to the local sights on tires, and then drives right across Lake Fanny Hooe—don't open the door!

The village itself is geared for the tourist trade, with many souvenir shops and concession-type stands. However, there are several nicer restaurants and some very suitable motel accommodations.

One more attraction worth the effort is Fort Wilkins State Park. The fort was built here in the 1840s to protect the copper miners (the industry that started the settlement) from the local Indians (who attached a religious significance to the copper the white men were stealing). The fort is located in the east isthmus of the harbor, behind the lighthouse and along the banks of the Fanny Hooe Creek. It's very much just a log palisade surrounding more log buildings that are still here and in good shape thanks to a WPA project during the FDR administration. The fort held an active garrison for only two years after it's completion. Then the troops were sent to fight the war with Mexico. Some troops were stationed here briefly during the Civil War, but for the most part this has mostly been an abandoned fort.

Harbor Grand Marais, Michigan
Location Outer Channel Light: L46°41.3'N, Lo85°58.5'W
Dockage Municipal Marina

Places to Stay Welker's Resort, Alvordson's Motel, Superior Hotel, Hilltop Cabins

Places to Eat Lake Superior Brewing Company & Dunes Saloon, Sportsmans Restaurant, Earl of Sandwich

Grand Marais (pronounced mur-ray') is a very isolated harbor on the north coast of Michigan's Upper Peninsula. This is a very sandy area with a wonderful beach and unfortunately, a sandy harbor that is in danger of silting closed. This is a DNR Harbor of Refuge, and extra efforts are being focused to prevent nature from reclaiming one of the prettiest harbors on Lake Superior. Think about it. Sand is only rock that's been pounded to smithereens by the surf. Many a nasty gale has crashed waves on this shore.

In fact back in the olden days of the late Victorian era, it was fairly common for ships to be forced ashore here. Those of you who know your maritime history will recognize Grand Marais as the site of one of the most decorated U.S. Life Saving Stations in the Great Lakes. Many of the service's most famous names served here at one time or another. The station and its buildings are long since gone, but the waves do pound on!

In town today you will find a quiet village with a handful of eateries and shops of the most functional nature. The big pastime here is fishing as Lake Superior serves up the big ones in these waters. But if you're looking for a pristine shore along the cold waters of this great inland sea, a place to relax and recharge during a quickly passing summer season, this is it!

Harbor Houghton/Hancock, Michigan
Location Along the Keweenaw Waterway traversing the Keweenaw Peninsula
Dockage Houghton County Marina, Houghton-Hancock Marina

Places to Stay Contact: Michigan's Keweenaw Tourist Council 906-482-5240

Places to Eat Gino's Restaurant 906-482-3020, The Ambassador 906-482-5054, Nutini's Supper Club 906-482-2711,
The Library Bar & Restaurant 906-482-6211

Houghton-Hancock are the famous twin cities of the Keweenaw Peninsula. The Keweenaw Waterway is the shipping canal that allows freighters to pass through the peninsula rather than brave the unprotected waters of Lake Superior. It's this shipping canal that separates the two cities.

The Waterway and the cities are deep in a gorge with high bluffs and cliffs surrounding the area. From here, at designated scenic lookout points along the highway, you can see both cities, the canal and much of the waterborne traffic.

This is also the home of Michigan Technological University (Michigan Tech). On the university's campus you can find the Seaman Mineralogical Museum, one of the finest displays of rocks, ores, and minerals you will ever see!

Of course the biggest historical claim to fame here is mining, mostly copper mining, as the Keweenaw was once one of America's principal sources of this valuable ore. Not far from town is the Quincy mine, a retired copper mine that has been opened for public tours. You can see the huge steam-powered hoist and shaft house, and you can even ride down into the mine shaft itself!

Another sight to see, or take, is the *Ranger III*. This is the boat run by the National Park Service that will take you out to Isle Royale for day trips. The preserved wilderness island is well worth the trip.

Harbor Isle Royale, Michigan
Location Buoy R"2" in Rock Harbor Channel: L48°05.5'N, Lo88°34.31'W
Dockage Rock Harbor Docks, Windigo Docks

Places to Stay Rock Harbor Lodge 906-337-4993

Places to Eat Rock Harbor Lodge

What can you not say about Isle Royale? This is a U.S. National Park located on an island in the northern reaches of Lake Superior. By all reasoning it should be in Canadian waters, but the border does a neat little jog to accommodate the U.S. claim to this pristine wilderness island.

Historically, the island was carved by the great glaciers that moved across the Great Lakes during the last ice age. Look at any map or aerial photograph of the island and you can see the long striations running southwest to northeast. It looks more like a rutted road in springtime than one of the nation's premier parks!

You can get to Isle Royal by commercial ferry boats leaving from various harbors around the shore such as Houghton-Hancock and Bayfield. For a complete schedule and locations, contact the park headquarters at 906-487-7150.

There really is a lot to do in the wilderness. Here you can observe nature close at hand, and we don't mean just bunny rabbits. You will see (and keep a respectful distance from) bears, moose and elk. The park has an excellent ranger staff to help you select a camping site and to offer help and suggestions for those not used to wilderness camping. From anywhere on the island you can enjoy breathtaking scenery, woodland trails, deep virgin forests and all the grandeur of Lake Superior.

There are also a number of historic lighthouses around the island, and a good number of shipwrecks too. Might I suggest reading *The Shipwrecks of Isle Royale National Park*, published by Lake Superior Port Cities (218-722-5002) or buying the video cassette *Isle Royale Lights* by Keweenaw Video Productions (800-382-6088). Isle Royale is the trip of a lifetime.

Harbor Knife River and Two Harbors, Minnesota
Location Knife River South Breakwall Light: L46°56'35"N, Lo91°46'40"W
Dockage Knife River Marina

Places to Stay Emily's 218-834-5922, The Byran House B&B 218-834-2950, The Country Inn 218-834-5557, Voyageur Motel 218-834-3644, The Superior Shores Resort 218-834-5671, Gowdy's Inn B&B 1-888-226-4614

Places to Eat Emily's, The Depot Cafe, Smokey Kendall's Bar, Russ Kendall's Smoked Fish House, Judy's Cafe, Shari's Kitchen, Betty's Pies

Knife River and Two Harbors are both located within five miles of each other just 30 miles from Duluth along the north shore of Lake Superior. These are both small places, but together they make a pretty neat destination.

The marina is in Knife River. They have a very modern marina with plenty of transient facilities. But there's not much of a town here. There's Emily's, which is a combination country store, eatery and B&B. There's also Smokey Kendall's Bar and a couple of other business. The big town is Two Harbors, just up the road. But the problem is Two Harbors doesn't have a recreational marina, yet. What they do have are some of the biggest ore docks this side of Duluth! This is a freighter town, and a perfect place to watch the giant ladies of the Lakes come in to fill up.

They also have a very historic lighthouse here that is still an operational aid to navigation. The grounds and some of the outbuildings are open as a museum, but the keeper's quarters is a private residence. Also on the grounds is the pilothouse of the ore carrier *Frontenac*. This is the newer pilothouse she received at a refitting part way through her career. The original pilothouse is on display at the Fairport Harbor, Ohio, Lighthouse Museum, which was the other end of the *Frontenac*'s usual route.

Historic downtown is an interesting place to visit, with lots of historic buildings. Of special note is the Sandpaper Museum. Sandpaper isn't *that* popular here, but the museum is inside the original corporate headquarters of the company that made sandpaper as their first product back at the turn of the century. This was the beginning of the Minnesota Mining & Manufacturing Company. You know them better today as 3M.

The Great Canal Race of 1871

by Bruce Jenvey

With a title like this, I'll bet you're waiting to read about steamships racing for local glory along a limited waterway. Well you're wrong. This race was between a canal that didn't exist and a train from Kansas. It involved the Army Corps of Engineers, the populations of two cities and a very important piece of paper. It is perhaps one of the strangest stories of life on the Great Lakes, and one that reminds us all never to underestimate the power of a people united. Intrigued? You should be!

It was the spring of 1871. In those days the only way into the Superior, Wisconsin/Duluth, Minnesota harbor was through the Superior entrance across the great sandbar at the mouth of the St. Louis River. Of course this put the Superior docks first in line for the waterborne commerce, and made it a difficult trip up the harbor to the docks in Duluth. The people of Duluth decided to carve their own canal through the sandbar near Little Portage along the north edge of Minnesota Point.

Of course the folks in Superior, Wisconsin, didn't like that much. Not only would it end their monopoly on the commerce, there was great fear that such a canal would change the course of the St. Louis River enough to cause the Superior entrance to silt itself closed. The north end of the harbor was shallow, swampy and contained several floating bog islands. If the river exited here, surely the bogs and swamps would re-form in the southern, the Superior end, of the harbor. The people of Superior even enlisted the help of the Army Corps of Engineers who quickly conducted a study that supported that fear.

But the people of Duluth pressed on with their plans. In response, the people of Superior took the matter to the highest authority: Army Headquarters at Fort Leavenworth, Kansas. The army court issued an injunction against the City of Duluth to prevent dredging a new canal, and they dispatched the all-important piece of paper by train to be properly served by an officer of the court.

But in 1871 words could travel faster than trains thanks to the telegraph lines. When the people of Duluth received word that the injunction was on its way, they made one of the most important decisions in Great Lakes history. The injunction prevented them from dredging a "new" canal, but what if a navigable canal already existed when the injunction arrived? It would be a different story then.

The decision was made to mobilize the population of Duluth. The train was coming and it would be a race to complete a canal before it arrived. As the story goes, church bells rang and the town closed down. Every man, woman and child mustered at the great sandbar with every digging utensil to be had. They worked without rest, and with the help of the river currents and the natural forces of water, they broke through to the big lake and let the mighty St. Louis carry the swampy silt and the bog islands out of the harbor and into deep water.

When the man with the injunction arrived in Duluth on April 29, 1871, he was met by a very dirty but enthusiastic crowd that lined the banks of the yet uncharted canal. It was only 40 feet wide and 5 feet deep but the crowd cheered as the tug boat *Frank C. Fero* steamed through the canal into the harbor. This navigation canal pre-existed the injunction, making the court order worthless.

Despite continued opposition from the people of Superior, the Duluth canal was improved and expanded to its current width of 300 feet. Yes, it's current width. If you enter this harbor under the famous Aerial Bridge, you travel through this very canal dug by the men, women and children of Duluth. And the Superior entrance? It seems the Army Corps of Engineers was wrong. The entrance never silted up and the bogs never formed in the south. This too is the same entrance that is still in use today.

ken miller

Harbor La Pointe, Wisconsin
Location Southwestern End of Madeline Island in the Apostle Island Chain
Dockage Madeline Island Yacht Club

Places to Stay The Inn on Madeline Island 715-747-6315, Island Inn 715-747-2000, The Madeline Island Motel 715-747-3000, Brittany Cottage B&B 715-747-3102 Bog Lake Outfitters 715-747-2685

Places to Eat The Clubhouse, Grampa Tony's, The Island Cafe, The Pub Restaurant & Bar

La Pointe, Wisconsin, is located on the southwest corner of Madeline Island in the Apostle Islands. This is a rustic island community that has learned to appreciate the simpler things in life.

The island's tourist trade comes here to find the many parks and campgrounds that are quietly nestled into the pristine scenery. Should communing with nature grow tiring for you, there are sights to see in town. The Lake View Schoolhouse is now a museum maintained by the Madeline Island Historical Preservation Association. This building was originally located at the north end of the island but was moved here and restored by the society. It's a classic example of what the rural American one-room schoolhouse was really like. It will also shed some light on the local culture and the way life was lived in a harsh environment.

You should also visit the Madeline Island Music Camp. Every summer, young band members from all over the area spend band camp here, and where there are bands there are weekly concerts. Call them for a current schedule at 715-747-2561.

Of course charter fishing is a very favorite pastime here too. Some of the best fishing in Lake Superior can be found in the rugged Apostle Islands and the shallow waters of Chequamegon Bay.

Harbor Marquette, Michigan
Location The Marquette Lighthouse: L46°32.8'N, Lo87°22.6'W
Dockage Cinder Pond Marina, Presque Isle Marina

Places to Stay The Landmark Inn 906-228-2580, The Tiroler Hof Inn 906-226-7516, Lac Vieux Desert Resort And Casino 1-800-583-3599

Places to Eat The Portside Inn, Vango's Pizza, Togo's, Cassia Calabria, The Sweetwater Cafe, Remie's Bar, The Vierling Restaurant & Marquette Harbor Brewery, The Border Grill, Babycakes!

Marquette is one of the oldest ports on Lake Superior. What was once a busy commercial harbor fighting for space with a handful of pleasure boats has dramatically changed in recent decades. There are now two harbors in Marquette. The southern harbor, or the old harbor or even the main harbor—depending on what you want to call it—no longer hosts the ore boats of the Great Lakes fleet. Instead there is a spacious, modern, recreational marina right in the heart of this picturesque old city. You can walk up the small bluff to the main business district in town and visit shops and brew pubs in your choice of direction. Most are in restored storefronts from the Victorian era. Palatial homes high on the bluff along the harbor's west shore are quite a magnificent sight.

You can also visit, from a distance, the old Marquette lighthouse. This red-brick school-house-style facility is not only a current aid to navigation, but it is still an active Coast Guard station too. That's why you can only get so close. However, at the foot of the bluff that leads to the lighthouse, is the Marquette Maritime Museum. This is a truly wonderful display of maritime lore on the greatest of the Great Lakes.

But where have all the ore boats gone? To Presque Isle Harbor just north of the center of town. And you can go there too. Modern ore loading facilities are lined up along the shore with several great vantage points for the freighter-watcher in your crew. There's also a very modern recreational marina here, and all in the center of the city's biggest, most wonderful park. All of Presque Isle is preserved as a naturalist's dream for you to enjoy.

Harbor Michipicoten and Wawa, Ontario
Location Michipicoten River Entrance Light: L47°56'00"N, Lo84°51'06"W
Dockage Buck's Marina, Harry McCluskie Municipal Marina

Places to Stay Contact: Wawa Tourist Information Center 1-800-367-WAWA

Places to Eat The Embassy, On Broadway, New Ace, Big Bird Inn Restaurant, Viking Restaurant & Tavern, Mr. Mugs Coffee & Doughnuts, Park Place Pizzeria Restuarant & Dining Lounge

Wawa is a small Canadian town along the north shore of Lake Superior. For many Americans, this is in the area we often call "The Great Gray," because on our charts there is no indication of settlement or transient facilities. However, this is not true and Wawa is just one of many examples.

If you come by car, Wawa is easy to find. It's a small town right on the Trans Canada Highway. Just look for the largest concrete Canada goose in the world and you're there. By boat this is a different story. You'll have to find Michipicoten Island, Michipicoten Bay, then the shallow river that leads to the area's only marina, Bucks.

But once you are there you'll find a community proud of it's mining heritage, its parks and its waterfalls. Yes, this is just a sample of what you'll find in Wawa. Actually it's about all you'll find in Wawa. If you come here for bright lights, you'll have to settle for the best display of northern lights you'll probably ever see. If you come for historic sites, you'll have to be content with the rotary blasthole drill in the park near the waterfront. If you come for rushing water and pristine woodlands, you will have come to the right place!

Lake Superior

Harbor Munising, Michigan
Location State Dock: L42°24.5'N, Lo86°39.1'W
Dockage The State Dock 906-387-2275 or 3178

Places to Stay Contact: Alger Chamber of Commerce: 906-387-2138

Places to Eat The Navigator, Dogpatch, Mainstreet Pizza, The Forest Inn, Sydney's Family Restaurant

Munising is a quiet harbor town on the north shore of Michigan's Upper Peninsula. It is located in a small bay situated behind the protection of Grand Island, and is the only natural refuge from open Lake Superior for quite some distance in either direction along the coast.

Because of this harbor, many ships and boats that were crippled out on the lake limped into the refuge of Grand Island only to sink in the clear shallow waters. Today much of the waters around Munising are protected by the Alger Diving Preserve—a favorite destination for sport divers. But even if you aren't a diver, the waters are clear and cold enough that viewing the wrecks over the side of your boat is not a problem. The first time Ken Miller was here he was afraid his keel would hit one of the wrecks—until he realized he was still in more than 30 feet of water! If you want to see the wrecks and let someone else do the driving and the narration, visit the Grand Island Shipwreck Tours on the west side of town. They have a glass-bottom boat that will float you directly over a good number of the many wrecks.

Besides shipwrecks you should also visit the famed Pictured Rocks that stretch along the shore to the east of town. These are beautiful limestone cliffs carved by nature over thousands of years to create fascinating formations and wondrous arches. You can buy tickets for the Pictured Rocks Boat Tours right in the center of town down at the pier.

Harbor Ontonagon, Michigan
Location West Breakwall Light: L46°52.8′N, Lo89°19.9′W
Dockage Ontonagon Municipal Marina

Places to Stay Northern Light Inn B&B 906-884-4290, Olde Convent B&B 906-884-4538

Places to Eat The Candlelight Supper Club, Syl's Country Kitchen, McMiles Restaurant, The Konteka Supper Club, Eadie's Hotel Bar & Grill

Ontonagon is a small Michigan town on the southwestern shore of Lake Superior's Keweenaw Peninsula. Today's visitor will find a quiet town with an average business district that makes no special effort to proclaim its history. Even the lighthouse at the harbor entrance, while a classic beauty, is closed to the public and has no historical society to look after its future. While a pleasant town to visit, you would have no idea that this was one of the most pivotal settlements in U.P. history.

This was originally the high holy land of the Chippewa people. While they populated much of this region, the Ontonagon area was considered the Mecca, the Jerusalem of their religious beliefs.

This was the home to what has since been called the Ontonagon Boulder—a huge boulder of pure copper naturally occurring and existing a short way up the Ontonagon River from Lake Superior. It was through this great boulder of copper that the Chippewa people spoke with their god. It was the center of their religion.

The land was deeded away by treaty in 1842 and in short order, a ship and a crew of men showed up and took the Ontonagon Boulder away. By fall of that year it was on display in Detroit for two bits a peek. Eventually it wound up in the Smithsonian Institution in Washington, D.C., where it remains today, never returned to its rightful owners or its rightful home.

The Ontonagon Boulder started the great copper rush in the Keweenaw. Walking down Main Street you can still see rails and ruts from the streetcars that once ran in Ontonagon. The rest is history.

The Wreck of the *Gunilda*

by Bruce Jenvey

Shortly after the turn of the century, William Lamont Harkness inherited his father's fortune of some 37 million dollars. This was a tidy sum, especially back then. It left the younger Mr. Harkness free to pursue his favorite pastime, yachting. He owned several but his pride and joy was the *Gunilda*.

She was the ultimate statement in luxury and unrestrained wealth. She was 198 feet overall, a graceful white-hulled beauty with gold leaf inlay around her nameplate and other conspicuous areas. Her living quarters were decorated with the finest framed tapestries, hand-woven rugs, sterling silver and bone china. Rare books and art objects were also said to be in abundance on board.

In 1910 Harkness brought his precious *Gunilda* into the Great Lakes for a summer cruise. So taken by the beauty of the inland seas, he vowed to return the next summer for an extended trip along the rugged north shore of Lake Superior. True to his word, he was near Rossport about mid-summer 1911 with his wife and children and other friends.

One day they were taking on coal and supplies at Jack Fish when the captain of the *Gunilda* decided it was best to hire a local pilot to help guide them through the rocky islands and shoals of Nipigon Bay. He had never sailed these waters before and had on board only American charts, not Canadian charts. He had negotiated with a local named Harry LeGault to ride along with them for the fee of $15 plus another $10 for his train fare back to Jack Fish.

When Harkness got wind of this he was outraged. They had charts and a competent crew on board. He felt the sum was outrageous and a complete waste of $25. They set off without Harry LeGault.

Upon entering the bay, the American charts showed a good 300 feet of water beneath them and the captain ordered full speed ahead in order to reach a prime anchorage by the end of the day. But shortly into the run they encountered something that wasn't on the American charts: McGarvey Shoal.

The yacht hit the granite rock with a tremendous shock and her momentum carried her up out of the water to where the bow was high and dry and pointed skyward, and her stern portholes were barely two feet above Nipigon Bay. Miraculously she had suffered little damage and was not taking on water. She was indeed soundly built. If she could be pulled off the rocks, she would float, and minor repairs could be made at a harbor of choice.

The guests and the extraneous crew were evacuated, the insurance company notified, and in time a salvage crew arrived to attempt to re-float the *Gunilda*. However, upon viewing the yacht, the salvage captain, one of the most experienced in the lakes, felt the need for additional barges to give lift to the *Gunilda*'s stern. He feared she might take a serious list one way or the other as she came off the rock.

But again Harkness wouldn't hear of it. This was yet just another example of how everybody was always trying to run up his bills and charge him more than was necessary just because he was rich. He said that she went on straight, she'll come off straight, and gave the order to proceed with the operation.

With great effort and after several tries, the tugs finally got the great yacht to move back off the rock, but after a few feet the *Gunilda* did the expected and listed hard to starboard. The angle put her starboard stern rail below the water. It seems that in their haste to re-float, and in anticipation of an easy recovery, no one had thought to close the stern portholes or seal the bulkheads. The yacht immediately began to flood at an uncontrollable rate. As her bow climbed higher in the sky there was nothing for the tug captains to do but cut the tow lines so they didn't follow her to the bottom. Progressively, geysers burst out her portholes up the length of the ship and it was all over in a few minuites. She slipped beneath the surface of Nipigon Bay and settled, upright, on the rocky bottom some 300 feet below.

As she disappeared from sight, Mr. Harkness was heard to sheepishly say to the salvage captain, "Well, they're still building others like her."

Harbor Rossport, Ontario
Location Battle Island Lighthouse: L48°45.1'N, Lo87°33.4'W
Dockage The Government Dock

Places to Stay The Willows Inn B&B 807-824-3389, The Rossport Inn 807-824-3213

Places to Eat Serendipity Gardens Cafe & Gallery, Forget-Me-Not Gift Shop

Rossport is located in the extreme northern section of Lake Superior, a short distance east of Thunder Bay. It is one of the more isolated destinations you can find in the Lakes, but still offers much to see and do for the tourist.

The Rossport Islands themselves are a treat and have long been a vacation destination for cruising boaters. Please see the associated stories about "The Wreck of the *Gunilda*" and "Who Was that Man with the Fresh Breath?" Also of special note is nearby Slate Island. This island was not formed by glaciers, as were the others. This one is the product of a meteorite impact on the earth—big enough to form an island!

In town, the Caboose Museum retells the history of this charming burg, especially as it relates to the trans-Canada railway. Also make sure you explore the Casque-Isles Hiking Trail and see beautiful Rainbow Falls Provincial Park.

In town there are two wonderful B&Bs and a small collection of shops. My favorite was the Forget-Me-Not Gift Shop which features a "husbands' waiting bench" out back, overlooking the beautiful Rossport Islands. You can sit here peacefully and enjoy the view while she forages for bargains inside.

Who Was That Man with the Fresh Breath?

by Bruce Jenvey

For several days in the mid-1930s, the Rossport Islands played host to one of their most prominent guests. While no official record exists, no supporting documentation, there are a handful of highly-prized photographs, and that is proof enough for anyone around these parts.

The visitor came by boat, aboard one of the most extravagant yachts ever seen around here. She was the 185-foot *Atlantic*, made famous by her stunning racing victories and record-setting trans-Atlantic crossings. She was also well-known because of the man who owned her, Gerard B. Lambert.

Lambert may not be a household name, but I'll bet you are familiar with his work. In 1921 he found himself in control of his father's small pharmaceutical company in St. Louis, Missouri. The company was going through hard times and Lambert was doing his best to market the meager handful of products his father, a chemist, had developed. One product was a mild antiseptic solution the senior Lambert had created in 1880. He had come up with the idea after reading about a daring young surgeon who was using carbolic acid to treat operative wounds. The new solution was named in honor of the surgeon, but it never really sold well.

In a now famous 1921 brainstorming session, while trying to think of ways to move this product, Lambert's ears perked up when he heard an elderly chemist sputter the word "halitosis."

"What?" demanded Lambert.

"Halitosis," repeated the chemist. "It's Latin for bad breath."

The rest is history. Lambert developed a whole ad campaign around this concept and in 1928 he sold his interest in the pharmaceutical company for a refreshing 25 million dollars.

Incidentally, the daring young surgeon was none other than Dr. Joseph Lister, and the antiseptic solution invented by Lambert's father was Listerine.

With the money conservatively invested, Lambert never felt the Great Depression and pursued his passion for yacht racing. He owned several ships but none as fast or as grand as the *Atlantic*, which he bought from the estate of the late Cornelius Vanderbuilt.

In the early 1930s Lambert was called out of retirement. It seems a small manufacturer of men's toiletries was in trouble and needed his skills. Instead of a salary, Lambert took stock options proportional to sales increases. When he again retired to yacht racing in 1934, his wealth was kept secret but reported to be several times over his original fortune. And why wouldn't it be? The company he had just saved was Gillette, and Lambert had helped them bring their newly designed safety razor to market.

So what's all this have to do with Rossport? The *Atlantic* was here in the mid-1930s, and some will even tell you it was the summer of 1936. In the spring of 1936, Lambert had married Grace Lansing Mull, a second marriage for them both, and they had immediately set off on an extended and secret wedding trip.

If Lambert were off on a honeymoon, what would his precious *Atlantic* be doing in the most secluded regions of the Great Lakes without him? And if you were an internationally known multi-millionaire and yachtsman, especially known along the eastern seaboard and in Europe, where might you go for some secluded privacy? The people of Rossport are convinced that smiling man at the rail of the big yacht was indeed Gerard B. Lambert himself.

Mr. Lambert passed away February 26, 1967.

ken miller

Lake Superior

Harbor Sault Saint Marie, Michigan
Location Northern End of the St. Mary's River at the Double Bridge
Dockage Charles T. Harvey Municipal Marina, George Kemp Downtonw Marina, Bellview Marina, Roberta Bondar Transient Marina

Places to Stay Contact: The Soo Chamber Of Commerce 1-800-MI-SAULT

Places to Eat Antler's Restaurant, Jeff's 50s Restaurant, Studebaker's, Ang-Gios, Abner's, Freighter's Restaurant

Sault Ste. Marie, Michigan, commonly called "the Soo," is located at the St. Mary's Rapids between lakes Superior and Huron. This was a gathering place of the native tribes for hunting and fishing long before it was considered a hindrance to navigation by European settlers.

In 1855 the first lock was opened here and the rest is navigational history. This became the busiest waterway in the world on a per tonnage basis. Some say it's only the second busiest, with the Detroit River being slightly busier. I'll let you count the ships!

Today you can stand next to the locks and literally watch the world float by as ships from nearly every nation lock through on their way to other ports. A glass-encased shelter is now lockside, allowing you to watch in comfort regardless of the weather.

Also in town are two most unusual and unique museums. Look up as you drive south of the locks and you'll see the Tower of History. This vertical museum retells the history of this area with special emphasis on the Native American contribution. Right nearby, at the waterfront, is the museum ship *Valley Camp*. This is a retired ore carrier that once was a regular visitor through the locks. Now she is open for tours and features intricate displays of nautical history. Here you will find one of the heavily damaged life boats from the *Edmund Fitzgerald*.

I have to mention one of the most fun restaurants in the entire U.P. Antlers is just down the road from the *Valley Camp* and is a rustic frontier-style eatery. Everywhere you look furry creatures of all sizes peer at you from the rafters and knotholes in a whimsical atmosphere. It's a taxidermist's dream but really amusing for the average tourist too.

73

Harbor Sleeping Giant National Park, Ontario
Location Thunder Cape Light: L48°08.3'N, Lo88°06.2'W
Dockage Silver Islet, Tee Harbour

Places to Stay Various Campgrounds

Places to Eat On your boat

Sleeping Giant National Park is located in the northern reaches of Lake Superior across the bay from Thunder Bay, Ontario. This is a rustic destination like none other in the Lakes! There are docks at Silver Islet and a fine anchorage at Tee Harbour. There are plenty of shore-side accommodations, but they all happen to be campsites. The entire Sibley Peninsula is a Canadian National Park and is a wonderful escape to nature with all its trails, lakes and yes, high cliffs. Some of the hiking trails take days to complete and are only for the most experienced backpackers. Others can be completed in an afternoon and are perfect for the beginner.

This park takes its name from the unusual stone formation at the southern end of the peninsula. If viewed from a distance you can clearly see the image of a man lying on his back, sleeping on the water. This is Nanabosho, the great giant that was the protector of the Ojibwa people. He was turned to stone by the Great Spirit in retribution for abuse of his mighty powers. Be sure to read the full story on the next page.

Physically, the giant is about five miles long and the rock formations that are his throat and chest are really eroded cliffs with sheer drops in excess of 75 stories! You can climb the giant, there are several trails that go up there. But these trails are on the list of those best taken by experienced hikers. The rangers will warn you that the stone that forms the giant's chest does get slippery at the very first drops of rain. Be careful!

In Silver Islet, you can shop and restock, but most of what is sold there is camping supplies. This was also the home of the first off-shore silver mine. You can read about that in the village or in the maps given to you by the rangers.

Legend of the Sleeping Giant

by Bruce Jenvey

As Native North American legends go, the Sleeping Giant is relatively recent and actually references European settlement along the shores of the Great Lakes. It is really an interesting legend, and one that for all practical reasons should make you pause and reflect today.

Nanabosho, the great giant, was the protector of the Ojibwa people. He led them to the bountiful Sibley Peninsula in northern Lake Superior so that they might prosper and be protected from their terrible enemy, the Sioux. One day, while sitting on the shore of this great water, Nanabosho scratched a rock and beneath its surface discovered silver. Silver was worthless to the Ojibwa people, but Nanabosho knew it would bring the white man in great numbers and they would lose this land.

He ordered his people to bury the silver on the tiny islet at the southern end of the peninsula and made them swear never to reveal its whereabouts. But all men are human and humans can be vain. One of the chieftains succumbed to temptation and fashioned himself a most glorious weapon from the silver and carried it into battle against the Sioux. This battle was his last and the Sioux found the silver weapon next to his fallen body.

A few days later Nanabosho watched a Sioux warrior canoeing his way across the lake, heading towards the peninsula. With him were two white men, one carrying the fallen chieftain's silver weapon.

The Great Spirit forbade Nanabosho to interfere, but the giant loved his people and raised a great storm on the lake, drowning the men in the canoe. As punishment, the Great Spirit turned Nanabosho to stone, and there he sleeps today, at the foot of the peninsula he saved for the Ojibwa people.

Please note, the legend refers to a sleeping giant, not a dead one. No one knows how long the giant is supposed to sleep. The legend gives no prophecy as to when the Great Spirit might awaken Nanabosho. Just always remember, Nanabosho had sworn to protect this land from the white man, and the first two that came here, he drowned. So when the storm seas boil and the shoals reach out for your hull, ask yourself, how soundly is the giant sleeping tonight?

Harbor Thunder Bay, Ontario
Location Light on Breakwater Main Entrance: L48°25.9'N, Lo89°11.7'W
Dockage Prince Arthur's Landing marina, Thunder Bay Yacht Club

Places to Stay Prince Arthur Hotel 807-345-5411, Circle Inn Motel 807-344-5744, Old Country Motel 807-344-2511, Venture Inn 807-345-2343, The Elms 807-344-0189, Lakehead University 807-343-8612

Places to Eat Port Arthur Brasserie & Brew Pub, Portside Restaurant, Eddy Lee's Chinese Restaurant, Pagota Garden, Harrington Court

Thunder Bay, Ontario, is located on the most northern shore of Lake Superior. Once called Port Arthur, the city has been a center for shipping grain, coal and other commodities for well over a century. If you like watching Canadian freighters, you won't find a town with more than this for hundreds of miles.

As an historical footnote to the shipping industry, the *Bannockburn,* Lake Superior's most famous ghost ship, set sail from here one afternoon around the turn-of-the-century and was never seen again. No wreckage was ever found.

This is a busy and active city with a whole shopping district to explore and fine restaurants to enjoy. There is no need to leave here hungry and poorly clothed. But it is also a very important city in Canadian history. This was the site of old Fort William, now completely restored as an open-air museum.

What was once a British stronghold on the north shore is now a fun-filled and educational spot to watch real craftsmen recreate the lost arts of daily life. You'll see coopers, blacksmiths, bakers, gunsmiths and voyageurs. Be sure to visit the canoe shed. Here they actually build the 24-foot North canoes and the 36-foot Montreal canoes used to traverse the Lakes centuries ago.

Harbor Washburn, Wisconsin
Location City Dock Light: L46°40.1'N, Lo90°53.0'W
Dockage The Washburn Marina

Places to Stay Redwood Motel & Chalet 715-373-5112, Washburn Motel 715-373-2331, Super 8 Motel 715-373-5671

Places to Eat The Steak Pit, Time Out Restaurant, Cantina del Norte, Sandie's Log Cabin Restaurant, C-Side Inn, Paisano's Family Restaurant

Whenever anyone thinks of Lake Superior they think of forbidding, rocky coasts and icy cold waters, even in the hottest of summers. What if I told you there was a place on Lake Superior where the beach was sandy and the water was warm(er)? Yes, there is such a place and it's called Washburn, Wisconsin, and you'll find it in the western end of the lake on beautiful, Chequamegon Bay.

The bay is shallow, hence the relatively warmer water, but once, the water was much higher and great waves pounded the stones along this shore into sugar-fine sand. Is it any surprise then that the town's two parks, Memorial Park and West End Park, are some of the most popular pieces of real estate in Superior's west end? West End Park also boasts a fine boat ramp, and both parks have campgrounds and picnic facilities. Memorial Park even has cable TV hook-ups for their campers.

Regardless of which park you visit, the Lakeshore Walking Trail connects the two in a mile-long lakeside stroll through the local foliage. If you want something a little more concrete to do, visit the Washburn Historical Museum and Cultural Center on East Bayfield Street. It's located in one of the most beautiful sandstone buildings you have ever seen. And the sandstone was locally quarried too. This was one of the many products that took the place of lumber after the sawmills faded away.

Another local product of interest was manufactured here under the DuPont name. It was unique to the area and gave the community a real blast of economic prosperity. The product was dynamite.

Harbor Whitefish Point, Michigan
Location Red Breakwater Light: L46°45.5'N, Lo84°57.8'W
Dockage State Harbor Of Refuge

Places to Stay Whitefish Bay Motel 906-492-3505, Weaver's Sunrise Cottages 906-492-3378, Cloud Nine Cottages 906-492-3434, Curn's Kitchen & Motel 906-274-5555, Howard Johnson Motor Lodge 906-492-3940

Places to Eat Yukon Inn, TJ's Restaurant, The Paradise Restaurant, The Paradise Bakery, The Little Falls Inn, The Fish House

Whitefish Point is not much of an exciting destination. There is no town here, the nearest civilization being in nearby Paradise. But you don't come here for what's here, you come for what didn't make it here.

Many freighters have hidden in the relatively calm waters of the bay while great northeasters raged out on Lake Superior. Just as many vessels have run for Whitefish Point as an angry lake boiled around them. Many never made it this far, the most famous of which has to be the *Edmund Fitzgerald*.

Out near the tip of the point is the Great Lakes Shipwreck Historical Museum, operated by the historical society with almost the same name. This is perhaps the greatest collection of Great Lakes shipwreck information, artifacts and history anywhere. While the town of Paradise offers nice places to stay and several nice eateries, a visit here without a significant amount of time spent in this fine museum would be a tremendous loss. Among things you will see is the bell from the *Edmund Fitzgerald* itself, on display, awaiting enough fund-raising to have it placed in a permanent shrine honoring the sailors she took to the bottom with her.

Also on premises is the old Whitefish Point Lightstation and its unusual skeletal tower. The light is still an active but automated aid to navigation. Ironically, due to a power failure, this light was dark the night the *Big Fitz* went down.

Lake Huron

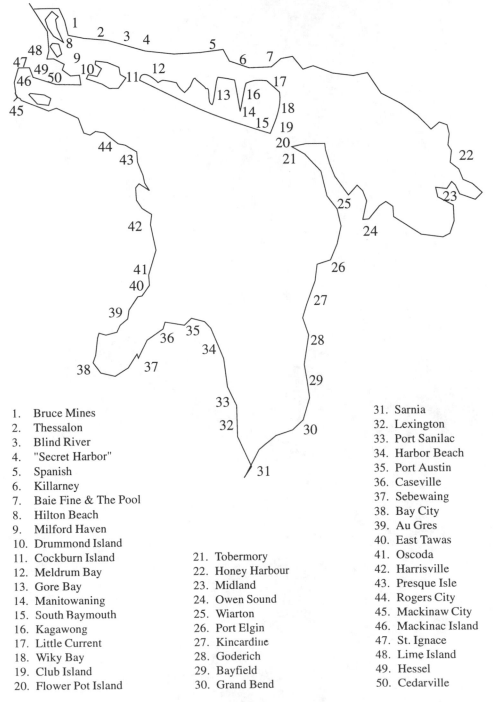

1. Bruce Mines
2. Thessalon
3. Blind River
4. "Secret Harbor"
5. Spanish
6. Killarney
7. Baie Fine & The Pool
8. Hilton Beach
9. Milford Haven
10. Drummond Island
11. Cockburn Island
12. Meldrum Bay
13. Gore Bay
14. Manitowaning
15. South Baymouth
16. Kagawong
17. Little Current
18. Wiky Bay
19. Club Island
20. Flower Pot Island

21. Tobermory
22. Honey Harbour
23. Midland
24. Owen Sound
25. Wiarton
26. Port Elgin
27. Kincardine
28. Goderich
29. Bayfield
30. Grand Bend

31. Sarnia
32. Lexington
33. Port Sanilac
34. Harbor Beach
35. Port Austin
36. Caseville
37. Sebewaing
38. Bay City
39. Au Gres
40. East Tawas
41. Oscoda
42. Harrisville
43. Presque Isle
44. Rogers City
45. Mackinaw City
46. Mackinac Island
47. St. Ignace
48. Lime Island
49. Hessel
50. Cedarville

Harbor "Secret Harbor," Ontario
Location L46°10.50'N, Lo82°41.56'W
Dockage Anchorage only

Places to Stay On your boat

Places to Eat On your boat

GLC's Bruce Preston has been no stranger to the famed North Channel for many years now. He has been in and out of more harbors up there than many of us have ever seen down here.

Together with his wife Phyllis, Bruce has "gunkholed" his way around much of the shoreline—wherever he could find enough draft for *Serendipity II* to float. On many occasions he used one cove in particular as a stopover between more conventional ports of call. This cove was so isolated they referred to it as their "secret harbor."

Just where is the Preston's secret harbor? Besides the obvious latitude and longitude coordinates, I can tell you that it is two-and-a-half miles southwest of Spragge and two miles directly south of the mainland and the Trans-Canada Highway. It's actually an unnamed cove off yet a larger also unnamed cove, and you have no chance of finding it without Canadian chart #2259.

So why go to all the trouble to get yourself so isolated? High rocky cliffs surround the anchorage. Rustic evergreens sprout right up from the rocks. The water is cold, but very clear. Water lilies bloom along the western shore. Wildlife comes right up to the shore to drink and is not too concerned with your presence. Do you need any more reasons than these?

Harbor Au Gres, Michigan
Location Au Gres River Entrance: L44°01'06"N, Lo83°39'55"W
Dockage Au Gres Marina & Campground, Au Gres Yacht Club, Au Gres State Dock, Harbortown Marina

Places to Stay Harbor Inn 517-876-8131, Au Gres Hotel 517-876-7217, Lutz's Au Gres Pinewood Inn 1-888-LUTZ-INN

Places to Eat H&H Bakery, Ma's Restaurant, Mike & Bridget Dunleavy's Eatery & Pub, Dave Wagner's Beartrack Inn, Marko's Pizzeria & Game Room

This is a quiet village along the north shore of Saginaw Bay. There's not a lot of excitement here but then, sometimes, that's what you go in search of—peace and quiet. The town is fairly unique among other Great Lakes harbors in that the village and the marina are a distance up the Au Gres river instead of being right at the lakefront. This means a well-protected harbor, but one you might pass by unless you were looking for it.

In town the State Docks are recently renovated and expertly maintained. They are also close to the village. There are all kinds of shops there to supply your needs and a few just to tickle your fancy. Besides a small amusement park and a man-made, well-stocked fishing pond (anyone can catch one here!), there is also the Sheep Factory. This unique shop actually does make sheep—in the form of slippers, wall hangings, coffee mugs and about anything else you wouldn't mind having sheep-shape. You can also find things in more conventional shapes too, like the shape of kitty cats, bunny rabbits and goats. They also sell hand-spun products and materials, and will even show you how the spinning wheel works. Be careful not to prick your finger!

There is also a very quaint museum in town. The Arenac County Historical Museum is located in a restored historical home right in the village. Here you will find exhibits representing the one-room schoolhouse, the old barbershop and the apothecary. There is also an excellent display on the local commercial fishing trade that is now long past.

Harbor Baie Fine and The Pool, Ontario
Location Okeechobee Lodge closed: L46°00.5'N, Lo81°40.5'W
Dockage Anchorage only

Places to Stay On your boat

Places to Eat On your boat

Baie Fine (pronounced bay finn) is perhaps the most well-known of all the cruising destinations in Canada's North Channel. Many will remember that the entrance to the Baie is guarded by the old Okeechobee Lodge. Sadly, the lodge (which was really a resort) has been closed since the untimely passing of Gord Blake, the beloved cantankerous man who built the lodge with his own hands. Eventually it is hoped the lodge will find a new owner and again be the only civilization in this remote section of the Lakes.

Baie Fine is a long and narrow passage that terminates in a small body of water called The Pool. It is the only fresh water fjord in the world. As you motor (boat motor, there is no access here by land yacht) down the Baie, you will see high rocky bluffs dotted with the occasional cottage here and there. The water is deep, and as Bruce Preston put it, it's also steep in that your depth sounder can read over one hundred feet as you motor within arm's reach of those limestone walls.

On the Preston's last visit to The Pool, they encountered yet again the large private yacht *Chanticlear*. This was the yacht of the famed Evinrude family of outboard motor fame. Prior to his death in 1985 it was not uncommon to see Mr. Ralph Evinrude and his wife, Francis Langford, the well-known radio star of the "Bickersons," enjoying coffee on the deck or on the porch of their cottage just up from the *Chanticlear*'s moorings.

The Pool has suffered in recent years from overuse and abuse at the hands of recreational boaters. Too much gray water is allowed overboard and the phosphates from soaps have encouraged the weeds to grow in various sections making anchoring impossible. Visit now and take everything out with you!

Harbor Bay City, Michigan
Location Saginaw Bay Light 1: L43°48.4'N, Lo83°43.1'W
Dockage Liberty Harbor Marina DNR, Jennison Boathouse, Brennan
Marine, Bay Harbor Marina, The Bay City Yacht Club, The
Saginaw Bay Yacht Club

Places to Stay The Holiday Inn 517-892-3501, For more, contact: Bay Area
Convention & Visitors Bureau 1-888-BAY-TOWN

Places to Eat Monique's Corner Lounge, The Stock Pot, Steamers,
The Lantern, The State Lunch, O Solo Mio, Mulligan's Pub,

Bay City is a major Michigan port at the most protected end of Saginaw Bay. Whatever you need, whatever you want, you can find it in this metropolitan area. They have everything from waterfront eateries housed in classic storefronts to historic sidewheelers on display at the docks.

You can also explore historic neighborhoods once populated by lumber barons who had a passion for building houses as big as their fortunes. You'll find most of these homes along Center Street, east of downtown. The best way to see these structures, and the rest of the downtown area, is aboard the Bay City Trolley. Tours start at the Bay County Historical Museum and you can call them for the trolley's schedule (517-893-5733).

In Wenona Park you can enjoy a summer concert on Tuesday or Thursday evenings while you watch the bay and river traffic. This is also the home of the city's newest attraction, the *Appledore*, a replica lakes schooner that will be used to teach history and ecology on a specialized schedule beginning in 1999.

Speaking of history, Bay City is famous for something the cruising boater uses almost every day: Range lights. The year was 1860 when young DeWitt C. Brawn, the fifteen-year-old son of the local lighthouse keeper, hung two lanterns in a line, one higher than the other, in an effort to help the schooners find their way into the tricky harbor. It didn't take the captains long to figure out how to line up the lights and soon the concept had been adapted all over the Great Lakes, the nation and the world.

Harbor Bayfield, Ontario
Location Rear Range Light: L43°43.1'N, Lo81°42.3'W
Dockage Village Marina, South Shore Marina, Harbor Lights Marina

Places to Stay Albion Hotel 519-565-2641, Bayfield Village Inn 519-565-2443, Camborne House 519-565-5563, Clair on the Square 519-565-2135, Clifton Manor 519-565-2135, Decoy Inn 519-565-2325, Little Inn of Bayfield 519-565-2611

Places to Eat Admiral Bayfield's Diner & Pub, Patty's Kitchen, Red Pump Restaurant, Albion Hotel, Spago's

Bayfield, Ontario, is a quiet Canadian crossroads just down the Huron coast from busy Goderich. The marina is a pleasant ten-minute stroll through a tree-lined path from town, and town itself is like a shaded walk in the country. If you've always heard that life in Canada moves at a slower pace, this is a great place to catch up to it all.

Several of the local restaurants are also inns, and provide "room and board" much as they have for the past century. A small selection of country stores represents Bayfield's business district. However, while it may not be the Mall of America, there are windows to shop and bargains to find. If you're looking for a quiet weekend, Bayfield is just one of several little-known stops on a trip up the shoreline.

Harbor Blind River, Ontario
Location Manitoulin Strait Light: L45°53.6'N, Lo83°13.5'W
Dockage Blind River Marina Park

Places to Stay The Northern Lights Motor Inn

Places to Eat Cortina Pizza, Chic Char II, Seventeen Restuarant, Carlo's,
The Iron Horse Inn

Blind River is one of the more civilized outposts in Canada's rustic North Channel. In this case, civilized means they have a modern marina and a motel that's open at least half the year. They also have a Tim Horton's along the highway that threads through town, but the business district itself is rather limited.

So why would you come here? If you're a boater, it's one of the first stopovers on an east-to-west cruise of the famed channel. It's also a modern and comfortable facility. But if you come by land yacht or want some time ashore, you can find lots to fill your time.

First, break out the hiking boots. There are several trails here of various difficulty, and each one offers peaceful scenery of the lake and the mountains (large hills?) that cover the area. Several of the trails actually begin in the village park, right in the center of town. These you can't miss. If you're looking for more challenging trails, you can find more information at the Blind River Tourist Information Centre on the east end of town, or you can call the Regional Travel Information Centre at 1-800-563-8719.

But wait, Blind River also has a very fine museum to visit. It too is on the east end of town and is called the Timber Village Museum. This facility has many outdoor and indoor displays that recount the years the logging industry helped feed the local economy. This is a very informative museum and well worth your time.

Lucky Ladies of the Lake
Two of Blind River's Own Ride Out the Tempest of 1913
by Bruce Jenvey

In early November 1913 the worst storm in Great Lakes history ravaged ship and shore for nearly five days. When it was over, hundreds were dead and a dozen lake boats had gone to the bottom. A full two dozen more sat as useless wrecks along the shore.

The carnage would have been less, certainly, had modern weather equipment been available. Back then the most reliable predictions came out of almanacs which were nothing more than historical averages. Lake captains tended to sail out into uncertain conditions rather than lose a valuable day of a limited shipping season. The general attitude was that you can't do anything about the weather, so worry about it when it happens.

"Happening weather" was tremendous understatement for the great storm of 1913. This storm's severity still captures the imaginations of those with an interest in Great Lakes lore. As recently as two years ago, two respected meteorologists were still attempting to solve the puzzle as to what meteorological events had taken place by studying the written accounts of eyewitnesses from various ports around the lakes. It has been generally accepted that four low-pressure cells converged over Lake Huron and joined forces in a freak occurrence. More recent studies discount this theory but still offer no concrete model. Whatever happened, southern Lake Huron took the worst of it leaving very few sailors to recount the ferocity of the tempest.

How bad did it get? Again, weather measuring devices were in their infancy or completely nonexistent in that era, but reports put sustained wind speeds in excess of one hundred miles per hour. The ice and snow that accompanied the storm was said to literally "explode" when hitting houses, barns or those foolish enough to venture out. Windows were destroyed not just by the wind, but by the large objects that were along for the ride. Entire buildings were obliterated by the ice and wind, or by the trees the ice and wind sent as destroyers. Those who could see the water told of waves that towered above the highest freighters. And this lasted for five days.

As I mentioned, eyewitness accounts of those who experienced this maelstrom from the water are few and far between, and many of those come from people on ships that were on the edge of the storm. Blind River was on the edge of the storm and I thought you might enjoy this account.

On the evening of Saturday, November 8, 1913, the storm had not yet made itself felt in the small lumber town of Blind River, Ontario. Seeing no reason to waste another night in port, Captain W.E. Pierce was preparing to get underway. His vessel, the aging lake steamer *Ogemaw,* was loaded to the hilt with prime lumber cut from the northern shores of Georgian Bay. As was the practice, once the hold was filled, more lumber was secured to the open deck in an effort to make every trip count the most, financially. But the *Ogemaw* would not be traveling alone. The schooner barge *C.A. Filmore* would be in tow, also loaded above her decks.

This lumber hooker-schooner barge combination was very common back then. Old sailing vessels, unable to earn a profitable living in competition to steam boats, would serve out the last useful years of their lives in tow behind aging lakers. When run as a combination they could justify their existence with a modest profit. Sometimes one steamer would tow several such schooners, and one by one cut them loose off shore from their intended ports. The schooners would then make their way to shore under sail, and when empty, rendezvous with their steamer on the open lake. This way one steamer could make deliveries to several ports in a fraction of the time of even a much newer boat. It made them profitable and kept the ships and their crews employed for a while longer.

But on this evening it was just the *Ogemaw* and the *Filmore,* aging hulks with wooden hulls and tired seams, that set out for Alpena. Within an hour of leaving Blind River the weather changed dramatically. The wind had shifted to the northeast and now screeched down on the sterns of the unsuspecting lumber boats. The seas built quickly making it impossible to turn around and claw back home. The seas mauled both vessels, smashing windows and companionways and slowly stripping their decks of valuable cargo.

After several hours Captain Pierce feared this storm might be the end of his ship, his barge, or both and began considering his options for survival. If he were to cut the barge loose (as was often the practice) it would spell certain doom for all eight men on the *Filmore*. To venture through the Mississagi Straits on the western end of Manitoulin Island, as was their original course, was now also suicide. Out on the open lake, the storm would claim both vessels within minutes.

The third option proved to be their salvation. Along the west end of

Manitoulin Island is Meldrum Bay, only a couple of compass points to the east of their current course. The bay would provide only limited protection from the wind in its current direction, but limited protection was better than what they had now.

It was a struggle against the seas, but Captain Pierce managed to guide both vessels into Meldrum Bay and there, in the relatively calmer waters, he managed to turn into the wind without losing the *Filmore,* and dropped both his anchors. The *Filmore,* still connected by the towing hawser, also dropped both anchors, and there they planned to ride out the weather.

Captain Pierce kept his engine engaged at "slow ahead" in order to take some of the strain off the ground tackle. But as the storm intensified throughout the day on Sunday, the 9th, he slowly nudged the throttle farther and farther ahead until the engine was at its maximum. Still this was not enough to keep the anchors from dragging across the rocky bottom of the bay.

By Sunday evening Pierce gave in to what he knew he must do and cut the *Filmore* loose. He hoisted anchor and set out on a last ditch effort to return to Blind River. On the open water he at least stood a chance. Back there in Meldrum Bay he was sure to be blown upon the rocks and smashed to pieces by the surf. The *Filmore* would have to fend for herself.

Clawing her way back to Blind River proved to be a monumental task for the *Ogemaw.* Ice and snow pelted the vessel without mercy, making visibility on that already black night completely impossible. Ice clung to those portions of her superstructure that struggled to stay above the heaving water. The waves ripped at this grand old lady of the lake, and bit by bit began stripping her of her deckhouse and pilothouse.

By the morning of the tenth the deckhouse was completely gone and not much remained of the pilot house. Several times during the night the thought to abandon the ship had crossed the captain's mind, but waves towering ten feet above the deck had made launching the lifeboats impossible. But now they could see the entrance to Blind River.

By lunch time they were secured to a dock and the crew was attempting to salvage what remained of their personal belongings from what remained of the *Ogemaw.* But the captain pushed for makeshift repairs and by Tuesday afternoon, when Georgian Bay had managed to calm itself slightly, the *Ogemaw* set out on a return run to Meldrum Bay and to the aid of the *Filmore.*

By now they were certain the *Filmore* was in ruins. If she hadn't blown ashore and been dashed on the rocks, surely the strain of riding anchor in this storm would have opened her seams allowing the cold lake water to rush in and take her. Captain Pierce wasn't going back for the *Filmore*, he was going back for survivors.

To the surprise of all, the *Filmore* was still afloat and riding her anchors quite well in the seclusion of Meldrum Bay. The *Ogemaw* hitched up her consort and continued on to Alpena to deliver what remained of their cargo before returning to Blind River for the winter and much needed repairs.

The *Ogemaw* and the *Filmore* continued to sail together out of Blind River for many more seasons before their final retirement. But wherever they went from then on, they were no longer just two tired lumber boats, they were recognized as those two "survivors" from Blind River.

ken miller

Harbor Bruce Mines, Ontario
Location McKay Island Lighthouse: L46°16.9'N, Lo83°46.8'W
Dockage Bruce Mines Marina

Places to Stay The Beacon Inn B&B 705-785-9950, The Bruce Bay Cottages 705-785-3473, Bavarian Inn & Restaurant 705-785-3447, Bobbers Restaurant & Hotel 705-785-3485

Places to Eat Bavarian Inn & Restaurant, Bobbers, B&D's Country Kitchen, Raising Dough, Country Cottage Ice Cream Cafe, Yancey's Meats

Bruce Mines is a small town at the eastern end of the North Channel. It's also right on the Trans-Canada Highway—right on the highway! In fact the main drag *is* the highway, making shopping in town an experience you pay attention to. You watch when you cross the street here!

The business district is a delight with an eclectic collection of small shops and friendly shopkeepers. Here you will find establishments like Janie's Orchard, The Victorian Attic, Maggie's Fashions and the Apple Creek General Store, just to name a few.

But once you're done shopping and dining, this place has preserved its history in a most interesting way. Mining was what this community was founded on. There are a number of old copper shafts all over town and in the surrounding area. The Simpson Shaft has been preserved and reconstructed as an example of what mining was like prior to 1850. Here you can see the tools of the mining trade in their natural setting and learn how this seemingly impossible task was accomplished. You can even go underground several feet in the shaft and feel what it was like to work here back then. To preserve the experience, there is no electricity down there, only candle power. See what you can, and imagine the rest!

Harbor Caseville, Michigan
Location Pigeon River Breakwater Light: L43°56'54"N, Lo83°17'15"W
Dockage Hoy's Saginaw Bay Marina, Caseville Resort, Riverside Marina, Municipal Dock & Charter House, Beadle Bay Marina

Places to Stay The Carkner House B&B 517-856-3456, The Belle Vista Inn 517-856-2500, The Lakeview Motel 517-856-2303, The Lodge At Oak Pointe 517-856-3055

Places to Eat Dufty's Blue Water Inn, The Bay Window Restaurant, The Caseville Dairy Inn, The Cozy Cafe, Hersel's on the Bay

Caseville, Michigan, is located on the southern shore of Saginaw Bay. This is a unique village in the sense that it has nearly always earned its living in the tourist trade. City fathers realized early on that the lumber that brought the barons and the lumberjacks would not last forever. In fact the very sandy soil of this area almost guaranteed that Caseville's lumber boom would be among the shortest—but that sand!

People soon realized that the barons and laborers of the lumber trade kept returning to the Caseville area to relax, even after the stock of pine thinned out. People loved the sandy beaches and cool breezes off the bay. A resort trade had begun.

Today, the modern harbor is in the center of town just a short stroll down the hill from the business district. Shops sell everything from fishing gear to swim toys to kites and all kinds of souvenirs. There's a first run movie theater and even an indoor amusement park/fun house for the kids. It's commercial, it's touristy, and it's a lot of fun!

Historically, the church on the north edge of the village is on the National Registry of Historic Places. But not only was this a place of worship, it also served as the local navigational aid. The extremely tall steeple was visible from a great distance on the bay. The one there now is a replica, the original having been struck by lightning once too often.

Lake Huron

Harbor Cedarville, Michigan
Location Buoy GC"31": L45°58'52"N, Lo84°20'55"W
Dockage Cedarville Marine, The Viking Boat Harbor

Places to Stay The Les Cheneaux Inn Bed & Breakfast 906-484-3422

Places to Eat The Landing, Popp's Deli

Cedarville is a quiet harbor on the eastern end of Michigan's Upper Peninsula. It's often considered a sister city to nearby DeTour by outsiders. But insiders will argue with you that both towns happen to be in the general community of the Les Cheneaux Islands; the particular town you are in is of little concern.

The Islands are among the most beautiful in the entire Great Lakes region. Heavily treed bluffs spring up from the deep waters forming a collection of islands uniquely carved by the glaciers. There are cottages to see here. Some are humble family getaways while others rival the summer palaces of the Czar himself. They are quite a sight to see.

In town you will find a small, concise business district with all the basic needs including a first-rate book store, Safe Harbor Books, where you may have bought this book!

There are two museums in town and both are "Don't miss" attractions. The Les Cheneaux Historical Society's Museum is located in the old school. Here you'll find a complete collection of records and photos detailing life in this, one of the Great Lakes' first resort communities.

Just down the road quite a ways is the Maritime Museum. Don't let the walk or its exterior appearance deter you. The walkway is lined with old wooden rowboats in various states of rot and decay. The building looks a little tired. However, inside, Ken Miller found one of the most complete and interesting collections of maritime artifacts he has ever seen. There is also a wooden boat-building school on the premises, preserving that part of our maritime past.

Lake Huron

Harbor Club Island, Ontario
Location The Island: L45°34.0′N, Lo81°36.0′W
Dockage Anchor or beach in the natural harbor on the east shore

Places to Stay On your boat

Places to Eat On your boat

If you're traveling by boat between Killarney in Lake Huron's North Channel and Tobermory, you might want or need a harbor in between. Our Bruce Preston, with years of exploring this area of the lakes, has often stayed in the natural harbor of Club Island.

This is a rustic destination with no facilities of any kind. You must be completely self-sufficient here. However, as the local waters are treacherous in times of limited visibility, this is an excellent sandy anchorage to enjoy until the fog burns off.

If you have a dinghy, go ashore and enjoy the natural aspects of this remote abandoned island. About the only thing you'll find are seagulls and the ruins of an old commercial fishing shack from the 1920s. Oh, and peace and quiet—there's lots of that here too.

Lake Huron

Harbor Cockburn Island, Ontario
Location Tolsma Bay Breakwater Light:L 45°57′35″N, Lo83°18′58″W
Dockage The Township Docks

Places to Stay On your boat

Places to Eat On your boat

Cockburn Island is a remote "cottage" island in the eastern end of the Canadian North Channel. Pronounced "coe'-burn", many describe the area as a ghost town, a fact bitterly disputed by the handful of regular residents. I say regular residents because by last count there were only two people who suffer out the winter here. To the rest of the handful, this is a summer-only community.

This is a destination for boaters only. No stores, no shops, no restaurants and no shoreside accommodations. No electricity at the docks and no water. You climb the hill with a jug and take all you want from the town well. There are a pair of pit toilets in the marina—end of facilities.

The steamers stopped docking here a long time ago and now, even the ferries have ended service. While the boater will find decent docks in the island's only settlement, Tolsmaville, that's about all there is. The locals are friendly and are more than likely to invite you in for tea or other beverages. What houses are here are called "camps" as they are only vacation homes in various states of upkeep. Down at the dock, tugboat traffic does come over from the mainland delivering products and services purchased by the islanders. They deliver services? When Ken Miller was there, he saw two old refrigerators being loaded off the tug and onto the dock, while one more was taken off the dock and onto the tug. The only refrigerator repairman is on the mainland—and he doesn't make house calls! Your refrigerator will be back in about a week.

If you get around the lack of conveniences, you will discover a very friendly and beautiful place in which to relax. I understand from Bruce Preston that berry picking is plentiful here. Just add cream and sugar, and have yourself a good old time.

Harbor   Drummond Island, Michigan
Location   Red Buoy "2" at Drummond Island Yacht Haven: L46°03.5'N,
Lo83°44.9'W
Dockage   Drummond Island Yacht Haven, Haviland Marina,
The Drummond Island Sport Center, Nate's Marina,
Fort Drummond Marine & Resort

Places to Stay   Anne's Attic B&B 906-493-5378, or contact: Drummond Island
Chamber 906-493-5245

Places to Eat   Northwood Restaurant, Bayside Restaurant

Drummond Island has often been called the American entrance to the North Channel. Nearly in Canadian waters and only American by the grace of a fragile peace treaty and a border drawn sometime after the end of the War of 1812, this was the site of the last British fort on American soil. The fort has long since collapsed back into the countryside and is now on private property.

A ferry runs regular car service back and forth to Michigan's U.P., or you can come by boat and stay in the Yacht Haven on the island's north shore. The proprietor here, Denny Baily, wears many hats. Besides being your harbormaster, of most importance to you, he is also the local U.S. Customs Official. You can meet all federal requirements for entering U.S. waters by having a little conversation with Denny.

While you're on the island be sure to stop by the Drummond Island Historical Museum just south of the Yacht Haven. Here you will find many Native American artifacts of local origin as well as the last of the relics from the old British fort. They even have one of the chimneys, torn down and reassembled on this site.

And if you're in the mood, you can also enjoy a world-class round of golf at The Rock, one of the wonderful facilities left behind when Dominos Pizza king Tom Monaghan abandoned his dream of a private resort on the island.

There are a lot of secluded roads to walk down where you can enjoy the rustic "up north" scenery. Just remember that much of the island is private property so please respect the privacy of the owners.

Lake Huron

Harbor East Tawas, Michigan
Location Tawas Point Light: L44°15.2'N, Lo83°26.9'W
Dockage State Dock, Jerry's Marina, Tawas Bay Yacht Club

Places to Stay Tawas Bay Holiday Inn Resort 517-362-8601,
East Tawas Junction B&B 517-362-8006,
Martin's Motel 517-362-2061, Bambi Motel 517-362-44582

Places to Eat Captain Coney, G's Pizza, Geni's Fine Foods

Tawas and East Tawas form one of Michigan's premier resort towns. Located at the northern entrance to Saginaw Bay, it is a natural depository for waterborne sand. In fact Tawas Point, which protects the harbor from the open waters of lake Huron and Saginaw Bay, is nothing more than a naturally occurring sand bar that has developed over tens of thousands of years.

Tawas point is now a State Park and home to the famed Tawas Point Lighthouse. The lighthouse is not only an active navigational aid, but a museum as well. Hours are limited and tours are given by members of the local Coast Guard Auxiliary. You can check with the harbormaster's office or the park's ranger station for the latest schedule.

Back in town, Tawas is a thriving community that enjoys tourism as it's prime industry. There are shops to explore and waterfront parks to enjoy. Also, there is sport fishing, and lots of it! If you didn't bring your own boat, there are commercial fishing charters in the harbor ready to take you out on the bay. Just check in at the Chamber of Commerce office on the main highway south of the harbor for all the latest schedules and boats available.

One more thing to do: Tawas, with it's sandy public beaches, is one of the finest places in the Great Lakes to build sand castles. If you haven't taken part in this pastime lately, it's high time you did!

Lake Huron

Harbor Flower Pot Island, Ontario
Location The Island: L45°18′N, Lo81°37′W
Dockage The Beachy Cove Government Dock (not in the yellow zone reserved for commercial tour boats!)

Places to Stay On your boat. This is a rustic island park

Places to Eat On your boat

Flower Pot Island is a small rustic destination just off the tip of Canada's Bruce Peninsula. This is a park. There are usually two park rangers on the island, but that is the only form of "facilities" you will find.

The harbor, called Beachy Cove, is on the island's southeast side and is the only docking facility on the island. Pleasure boaters may tie up at the small dock along the beach if your draft allows, or there is room for about two cruising vessels on the far end of the ferry dock. Do not tie up in the yellow area reserved for the ferry! You are truly on your own here. There is no electricity, dockside water or harbor lights of any kind.

This is also a camper's haven. A good number of rustic camp sites are scattered across the island providing the camper with a solitude he will be hard pressed to find anywhere else. The ferry that arrives several times a day from Tobermory is the camper's link to the mainland.

Surprisingly, there's lots to do here! A system of hiking trails takes you across and around the island past everything a naturalist would love to see. There are rare birds that make this island home as well as abundant growth of all kinds of plants and ferns. The geologist in your crew will be thrilled here too. Natural erosion has exposed rock stratification and created unusual formations. The rock formations are very impressive, especially the two that look like giant flower pots, from which the island takes its name.

Harbor Goderich, Ontario
Location North Breakwater Light: L43°44.4'N, Lo81°44.1'W
Dockage Snug Harbor Municipal, Maitland Valley Marina, Howman's Inlet Marina

Places to Stay Bedford Hotel 519-524-7337

Places to Eat The Bedford Hotel, Laurie's Restaurant, Joe's landing, Pearl's Chinese Food, Robindale's

Goderich is an interesting Canadian town with an even more interesting past. Many years go, salt was discovered as an exportable substance—so they opened a salt mine! While salt is still one of the city's chief exports in its busy commercial harbor, agricultural grain is also now a major part of the economy.

A regular flow of freighter traffic comes and goes from the harbor, but for an interesting stroll, look for the freighter that never leaves. The city has long maintained a retired steamship to use for surplus grain storage. In the fall, the ship is tied up on one side of the docks, and as the grain is slowly shipped out of the elevators over the course of the winter and spring, the old freighter is towed over to the elevators for unloading. At the time Ken Miller last visited this harbor, the boat was the *Cedarglen*. But the philosophy of this program says that as a newer steamship is retired, she replaces the "silo ship" and the old incarnation is sold for scrap. Right after Ken's visit, they changed ships. Hard to tell what it is now, but rest assured it is there.

Other sights to see include the Marine Museum in the park at the beach. The museum itself is really the old pilothouse from the *S.S. Shelter Bay*. The auxiliary wheel and spare propeller blades are on display here too.

Also, climb the high bluff to yet another park and visit the Goderich Light. From up here you have a commanding view of the harbor and the lake, as does the light from the old beacon. In the same park you will find a rather crude fountain running constantly. This is very tasty, ice-cold spring water and is the last vestige of Goderich's attempt at the mineral spring spa/resort trade that was so popular in the late Victorian era. Nearby is the historic old train station.

Harbor Gore Bay, Ontario
Location Red Buoy JE2: L45°55.3'N, Lo82°27.5'W
Dockage The Government Dock

Places to Stay Seradon House B&B 705-282-3324, The Bed & Breakfast 705-282-2437

Places to Eat Red Roof Tea Room, Gordon's Lounge, Twin Bluffs Bar & Grill, Gallery Drive Inn, B&J Bakery

Gore Bay is a quiet village in Canada's North Channel cruising grounds. *GLC*'s Ken Miller has often used this harbor as a place to relax after a long week's passage or after fighting a turbulent lake. There's a wonderful park with picnic tables right next to the launch ramp that is often used on weekends as a local flea market.

The village itself is a short walk up the road and there you will find all town services including a bank and local eateries. It's a peaceful place to explore.

Nearby are the famous Benjamin Islands, a remote anchorage accessible only by boat.

However, you'll be missing a lot if you don't take the walk out of town to Janet Head. Those who come by boat round this on the way in. There's a very nice park there with an entire maze of walking trails to discover. But there's also a wonderful old lighthouse. The light is an operating aid to navigation, and while the grounds and camping and picnic sites are open to the public, the lighthouse is not. It's a very typical Canadian lighthouse of this era, made of wood with a square tower. A great photo opportunity and a nice romantic evening can be found here.

Harbor Grand Bend, Ontario
Location Harbor Entrance Light: L43°18.8'N, Lo81°45.9'W
Dockage The Grand Bend Municipal Harbor Dock,
The Grand Bend Yacht Club, The Manore Marina

Places to Stay Bonnie Doone Manor-on-the-Lake 519-238-2236, The Oakwood Inn 1-800-387-2324, The Colonial Hotel, and many others

Places to Eat Grammie's Pizza Plus, The Oakwood Inn, Coral Reef Inn, The Colonial Hotel

Grand Bend is in the southern end of Lake Huron, along the Canadian shore. This is one of Ontario's oldest resort towns. The wide sugar-sand beaches and cool lake breezes have been attracting tourists to this relatively remote shore for decades. The Oakwood Inn, one of the community's finest resorts, was built in the mid-1920s to accommodate a thriving resort economy.

The beaches here are among the finest in the lakes. The sand is virtually white and the public beach areas are very wide and stretch way down the shore. There are organized volleyball tournaments as well as other beach events with name-brand sponsors.

The town is a tourist haven. There are restaurants of every kind, everywhere. After that, you will notice a large amount of gift and souvenir shops and the ever-popular arcades. Rock and roll music forces its way out of overcrowded bars. There is a decided carnival-like atmosphere in town. And of course the dress code of the day is whatever you were wearing on the beach that morning.

But Grand Bend does have more to offer than just resort life. The Pinery Provincial Park is a protected naturescape of towering dunes, wetlands and ancient river beds. There's also camping here and a good opportunity to study nature. Just outside of Grand Bend is the Huron County Playhouse, presenting professional live theatre in the country. Their selection of productions is always intriguing.

Also, don't miss the Lambton Heritage Museum just south of town. It's an interesting presentation of life along these shores—even before there was beach blanket bingo.

Lake Huron

Harbor Harbor Beach, Michigan
Location Harbor Beach Lighthouse: L43°50.7'N, Lo82°37.9'W
Dockage Harbor Beach Marina 517-479-9707

Places to Stay Deborah's Wellock Inn (B&B)517-479-3645, Randolph's Family Motel 517-479-3325, State Street Inn 517-479-3388, Jill's International B&B 517-479-6589

Places to Eat The Sunrise Cafe, Al's, Randolph's, Ernesto's Pizzeria

Harbor Beach is a good-sized (2,500 residents) community on the Lake Huron shore of Michigan's thumb. Its large rip-rap break-walls topped-off with a classic lighthouse encircle the world's largest manmade harbor. This harbor of refuge was built for passing freighters in the late 1800s. But as freighters grew, the commercial traffic dwindled until only the occasional coal carrier enters today to service the giant electric plant in the harbor's heart.

Originally the town was known as Sand Beach, changing its name after the great forest fire of 1881 and the construction of the harbor. The town's history is portrayed on a series of murals on the exterior walls of the Community Center. It's a large two-story brick structure housing the library, the movie theater and a gymnasium.

Other sights worth seeing around town: The Grice House Museum near the marina is a farmhouse and schoolhouse filled with relics that recreate daily life in the area. Also visit the Frank Murphy Museum on South Huron Street. Frank Murphy was a favorite son of Harbor Beach whose career ranged from hometown attorney to Governor of Michigan and U.S. Supreme Court Justice. The museum preserves photos and other memorabilia from his career.

The are a good number of shops to explore in the downtown area including a Hallmark shop, two hardware stores, a bicycle shop, a full-service old-style drug store, a new/used book store and a very-well-stocked craft and gift shop, among others.

Several very good eateries are in town but of special note is Ernesto's Pizzeria. Ernesto's has been selected by the *GLC* staff as having the best pizza on all of Lake Huron!

Harbor   Harrisville, Michigan
Location   Outer Breakwall Light: L44°39.7'N, Lo83°16.9'W
Dockage   Harrisville Municipal Marina 517-724-5242

Places to Stay   Red Geranium Inn B&B 517-724-6153, Silver Creek Lodge B&B 517-471-2198, Widow's Watch B&B 517-724-5465

Places to Eat   The Pizza Parlor, Bob's Pizza Station, Muelbeck's Bravarian Inn

Harrisville is located on the northern Michigan shore of Lake Huron and is a nice cruising stopover north of Saginaw Bay. The town today is a small village with a few shops and stores, and one bank. But what is here has been here for a very long time.

Harrisville was one of the first big boom towns in Michigan during the early days of the lumber boom. At one time a gigantic dock stretched out into the lake for steamships to load lumber from the town's main employer, the Harris Lumber Mill. As the land was cleared, agricultural products became an exportable commodity and began to fight for dock space with the lumber mill. Eventually another dock was built. But as roads developed and the lumber business died, Harrisville shrank to a permanent core of its former existence.

Today you will find many old buildings with false fronts—some abandoned, some revitalized into attractive business, some barely being maintained. You'll also find the old mill pond and the ruins of the original mill. And while you're exploring the rest of the town and its past, see if you can find the old train station. I won't tell you where it is, but it's not where you would expect it to be. My thanks to *GLC*'s senior editor Ken Miller, who not only wrote this story originally in our May, 1995 issue, but who also found the train station.

Harbor Hessel, Michigan
Location West Entrance Buoy: L45°57.8'N, Lo84°27.1'W
Dockage Hessel Municipal Marina

Places to Stay Law Cabins 906-484-3924, Lindberg Cottages 906-484-2440, Loreli Lodges Log Cabins 906-484-2636, Heron's Point Resort 906-484-2623, Sunset Resort 906-484-3913

Places to Eat The Hessel Bay Inn

Hessel is a sleepy little harbor in northern Lake Huron at the eastern end of Michigan's Upper Peninsula. This is a rustic destination but not lacking in any sense. There is only the municipal marina for transient dockage. There are cottages and cabins to rent if you're looking for shore-side accommodation. The Hessel Bay inn is the only eatery in town, but the food is good and the view is wonderful. Like Ken Miller said, you won't lack for the necessities of life here.

But wait, there's more. Hessel is also home to one of the most famous boat shows in all the Great Lakes. But put your checkbook away. The Hessel Antique Wooden Boat Show is an opportunity for the proud owners of classic runabouts to show off their brightwork and chrome engines. Every kind of classic craft imaginable is represented here. For a schedule of events call the Les Cheneaux Historical Society at 906-484-2821.

As long as you've got the Historical Society on the phone, get directions to their museum. It is one of the finest in the Upper Peninsula and brings to life a history very much forgotten by the general population. These beautiful Les Cheneaux Islands were enjoyed for their rustic scenery long before modern tourism took over. Over a hundred years ago these islands were dotted with luxury hotels and resorts along the lines of the Grand Hotel on Mackinac Island. Here you can anchor, picnic, and enjoy the deep waters between the islands.

Harbor Hilton Beach, Ontario
Location Breakwater Entrance: L46°15.62'N, Lo83°53.32'W
Dockage Hilton Beach Marina

Places to Stay Hilton Beach Hotel 705-246-2204, Hilton Harbor Resort 705-246-0063

Places to Eat Chez Jeannine Restaurant, Hilton Beach Hotel's Dining Lounge

Hilton Beach, Ontario, is located on the northeast corner of St. Joseph Island at the western end of Canada's famed North Channel cruising grounds. This is a small rustic town with only the very basic amenities. Sandra Swanson listed the local post office and the local automotive repair facility here when she discussed the local shopping experience. It's that small!

But there are a few unique experiences to share here. First of all, is the very beautiful scenery. The second experience to enjoy has to be the laid-back life style. Things do not move fast here! Third on the list has to be the riding lawn mowers. Yes, most locals show up at the post office aboard their riding lawn mowers. It seems it's cheaper to ride the John Deere to town than drive the car.

But above all, the most fun thing to do in Hilton Beach is to watch the tourists dock, and the old men score their efforts. The local hotel is at the end of the main dock. A row of rocking chairs sits on the deck of the hotel. On any given afternoon the old men rock away the hours and watch the transients dock. After a new boat comes in, they hold up cards much like the Olympics and score the skipper. But don't let that make you nervous!

Harbor   Honey Harbour, Ontario
Location   Canadian Chart #2202, Southeast Corner of Georgian Bay
             near the terminus of the Trent-Severn Waterway
Dockage   Honey Harbor Boat Club, Admiral's Marina,
             South Bay Cove Marina

Places to Stay   South Bay Cove Marina 705-756-3333, The Elk's Hide-A-Way
                    705-756-2993

Places to Eat   Numero Uno, Delawana Inn, Top of the Cove Restaurant

Honey Harbor is not really a community, it's an extension of Port Severn, Ontario, near the northern terminus of the Trent-Severn Waterway. You just leave the last lock, come out around the corner to your right and you're there, sort of. You can also take the bridge over from Port Severn.

Either way you'll find more of a resort community than a retail-oriented business environment. There are resorts here at which to stay and a couple of marinas. If you look around real hard you'll find the post office, a general store and even a library. There's also a bed and breakfast that triples as the local bakery and the pizzeria! One of the nicest facilities here has to be South Bay Cove Marina. You can park your boat, enjoy fine dining, Cuban cigars, the morning paper and even cable TV at your dock.

While there may not be a lot here, that's the idea. You are in the extreme southern reaches of Canada's Georgian Bay. Most of what is around you is solid rock, peppered with determined trees and hardy plant life. The sunsets here are breathtaking, and according to our own Don Stockton, the sunrises aren't too shabby either. You come here to relax, and the isolation and majesty of these surroundings make this a perfect place to do just that!

But don't take our word for it. A well-known American entrepreneur spent many summer holidays here with his family. At his passing he left his boat to the keeper who had maintained it for him in his absence all those years. The boat is still here, named the *Kittyhawk*. The man was Orville Wright.

Harbor Kagawong, Ontario
Location Northern Marina Wharf Light: L45°54'34"N, Lo82°15'39"W
Dockage Northern Marina, The Government Dock

Places to Stay The Bay View B&B 705-282-0741, The Bridal Veil B&B 705-282-3300

Places to Eat Kagawong Stonehouse Restaurant & Bar, Farmer's Market

Kagawong is a rustic remote harbor on Manitoulin Island in Canada's North Channel. There is not much here—a couple of B&Bs and a couple of restaurants are about all you'll find. There are two very nice historic buildings in town. St. John's Church and the Old Pulp Mill, which is now a community center. You can charter a boat here at Maple Ridge Yacht Charters (705-282-3330) or restock your galley at the local grocery store. If you come for exciting shopping and night life, you will have made a terrible mistake.

However, if you come to see some of the most wonderful, rustic scenery of the Canadian Shield, you couldn't have picked a better stop. The harbor of Mudge Bay is beautiful. The rocky shoreline surrounding the area is splendid. But the most beautiful place in town is nearby Bridal Veil Falls. You can follow the creek from the marina back into the woods a short distance to where the woods opens to a lovely grotto with a gentle waterfall running year round. It's not Niagara, but these and the wild raspberries you may find along the way may very well be the highlight of your North Channel visit.

Harbor Killarney, Ontario
Location Killarney West Light: L45°58'20"N, Lo81°29'20"W
Dockage Municipal Dock, Sportsman's Inn, Killarney Mountain Lodge, Gateway Marine, Killarney Marine & Rigging

Places to Stay Sportsman's Inn 705-287-2411, Channel View B&B 705-287-2797, Killarney Mountain Lodge 1-800-461-1117

Places to Eat Mr. Perch

Killarney is located in the heart of Canada's well-known North Channel in northern Lake Huron. This is a typical teaming hub of activity in the famed rustic cruising grounds.

The best things to do here involve enjoying nature and the area's most spectacular scenery. In fact Killarney Provincial Park is close at hand and there are a number of local businesses ready to meet your needs when it comes to enjoying the great outdoors. You can hire about any level of assistance you want from completely guided wilderness packages to bike rentals, kayak rentals and simple map sales. Either way, the park is something to see and promises to bring the naturalist great joy.

If you prefer to stay in town you can shop at the General Store, although most of what they sell relates to exploring the park. Or you can have lunch at Mr. Perch.

Mr. Perch is perhaps the most famous restaurant in the North Channel. It's an old yellow school bus that no longer runs. It's parked permanently near the docks and folks line up every day for what many claim to be the finest fish and chips on the planet. You buy them right through the open window and enjoy them wherever you wish.

Lake Huron

Harbor Kincardine, Ontario
Location Kincardine Harbour Mouth: L44°10'42"N, Lo81°38'38"W
Dockage Government Dock, Kincardine Yacht Club

Places to Stay Harbour House B&B 519-396-8787, Victoria B&B 519-396-4423, Lakefront B&B 519-396-4345, Wickens House 519-396-3163

Places to Eat Contact: Kincardine Tourist Information Center 519-396-2731

Kincardine, Ontario, is a wonderful mix of old and new. Located on the Lake Huron shore of the southern Bruce Peninsula, there has been an active harbor here for over 150 years. The harbor even looks old (though perfectly maintained). The lighthouse that dominates the dockage area is typical of the Canadian wood-style construction, but is unique in its location. This is an eight-sided wooden tower built on top of a rather ordinary stone structure. The stone structure served as the keeper's quarters then, and as a museum now. Originally, before it was part of a lighthouse, this building was the Walker and Henry Distillery.

Up the bluff from the very old harbor is a very new and modern town. Here you'll find every modern convenience you can imagine and shops of all kinds to explore. But it's not all new. You will find the Malcom mansion in town, a perfectly restored Victorian structure that is now home to Chamber Music Kincardine, a group that offers live performances in the spring and fall of the year. You should also visit the Bluewater Summer Playhouse to see some of the best summer-stock theater on this shore. Call them for a current schedule at 519-369-5722.

Every Saturday evening there's a parade through the center of town featuring the Kincardine Scottish, the local bagpipe band. These folks are something to see! After the parade, one piper goes down to the waterfront and performs a solo concert as the Phantom Piper, in memory of Donald Sinclair. Many years ago Sinclair and his family were on a boat in a storm trying to find the harbor. He played the pipes on the deck and to their relief a piper on shore repeated the refrain. They followed the sound and were saved. After that, every night, Sinclair would "pipe the sun down" in the harbor in thanks for the piper who had saved him. Today the tradition lives on.

Harbor Lexington, Michigan
Location West Breakwater Light: L43°16.1'N, Lo82°31.8'W
Dockage Lexington Municipal DNR Dock

Places to Stay Britannia House B&B 810-359-5772, The Governor's Inn B&B 810-359-5770, The Powell House B&B 810-359-5533

Places to Eat The Cadillac House, Wimpy's Place, Steiss' Village Inn, L&J Restaurant

Lexington, Michigan, is one of Lake Huron's fastest growing and more popular destinations. Located just twenty miles north of Port Huron in the southern end of the lake, this once sleepy, forgotten lakeshore village has experienced a tremendous rebirth in tourist trade.

This is a State of Michigan DNR Harbor of Refuge with a most adequate stone breakwall protecting the harbor from the open lake. There is a playground right next to the marina and a sandy area just outside the breakwall, used as a beach.

To get to the village, there are two routes. Walk up the street which is a very steep hill, or take the multi-tiered stairway that begins in the park and ends on top of the bluff behind the main drag. The stairway also has resting platforms which are really vantage points from which to enjoy the wonderful expanse of Lake Huron. I've stood there and watched storms roll in off the lake. As long as you take cover soon enough, it's a wonderful experience.

The village is full of small shops and boutiques selling resort clothing and unusual collectibles. One shop called Weekends sells only things you might want to fill your spare time with, over the weekend! They also often have live entertainment of the gentle kind in their garden down the back stairs. When I say entertainment, they have hosted anything from harpists, flutists and the occasional piano player. There are also a number of very good restaurants in town. At the top of this list put the locally famous Cadillac House, located at the top of the hill at the traffic light (yes, they have one).

Harbor Lime Island, Michigan
Location Rocks at Harbor Entrance: L46°05.2'N, Lo84°00.8'W
Dockage Along the old coal dock

Places to Stay Rustic destination, contact: Michigan DNR's Soo Office at 906-635-5281

Places to Eat On your boat

Lime Island is a rustic destination located in the St. Mary's river between Lakes Huron and Superior. Facilities have just begun to develop here. Currently, cruising boats can tie up at the old coal dock if space is not available at the limited number of finger docks. Wherever you tie up, it's currently free.

The area of the coal dock has been seeded and now is a very nice picnic area for all to use. Freighters glide by just two hundred feet from the mouth of the harbor making for a picturesque setting. The pile of rocks near the harbor entrance is all that remains of the *Rome,* a steamship that burned to the waterline in 1909. The local islanders filled the wreck with limestone, creating the harbor's first breakwall.

Around the island, old buildings are starting to be restored as sort of an open-air museum. Also, wooden boardwalks have been built to accommodate hikers and campers. There are a number of tent platforms along the boardwalk trail ready for campers to use without damaging the natural environment. There are also a very limited number of rental cabins on the island, but you will have to contact the DNR at the number above concerning availability. There is an old farmhouse on the island that was dragged here from the mainland, across the ice in the winter of 1910. There have been suggestions offered that the farmhouse would make a perfect bed and breakfast.

Lime island was a center for the production of lime in this end of the Lakes, and on-going archeological digs continue to locate more historic industrial sites.

Harbor Little Current, Ontario
Location Narrow Island Light: L45°59'27"N, Lo81°58'43"W
Dockage Little Wally's Dock Service, Boyle Marine, Harbor View Marina, Spider Bay Marina

Places to Stay Bridgeway Motel 705-368-2230, Hawberry Motel 705-368-3388, Anchor Inn 705-368-2023, Little Current Motel 705-368-2882, Wagon Wheel Motel 705-368-2805

Places to Eat Old English Pantry, Anchor Inn, Senorita del Salsa, Edgewater Inn, Garry's Family Restaurant, Manitou Chicken Hut

Ken Miller, who has visited this destination many times, has always described it as the "Hub of the North Channel." That's because of its central location and well-rounded business district. The North Channel is famous for wilderness-like anchorages and rustic scenery. Yet just a few hours away by very slow boat, you can be in a pocket of civilization to recharge your batteries (literally) and restock the galley.

The cruising boater will find everything he needs here from showers (at just $1.50 each) to ice cream (about the same price), and of course everything in between. There are also restaurants, a small collection of shops and a very nice walkway along the Government Dock.

The best way to describe Little Current is as a trading post. It provides many of the services that were needed back in the frontier days, except now they take cash and credit cards instead of beaver pelts.

Harbor Mackinac Island, Michigan
Location The New Round Island Passage Light: L45°50′37″N, Lo84°36′55″W
Dockage The State Docks

Places to Stay The Grand Hotel 1-800-33-GRAND, Chippewa Hotel 1-800-241-3341, The Hotel Iroquois 906-847-3321, The Windermere 906-847-3301, The Lakeview Hotel 906-847-3384, The Island House 906-847-3347, The Pontiac Lodge 906-847-3364, many more

Places to Eat The Pink Pony, Harborview Dining Room, Horn's Gaslight Bar, The Carriage House, The Governor's Dining Room

What can you not say about Mackinac Island? This is perhaps the choice dream destination for boaters in the Great Lakes, and the correct pronunciation is Mackinaw. The heart of town is filled with fudge shops, souvenir stores and all kinds of bars, pubs, eateries and restaurants. Among the most famous are the Pink Pony Bar (if you're a sailboat racer) and the Grand Hotel (if you're a fan of decadent luxury).

The island has a long and historic past. The fort at the top of the hill was built by the British, ceded to the Americans after the Revolution, recaptured during the War of 1812, and again given back to the Americans in the Treaty of Ghent. Today the fort is a major tourist attraction with costumed interpreters and demonstrations of firearms and cannons from the nineteenth century.

This is also the site of the famous experiments by famed Dr. William Beaumont, the first man to observe the digestive process in a living human—courtesy of a rough and tumble French Canadian who was shot in the stomach in a bar fight. The wound failed to heal correctly and allowed the good doctor to see directly into the human stomach.

On a more settled note, the lighthouse on the small island across from the harbor is the Old Round Island Light. If it (and several other sites around town) look familiar to you, it's because the romantic movie *Somewhere In Time* starring Christopher Reeve and Jane Seymour was shot on location here. The famed Grand Hotel and the lighthouse figured prominently in the film as they do in the daily life of the island.

Harbor Mackinaw City, Michigan
Location Outer Breakwater Light: L45°46.9'N, Lo83°43.2'W
Dockage Mackinaw City Municipal Marina

Places to Stay Starlight Budget Inn 616-436-5959,
Also, contact : Mackinaw City Chamber 616-436-5574

Places to Eat Audie's, Scalawag's Whitefish & Chips, The Admirals Table,
Crossroads Restaurant & Lounge, Mario's Ristorante

Mackinaw City is one of the premier destinations on the Great Lakes and is located at the tip of Michigan's mitten at the southern end of the Mackinac Bridge. This is a great departure point for harbors in the U.P., on Mackinac Island, or really—this is a fine place to stay in its own right!

There are now effectively two main streets in town. The old main drag, Division Street, is filled with gift shops, a couple of small museums, a couple of famous bars and some pancake restaurants. It has retained the same small-town charm for decades. Running parallel with that is the new Mackinaw Crossings development. This Disney-like village is home to shops and eateries filled with up-scale collectibles and attractions. Both are interesting shopping experiences.

The biggest attractions to see include Historic Fort Michelimackinac on the west end of the bridge entrance. This was originally a fortified French trading post that was later captured by the British and operated as a military stronghold. A massacre of the fort's garrison at the hands of the local Indians forced the British to retreat to Mackinac Island and build a fort there. Today the fort is an open museum with costumed interpreters recreating daily life as it was so many years ago.

Also, visit the historic Mackinaw Point Lighthouse. This is a grand old structure and is preserved on park grounds at the foot of the bridge. The light is currently dark, made obsolete by improved offshore aids and the lights of the Mackinac Bridge.

Watch this destination for the new Great Lakes Lighthouse Museum to be built on the old State Dock. It will include this lighthouse as part of its facilities. To find out more about this exciting new attraction call 616-436-3333.

Harbor Manitowaning, Ontario
Location The Manitowaning Light: L45°44'42"N, Lo81°48'29"W
Dockage The Municipal Marina

Places to Stay The Manitowaning Lodge 705-859-3136

Places to Eat Norisle Bistro, Manitowaning Lodge Dining Room, Wayside Restaurant, Schooner's, Van's Drive-In

 Manitowaning is a quiet Canadian harbor in the eastern end of the North Channel. But for such a small place they sure have packed in a lot of neat things to see and do.

As you enter the harbor you will see an unusual lighthouse. Unusual in the Lakes but a common sight in the North Channel. All it is, is a four-sided wooden pyramid with a couple of windows and a lantern room. Not very exciting but very well built. This one has been here since 1886.

In the harbor you can't help but notice the ship tied up along the harbor wall. This is the *Norisle*. For many years this was the slow but steady steamship that made the regular ferry run between Tobermory and South Baymouth. In 1974 she was replaced by the *Chi-Cheemaun* and retired here. Now she is a floating museum (when's the last time you saw the inside of a real steamship with a triple expansion engine?) and also a very fine restaurant. You can spend the afternoon exploring the ship and it's state-rooms, and the evening dining in the Norisle Bistro.

Right next to the *Norisle* is the old warehouse for the old roller mill that's just up the street. The warehouse has been refurbished and is now home to the Burns Wharf Community Theatre. Here you will enjoy all kinds of live stage productions during the summer season. The roller mill is now a museum open to the public. Other old buildings of note include the old town jail and sheriff's office which is also a museum, and St. Paul's Anglican Church at the top of the bluff. St. Paul's in now completely restored and is the oldest Anglican church in Ontario.

Harbor Meldrum Bay, Ontario
Location Mississagi Strait Light: L45°53'36"N, Lo83°13'30"W
Dockage Meldrum Bay Marina 705-283-3252,
Whitesea Cottages and Charters 705-283-3450

Places to Stay Whitesea Cottages and Charters: 705-283-3450, Meldrum Bay
Inn, Meldrum Bay Bed & Breakfast

Places to Eat Sunrise Grill, Meldrum Bay Inn

Meldrum Bay is a quiet rustic harbor on the northwest corner of
Canada's Manitoulin Island. For many cruisers, this is the easiest
entry and quickest access to the famed cruising grounds of the
North Channel.

Eateries are rather limited. The Sunrise Grill is casual dining outdoors
while the Meldrum Bay Inn offers a dining room. Also, townsfolk bring
fresh homemade baked goods down to the docks daily and sell them to
the boaters, a tradition that dates back to the days of the passenger steamers in this part of the lakes.

There is not much to do here either, but what there is, is certainly in
the "Don't miss" category. The Net Shed Museum at the waterfront displays rare photographs and artifacts that retell the hamlet's past as a fishing village and sawmill town. The wreck of the barge *Winslow* is at the end
of the stone jetty near here and is very popular with SCUBA divers. You
can also take a dinghy tour of Meldrum Bay and discover sites and locations not visible to the casual observer including two sawmills and other
shipwrecks. Maps are available at the Net Shed Museum.

Lighthouse buffs will enjoy the Mississagi lighthouse just five miles
west of the village. The lighthouse is open to visitors from mid-May to
mid-September and there is no admission charge. The light dates back to
1873 and is reportedly one of the several alleged wreck sites of the *Griffin*.
This was the first sailing ship on the Great Lakes and belonged to the
famous explorer La Salle. The ship, along with a treasure of furs and pelts,
disappeared without a trace in 1679.

Lake Huron

Harbor Midland, Ontario
Location Midland Bay Shoal Light: L44°45.7'N, Lo79°53.5'W
Dockage Midland Town Dock, Midland Marina, Bayport Marina,
Wye River Heritage Marina

Places to Stay Best Western Highland Inn 705-526-9307, Comfort Inn 705-526-2090, Chalet Motel 705-526-6571, Park Villa Motor Motel 705-526-2219, Shamrock Motel 705-526-7851

Places to Eat Boat Works Restaurant & Bar, Mario's World Famous Eatery, Riv Bistro, Sha-Na-Na's Dine-N-Dance, Dobbie's

Midland, Ontario, is one of Canada's nicest small cities. Located on the southern shore of Georgian Bay, their waterfront area has a more park-like appearance than some towns' parks! This is a neat and clean, well-maintained community and here's a word to the wise: They do expect the same from their tourists! If you don't remove your ball cap at the dinner table, don't be offended if your waitress asks you to do so.

Midland has a long history from grist mill settlement to lumber town to agricultural center, and even to a shipbuilding capitol. But today the town depends more on tourism, and the history they like to share the most took place before these shores were called Midland.

Visit the Huronia Museum and Huron Indian Village while you're here. This is perhaps the most complete display of native life with the Huron Tribe anywhere. There are artifacts to see as well as re-created structures and facilities to tour. The Huron Indians were among the fiercest tribe ever to walk the shores of any Great Lake—this lifestyle is what they so strongly defended.

Later came the Jesuits and you can see how they lived by visiting Sainte Marie Among the Hurons. This is an interactive museum complete with costumed interpreters who re-create daily life as it was in this seventeenth-century French mission.

Other sites of interest include the Martyr's Shrine and the Wye Marsh Wildlife Centre. I also want to be sure to mention the local sight-seeing cruises aboard the *Miss Midland*. Here you can tour the beautiful 30,000-island area while someone else drives. The tour ship is completely handicap accessible and the sunset cruise includes entertainment and dancing.

117

Harbor Milford Haven, Ontario
Location Kosh-Ka-Wong Point Light: L46°08.0'N, Lo83°48.5'W
Dockage None, anchor in the natural harbor

Places to Stay On your boat

Places to Eat On your boat

This is another of those rustic natural harbors in the northern reaches of Lake Huron of which *GLC*'s Bruce Preston is so very fond. There are no facilities here. No docks, no electricity and no water. You must be completely self-sufficient on your boat.

But that has never stopped Bruce and Phyllis from enjoying themselves and their surroundings. The Preston's believe this is one of the finest anchorages from which to view the northern lights. From here they dance across the sky and almost touch the water.

While there are a few private cabins and "camps" on the island, there is an abundant amount of wildlife to watch from the comfort of your dinghy or anchored boat. Deer come right up to the shore to drink, birds of all kinds find homes in the thick trees and many more of Nature's creatures wrestle their existence from the land or the water in full view.

The Prestons also mention the stars here—there are a lot of them, and they have yet to count them all.

Harbor Oscoda, Michigan
Location North Breakwall Light: L44°24′25″N, Lo83°18′58″W
Dockage Main Pier Marina, Bunyan Town Marina, North East Michigan Marina, Fellows Marina, Oscoda Yacht Club

Places to Stay Contact: Oscoda & Au Sable Chamber 517-739-7322

Places to Eat Wiltse's Brew Pub, The Pack House, Ye Old Toby Jug, Charbonneau's Family Restaurant

Oscoda is a very active recreational fishing harbor on the eastern coast of Michigan just north of Saginaw Bay. Sailors beware, there is a fixed highway bridge over the river that will permit only the shortest of day sailors to pass. However, there are transient facilities at the mouth of the river and the bridge is arched and high to accommodate most large powerboats found at the local yacht club on the other side of the bridge.

Once docked, the town is a nice walk up the highway, over the bridge. The local chamber is working on a courtesy van that will dash you into town and back with a simple phone call, but availability is season to season. You can stop in at the chamber office right in the parking lot of the marina and at the very least, they will hook you up with the local public transit.

There are lots of stores in town including a Hallmark shop and two, count 'em, two hardware stores! Of course there are a good number of other shops to explore and some wonderful eateries to enjoy. Don't miss the Pack House located in an historic structure on the north edge of town, and Charbonneau's Family Restaurant on the river. Charbonneau's Swiss steak is the best I have had in a long time!

Also, don't miss the beautiful Au Sable Riverwalk through the trees and deep ravines inland from the lake. Historically, Oscoda and her twin city Au Sable were burned to the ground during the great forest fires at the turn of the century. While Oscoda recovered, Au Sable exists today pretty much in name only.

Harbor Owen Sound, Ontario
Location Harbor Channel Buoy, T-12: L44°35.2′N, Lo80°56.1′W
Dockage Georgian Yacht Club 519-376-0047, West Bank Boat Launch
519-376-9890, Owen Sound Marina 519-3761-3999

Places to Stay The Gallery House B&B 519-371-6186, The Company Motor Inn
519-371-2266, The Destination Inn 519-371-9297, Holiday Inn
529-376-1551

Places to Eat Baker Bob's, The Peking Garden, Harrison Park Inn,
Pepi's Italian Dining, Stephanie's Fine Dining,

Owen Sound is a small quaint city on the southern shore of Canada's Georgian Bay. You'll find a thriving downtown district with wonderful shops and stores in perfectly maintained storefronts just a short walk from the marina. And what a walk it is! The Inner Harbour Walkway connects downtown with Kelso Beach and all points in between.

Walking is considered excellent exercise here and this walkway is just the beginning. Break out the hiking boots and explore the famous Bruce Trail, a naturalist's escape that takes you past Indian Falls, Jones Falls and the most popular stop on the trail, Inglis Falls.

As long as you're walking, Owen Sound has a number of museums to visit too. The Billy Bishop Heritage Museum is really the boyhood home of the famous WWI flying ace. Here, many of the Bishop family belongings and furnishings from that era have been preserved, making this museum an excellent snapshot in time.

Also, visit the Tom Thompson Memorial Art Gallery. Tom Thompson was one of Canada's most revered naturalist painters and a member of the famed Group of Seven who set trends and broke rules for Canadian expressive art a century ago.

The city also offers the County of Grey-Owen Sound Museum and the Owen Sound Marine-Rail Museum. Both do an excellent job at representing their respective historic specialties.

Owen Sound is a friendly place to visit, vacation—even live. Ask anybody who's there!

Harbor Port Austin, Michigan
Location Breakwater Light: L44°03.2'N, Lo82°59.6'W
Dockage Port Austin State Dock

Places to Stay Garfield Inn 517-738-5254, Questover Inn B&B 517-738-5253, Lake Street Manor B&B 517-738-7720

Places to Eat The Garfield Inn, The Bank, The Farm, Chuck & Jane's Restuarant, The Sportsman's Inn, Captain's Quarters, Kornetti's Kitchen, My Brother's Place

Port Austin is easy to find. It's located at the very tip of Michigan's thumb guarding the entrance to Saginaw Bay. If you come in off the water you will be greeted by the historic Port Austin Reef Light. This unique offshore lighthouse is not built on a crib. Instead it's built right on the granite and sandstone reef. You step off the lighthouse, you get wet. You get too close, you get sunk.

If you approach by highway you will first encounter some of the older and more majestic buildings in town. I say majestic because one of the first is the historic Garfield Inn. This perfectly restored Victorian mansion is not only a classic representative of its era, but it is also one of the best restaurants in town and provides first-class accommodations too. The name comes from James Garfield, a regular visitor here in the years before he was elected president. It is rumored that the visits of this congressman-clergyman-turned-president were to accommodate a romantic affair, but back then, people didn't publish the details of such things.

Another landmark in the area is The Bank. Nope, it's not the one they have now with the drive-up window. This one dates back well into the Victorian era and now serves the community as one of its finest restaurants. What, your bank doesn't serve up prime rib and shrimp scampi? Too bad!

Keeping with the trend of simplistic names is another of Michigan's best eateries: The Farm. It really used to be a farm but now its reputation for fine dining is known throughout the Lakes.

Once you tire of eating and admiring old buildings, Port Austin is famous for its beach and local perch fishing—among the finest on the lakes!

Harbor Port Elgin, Ontario
Location Lower Range Light: L44°26′39″N, Lo81°24′13″W
Dockage Port Elgin Municipal Docks

Places to Stay Gowanlock Country Guest Home 519-389-5256,
Spruchall B&B 519-832-9835

Places to Eat Kleo's Family Restaurant

Port Elgin lies on the Lake Huron shore of Ontario's Bruce Peninsula approximately twenty miles north of Kincardine. If you want to sound like a local, or at least an informed tourist, Elgin is pronounced with a hard G as in again, not a soft G as in the alcoholic beverage.

While the village is close at hand and offers provincial shops and restaurants to enjoy, and while there are certainly shady, picturesque residential neighborhoods to enjoy, the real attraction is the harbor itself. They have one of the nicest sand beaches on this shore, bar none. Also, there is lots of activity at the beach including all kinds of concessions and even a gift shop. But the biggest attraction has to be the Port Elgin & North Shore Railroad. This is a miniature 24-gauge steam train that takes train buffs of all ages on a one-mile ride around the harbor and back. The cost is just $3 Canadian. A scenic bargain.

Port Elgin also gets my vote for the most caring city in Canada. On the night we lost our good friend and co-founding editor Jon Kaplan in a tragic car accident, it was the Port Elgin police that located *GLC*'s Ken Miller in the marina. They then stationed an officer to keep a watchful eye on Ken until I could arrive by automobile to rush him home for the funeral. I arrived at 6 A.M. and called the police station for directions to the marina. I never got directions, I got a police escort to the harbor, the marina and right down the dock to Ken's boat. They did this out of caring and we have never forgotten their kindness. This is a community who takes care of their own, and those who come their way. You will be safe here.

Lake Huron

Harbor Port Sanilac, Michigan
Location Port Sanilac Light: L43°25.8'N, Lo82°32.4'W
Dockage Port Sanilac Harbor Commission Docks, public
Port Sanilac Marina, private

Places to Stay Raymond House B&B 810-622-8800

Places to Eat Mary's Diner, Sanilac Bakery & Deli, Raymond House Inn,
The Bellaire

Port Sanilac is just thirty miles up Michigan's Lake Huron coast from Port Huron. This small village has the honor of being the very first Michigan DNR Harbor of Refuge, dedicated in 1951. You'll find pictures of this event in the newly updated harbormaster's office on the hill.

There are a few small shops to explore in town, but at the top of your list put the Lake Huron Shipwreck and Maritime Center. This is a recently opened non-profit museum located in a small store front near the center of the village. It brings back to life the maritime history of the Sanilac Shores area and displays artifacts from some of the more famous wrecks now protected in the Sanilac Shores Diving Preserve

If you come to town with SCUBA tanks, this is one of the most popular diving sites in the Great Lakes. This is also one of the shores hardest hit by the Great Storm of 1913—to this day the most vicious storm to ever rip the Great Lakes. The wreck of the *Regina* is just a few miles from the harbor and less than three miles off shore. She disappeared without a trace during the big storm and was not discovered until the mid-1980s.

Also don't miss the local lighthouse. It's a private residence and has been for a very long time, but the Coast Guard has access to the tower to maintain the automated light. It's a classic shoreside beacon on the bluff just on the south side of the harbor. A tree lined street leads up to the white picket fence that surrounds the grounds.

Harbor Presque Isle, Michigan
Location Red Nun Buoy #2: L45°20.5'N, Lo83°28.5'W
Dockage State Docks inside the breakwall 517-595-3069

Places to Stay On your boat

Places to Eat The Portage Restaurant

Presque Isle, Michigan, is just one of many places with this same name in the Great Lakes. It's French for "almost an island," and it seems they found several places like this in their explorations. There's a joke that goes, wherever the French went they named it Presque Isle. Right behind them came the British and they named every place York (Toronto was originally called York too). Then came the Americans and they named every place McDonalds.

All humor aside, Presque Isle is a Michigan DNR Harbor of Refuge not far from Alpena. There's really nothing to do here but relax and take in the scenery, with the exception of visiting the lighthouses.

There are two. Both are open as museums. The Old Presque Isle Lighthouse dates back to 1840 and is just a short walk from the docks. The New Presque Isle Lighthouse is more in the center of the small peninsula and was commissioned in 1870. There is a wonderful collection of old ships' bells and whistles at the newer lighthouse. Incidentally, both are reputed to be haunted!

A mysterious light comes on in the lantern room of the old lighthouse without electricity or explanation. In the new lighthouse the sobbing sounds of a woman can be heard late at night—supposedly the cries of a past keeper's wife who was repeatedly locked in the keeper's quarters while he strayed off to visit his mistress.

Lake Huron

Harbor Rogers City, Michigan
Location Harbor Channel Lighted Buoy 1: L45°25.5'N, Lo83°48.4'W
Dockage Rogers City Municipal Marina

Places to Stay Contact: The Rogers City Chamber 517-734-2535

Places to Eat Nowicki's Sausage Shoppe, Black Bear Cafe, The Buoy
Restaurant, Jason's Gaslight Lounge,
The International Bar & Grill

Rogers City, between Cheboygan and Alpena, Michigan, has always been a town of people who worked the lake. Yes, there is a very nice recreational harbor here, now complete with a new southern breakwall that does much to smooth out the waves in a big blow. There is also a wonderful business district that curves up from the marina and includes restaurants, hotels and small shops. But this is not a town dedicated to the tourist trade. These are people who work the lake.

There are a good number of fishing charters in the recreational harbor, and that's about as commercial as things get. (And tell me these guys don't work hard for their money!) Many more bread winners work in nearby Calcite Harbor where the big freighters come in to load up with limestone for the cement trade. Then there are a good number of citizens who actually work on the ships themselves. This has always been a good seafaring town.

And because of that, there is a memorial in the park to honor the dead of the *Carl D. Bradley*. The *Bradley* was a 638-foot bulk carrier that was broken in half by a vicious Lake Michigan Storm in 1958. There were only two survivors. Of the 35 crewmen on the ship, fully 25 of them lived in Rogers City. This tragedy left many broken families in this town and eventually led to the dedication of the memorial.

One more sight to see in the area is the Presque Isle County Historical Society Museum on the south side of town. It is located in the home of former Michigan Limestone Operations president, Mr. Carl D. Bradley himself.

Harbor Sarnia, Ontario
Location Entrance to Sarnia Bay Marina: L42°56.5'N, Lo82°24.6'W
Dockage Sarnia Bay Marina, Sarnia Yacht Club, Lake Huron Yachts

Places to Stay The Drawbridge Inn 519-337-7571, The Harbourfront Inn 519-337-3888, Holiday Inn 1-800-265-0316

Places to Eat Kelsey's, Stokes Bar & Grill, Samuel's, Brittany Arms English Pub, Ups and Downs English Pub, Giresi's Pizza

Sarnia sits on the Canadian shore across from Port Huron, Michigan, at the southern end of Lake Huron. A small city, but one well-equipped with several modern marina facilities.

The business district is a pleasure to visit too, with perfectly landscaped office buildings and more glass and steel than you will find anywhere else along this area of the shore. It's a very cosmopolitan atmosphere with all the leading shops and retail stores close at hand here and in the Eaton Centre Mall.

The waterfront is managed by the St. Clair Parkway Commission and maintains several landscaped parks and waterfront picnic areas. Perhaps the most used park in all of Sarnia is Centennial Park which is the scene of several festivals over the summer season. For an upcoming schedule of events, contact Sarnia Community Services at 519-862-2291.

Of special interest, they have an annual celebration called Rum Runner Days, remembering all the liquid product exported across the river during the existence of Prohibition.

Harbor Sebewaing, Michigan
Location Sebewaing River Channel Entrance: L43°45.1'N, Lo83°31.3'W
Dockage Sebewaing Harbor Marina

Places to Stay Contact: Sebewaing Chamber of Commerce 517-883-9676

Places to Eat The Sugar Creek Restaurant

Sebewaing is a small town along the southern shore of Lake Huron's Saginaw Bay. This is shallow, marshy water that doesn't accommodate big sailing vessels very well. In fact when the first settlers came here in 1851 they were put off the ship on Lone Tree Island at the mouth of the river. The party of 40 men, women and children stayed here for three weeks until local boats—mostly canoes belonging to the local Native Americans—could be procured to bring them ashore.

With dredging and hard work, the harbor had become prosperous in the late 1800s. Still, the river was narrow enough that ships couldn't turn once they entered. A pair of turning slips were dug allowing boats to reverse direction much like you would in your neighbor's driveway. Remember, much of this traffic was sail powered and had to be pushed into and out of the turning slips with pike poles.

Today this is a quiet village with "frontier" storefronts housing shops directly out of some Norman Rockwell painting. There's even a dime store that still sells penny candy!

There are also two museums in town to note. The Historical Museum is located in the old City Hall and faithfully presents the community's past to its present visitors. The Great Lakes Lore Maritime Museum is relatively new and is dedicated to the 100 plus years of shipping in the harbor.

Also note the historic old firehouse (Firehouse #1) in the heart of town. This is indeed a wooden firehouse. The tower is called a "hose tower" and was very important to those who maintained the equipment over a century ago.

Harbor South Baymouth, Ontario
Location South Baymouth Range: L45°33'28"N, Lo82°00'48"W
Dockage South Baymouth Marina

Places to Stay South Bay Resort 705-859-3106, Happy Acres B&B 705-859-3453, The Buck Horn Motel 705-859-3635, The Wigwam 705-859-3646, The Huron Motor Lodge 1-800-387-2756

Places to Eat The South Baymouth Cafe

South Baymouth, Ontario, is on the southeastern corner of Lake Huron's Manitoulin Island. There's not a lot here. It's really rather rustic and quaint. There are a couple of nice eateries and some really nice scenery to see. So why is it here?

This is a really well-protected harbor along a particularly hazardous shore. It's the closest point to the Canadian mainland coming across Georgian Bay from the Bruce Peninsula side. Put two and two together—this is a ferry port. For many years the old steamship *Norisle* plied the waters between here and Tobermory. That trip took hours as the old ship with its triple expansion steam engine could only generate a cruising rpm of 92 and a top speed of about ten knots. Today the *Norisle* is a museum ship and restaurant in nearby Manitowaning, having been replaced by the bigger, faster *Chi-Cheemaun* in 1974.

The ride on the *Chi-Cheemaun* is one of the highlights of your visit here. But if you neglect to visit the Little Red Schoolhouse Museum and take advantage of some of the best charter fishing in northern Lake Huron, you're just not in the spirit of things!

Lake Huron

Harbor Spanish, Ontario
Location Harbor Entry Buoy "UV2": L46°10.9'N, Lo82°22.2'W
Dockage Municipal Marina, Vance's Marina

Places to Stay Vance's Motor Inn

Places to Eat Vance's Motor Inn, Cheryl's Bakery & Coffee Shop

Spanish is a small settlement in the Canadian North Channel, a short distance east of Blind River. Because it is on the mainland and not one of the islands, this makes it a really convenient land yacht destination too. In fact the Trans-Canada Highway runs right through town.

Those who haven't visited Spanish in some time are in for a surprise. First, there is a new marina in town. One hundred and forty slips await anybody (and their brother) to tie up for the night, the week or the whole season. Downtown is different too—not that there is much of a downtown. After all, this is the smallest town in the North Channel. But downtown is a collection of about eight stores. The sidewalks are all new and so are the street lights. Decorative park benches are conveniently located as is the park in the center of town. Here there are shade trees and picnic facilities.

It's a quiet place. But the big attraction here is the surrounding country side. This is the exposed area of the Canadian Shield, geologically speaking. Just within minutes of the harbor are rocky islands that are sheer cliffs above and below the water. When Ken Miller traveled through here he was surprised at huge mountainous boulders that jutted up from the water right next to his boat, and all the time his depth sounder never went below 100 feet. This is rustic wilderness, this is the Grand Canyon filled with water.

Harbor St. Ignace, Michigan
Location Historic Coast Guard Cutter *Maple*: L45°51'58"N, Lo84°40'06"W
Dockage The St. Ignace Marina DNR

Places to Stay Colonial House Inn B&B 906-643-6900, The Boardwalk Inn,
Many more, contact: St. Ignace Chamber 1-800-338-6660

Places to Eat Many, many, many

St. Ignace is perhaps the oldest city in the Great Lakes (there is some controversy), founded in 1671 by Father Jacques Marquette, better known as Pere Marquette. The Jesuit priest was a well-known missionary and explorer in the Great Lakes region. When he died in 1677 he was eventually interred here beneath the foundation of the church he helped found. But eventually the grave site and the church were lost until rediscovered by archeologists in the late 1800s. Now there is a monument marking the gravesite situated in a quiet, shaded park.

The park itself is part of the Huron Walkway, a waterfront park-like pathway that finds its way along the shore and gives the visitor several quiet resting spots at which to enjoy the view and the solitude.

Among things not to miss in town, right next to the municipal dock, is the Coast Guard Cutter *Maple*. The *Maple* is retired now and has been converted into a first-class museum ship. Tours are available depending on the schedule of the volunteer caretakers.

Also don't miss the Museum of Ojibwa Culture next to the Marquette Mission Park. This is along that Huron Walkway mentioned above. In the museum, you will find some really tremendous displays of the history of the Ojibwa People in the Straits. Around the grounds are more displays showing the events of daily life among these people.

One more thing to notice about the Straits is that big bridge from the lower peninsula. "Big Mac" is the largest suspension bridge in the world and brings millions of tourists from the lower peninsula each year.

Harbor Thessalon, Ontario
Location Thessalon Range Light: L46°15'14.3"N, Lo83°33'04.2"W
Dockage The Municipal Marina

Places to Stay The Carolyn Beach Motel 705-842-3330

Places to Eat J.R. Cafe, Ole Cook House, Jimmie's Restaurant, Rickie's Delights, The Carolyn Beach Motel

Thessalon is located at the very western end of the Canadian North Channel. Since most boaters prefer a west to east crossing, this harbor is often referred to as the place where the North Channel begins.

This is a very quiet community in what amounts to the Canadian outback. Yes, its a commercial harbor and a number of freighters do come and go hauling rock and gravel from the quarry across the bay. There is also a good commercial fishing industry here, and if you approach the tugs as they return, most of them well sell you a very fresh fish to cook up for your supper.

Community Day is a Canadian holiday that takes place every weekend during the month of August. Community Day is a great time to visit Thessalon. It's really quite a celebration. There's a parade, but since it's rather short, they usually run it twice. Yes, the lead band turns the block around Main Street and leads everybody through the parade route again. Instant replay!

There are also all kinds of games and activities that take place then too including softball games, kid's games and of course the ever-popular Cow Pattie Bingo. A cow is placed in a fenced area in the park where the ground has been covered with a taped grid pattern. You can buy a square and let the chips fall where they may.

Harbor Tobermory, Ontario
Location Cove Island Light: L45°19'37"N, Lo81°40'07"W
Dockage Little Tub Harbor, Big Tub Harbor

Places to Stay Harbourside Motel 519-596-2422

Places to Eat The Crow's Nest, Ferry Dock Restaurant, The Sweet Shop

Tobermory is located at the end of Canada's Bruce Peninsula. Here you will find beautiful rustic scenery and high limestone cliffs all the way up the coast. The famed Bruce Hiking Trail and the Bruce Peninsula National Park allow you to experience this scenery first hand. The trail winds its way up the peninsula and ends in the harbor town of Tobermory.

The village itself has a small but busy business district based on its tourist economy. What brings the tourists to Tobermory? Two things:

One, the *Chi-Cheemaun* literally brings them to town, and takes them out again too! This is the well-known car ferry that can transport you and your automobile across the opening of Georgian Bay to South Baymouth on Manitoulin Island. It can save you hundreds and hundreds of miles of drive time trying to get there from the other direction.

Also, Five Fathoms National Marine Park brings the tourists here. This rough and rustic coast has claimed many ships from the surface ever since man first ventured out onto these waters. There are many shipwrecks and the water is cold and clear. You can see the wrecks from one of the many dive charters available in town, or there are even glass bottom boat tours for those who don't SCUBA dive. There is a tremendous part of Great Lakes history here for first-hand viewing. Tobermory is also one of several communities that claim to be the final resting place of the famed *Griffin*, the ship of the famous explorer La Salle that disappeared without a trace in 1679.

Harbor Wiarton, Ontario
Location Harbor Light: L44°44′50″N, Lo81°08′20″W
Dockage The Wiarton Marina, Bluewater Park

Places to Stay Maplehurst B&B 519-534-2110, Gadd-About B&B 519-534-5282, The Hillcrest 519-534-2262, The Green Door B&B 519534-4710, Bruce Gables B&B 519-534-0429, The Bayview 519-534-5013, The Cedarholme 519-534-3705, Cobble Ridge 519534-0432

Places to Eat The Anchor Inn, Pacific Inn Restaurant, Spirit Rock Family Restaurant & Hotel, Station Roadhouse, Windmill

Wiarton, Ontario, is located in the southern reaches of Lake Huron's Georgian Bay at the farthest end of Colpoy's Bay. This long narrow bay is framed by high limestone cliffs and is a most impressive sight whether you come by land or sea. The highway runs along either shore of the bay as does the famed Bruce Trail, a hiking trail that connects this community with the rest of the rustically beautiful Bruce Peninsula. If you are doing this trip by land yacht, Wiarton is a wonderful starting point from which to explore the Bruce. If you came by boat, you have already come around "the point," and will now have the pleasure of retracing your steps, town by town.

Wiarton is a good-sized town with a colorful past. It was once the very hub of the emerging Canadian economy. Well over a hundred years ago, this was a working harbor for lumber, agricultural products and even tourism. Steamers and schooners formed an endless parade of commerce. But when the railroad and the highways shifted the means of transport, the town of Wiarton voted not to participate and let the transport hub shift to other communities. They wanted a return to the quieter days of the past and for many years that's exactly what they got.

Wiarton's economy is growing again, this time based solely on tourism and the personality of an albino ground hog named Willie. Yes, Wiarton has their own mid-winter ground hog festival at which Willie is the guest of honor. All the town dignitaries show up in tuxedoes and all of Canada is invited to watch Willie's weather prediction for the balance of the season. This is something to see. The importance of the event is surpassed only by its charm.

Lake Huron

Harbor Wiky Bay, Ontario
Location Marina Entrance Buoy: L45°48'N, Lo81°43'W
Dockage Wiky Bay Marina

Places to Stay Contact: The Paa-Yaa-Daa Tourism Group 705-859-3001

Places to Eat Pat's Cafe, J.J.'s Restaurant & Pizza, Patsy's Family Restaurant, Andy's The Coffee Shop

Wiky Bay is on the eastern end of Manitoulin Island on the outer fringes of Canada's North Channel. The bay appears on your charts as Smith Bay and the community is more properly known as Wikwemikong Bay First Nation. This is what we would commonly call an Indian reservation, and it's a very special one. This is one of only a handful of unceded reserves in all of North America. Unceded means it was never handed over to the European settlers by treaty and then given back to them by yet another. This land is theirs and it has been since the beginning of recorded history.

Wiky Bay is a treat to visit. The marina facilities have been recently remodeled and are a modern example of what a rustic recreational harbor should be. Ephriam the harbormaster will make certain you are well taken care of and will help you get around to the many sites to see here. What can you see in a peaceful, quiet Indian reservation like this?

At the top of your list put the De-Ba-Jeh-Mu-Jug (The Story Teller) Theatre Group. This is live theatre usually performed outdoors within the ruins of the Holy Cross Mission's parish school. The Church and the grounds are wonderfully maintained, but the school burned quite some time ago and was never rebuilt. The theatre group calls it home now and gives regular performances of plays that tell the history and the many stories of this culture. What once began as a local cultural expression has risen to high artistic acclaim. "Don't miss!"

You can also see the annual Pow Wow, one of the biggest in North America, and the Three Fires Music Festival among other special events scheduled throughout the year. The Paa-Yaa-Daa Tourist Group can give you the latest schedule: 705-859-3001.

Lakes Erie & St. Clair

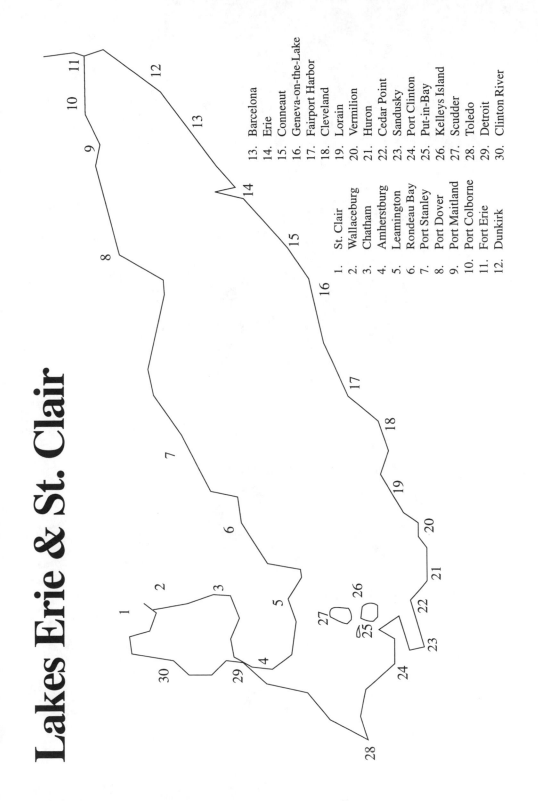

1. St. Clair
2. Wallaceburg
3. Chatham
4. Amherstburg
5. Leamington
6. Rondeau Bay
7. Port Stanley
8. Port Dover
9. Port Maitland
10. Port Colborne
11. Fort Erie
12. Dunkirk
13. Barcelona
14. Erie
15. Conneaut
16. Geneva-on-the-Lake
17. Fairport Harbor
18. Cleveland
19. Lorain
20. Vermilion
21. Huron
22. Cedar Point
23. Sandusky
24. Port Clinton
25. Put-in-Bay
26. Kelleys Island
27. Scudder
28. Toledo
29. Detroit
30. Clinton River

Lake Erie

Harbor Amherstburg, Ontario
Location Duffy's Docks: 42°05.9'N, o83°06.8'W
Dockage Duffy's Docks, Walter Ranta Marina, Bois Blanc Island Marina

Places to Stay Duffy's 519-736-2101, Blue Haven Motel 519-736-5404, The Honor's B&B 519-736-7737, Patrician Inn B&B 519-736-1549

Places to Eat Duffy's, The Gordon House, Rosa's Italian Family Restaurant, The Bullock Tavern

Amherstburg, Ontario, is located along the Canadian shore where the Detroit River empties into Lake Erie. The village and the docks are on the up-bound freighter channel just behind Bois Blanc Island. Pronounced Bob'-Lo, this was once the site of a very popular amusement park.

Downtown Amherstburg is more than provincial, it's nearly colonial. A line of shops and eateries grace Dalhousie Street along the river front, the traditional main street of town. A more modern commercial district heads away from the river at the north end of Dalhousie, near the entrance to the King's Navy Yard.

The King's Navy yard is a perfectly landscaped river-front park. Blossoms, blooms and cannons dot the fine trimmed lawns that have won national awards for their beauty. And yes, I did say cannons. During the War of 1812 this was the greatest British stronghold on the Lakes. The Navy Yard was just that, a British shipbuilding and maintenance facility where the most powerful warships on the lakes were based. Next door is Fort Malden, where the British army protected the navy while the navy protected the fort.

All that changed in the fall of 1813 when Commodore Perry beat the British fleet in the Battle of Lake Erie causing the British to burn the fort and the Navy Yard and retreat up the Ontario peninsula. Be sure to read the associated story about "The King, The Chief and The President" to find out why Ontario is not a U.S. state today!

Amherstburg is one of the most charming and historically important destinations in all the Great Lakes. "Don't miss!"

Very Real Estate:
The King, The Chief and The President
by Bruce Jenvey

The Amherstburg area has played an important role in North American history. It's true. Besides changing our maps, our politics and our nationalities, this small piece of land directly changed the lives of a king, a chief and a U.S. president. It's quite a story so you might want to gather the younger crew members together and read this one out loud.

From the beginning of recorded history the Great Lakes have been the grand prize everyone wanted to control. To Native Americans, this was the richest hunting and fishing grounds in existence. When the Europeans came, they saw it as the source of great natural resources from food to lumber to furs. As a young American Nation was born, it was seen as part of a great foundation to help build a powerful and independent country. Even today we are fighting over the resources of these lakes, both natural and economic.

Before the American Revolution, when the British were the supreme power in the Lakes, they controlled the traffic between the upper and lower regions from their stronghold at Fort Wayne in Detroit. The river was narrow there, the land was flat, the control was good. But the Jay Treaty of 1799 gave Detroit and the fort to the Americans. To retain their position of regional power, the British crossed over to the Canadian side and moved downriver to a point where the river flowed into Lake Erie. Here the visibility wasn't as good, but the river was even narrower. From there a medium-sized garrison with a few ships could control the entire river. And whoever controlled the river controlled the Lakes. This selected tract of land eventually became known as Amherstburg, home to Fort Malden and the King's Navy Yard. For several years things went as planned: the British controlled the traffic on the Great Lakes.

You have probably read in school history books that the War of 1812 was declared in reaction to the British policy of stopping United States ships, searching their crews for deserted British sailors and pressing into service anyone they believed might be a fugitive British subject. We were all taught that this happened on the high seas, but did you know it also happened on the Detroit River right under the protective guns of Fort Malden, on ships built right there at Amherstburg?

After war was declared the British launched several successful invasions and campaigns in the Great Lakes from their base at Amherstburg. The British divided the American forces between the Great Lakes and the East Coast and hampered American strategy. They were winning the war.

Finally, in a scheme of questionable sanity, the American forces sent young Oliver Hazard Perry to the Great Lakes with an impossible mission: To take control of the shipping lanes and end British control of the lakes. Perry wasn't even a full naval captain yet. He took the title of commodore as he would be in charge of the American fleet on Lake Erie. The real American fleet on the Great Lakes was at Sackets Harbor in eastern Lake Ontario below Niagara Falls, and with no canal yet built, these ships could not reach the upper lakes. So Perry was to be commodore of a fleet that didn't exist. He had to build his own ships.

He set up a shipyard on Presque Isle at Erie, Pennsylvania, and began to build ships out of the only thing he had—green lumber. These ships would be weak, built of unseasoned timbers, but there was no time to season the wood. To compensate, he built more than twice the number of ships the British had. In fact while he was in the process of building these green ships, Captain Barclay, the senior British officer in charge at the Fort Malden complex, twice brought his fleet within cannon range of Perry's shipyard in order to keep an eye on him. While it was within his power to destroy the ships, the yard and the entire American effort on the lake, no one knows why he never took the opportunity. He could have done so in complete safety. You see, the British ships were armed with long-range highly accurate rifled cannons. The best the Americans had and what they were installing on their ships were short-range less accurate cannonades, but again, Perry had twice as many as the British.

The summer and fall of 1813 was the most pivotal time for the Great Lakes theater of war. Perry completed his fleet and sailed it out across the lake to South Bass Island where he established a base of operations. From there, with a superior number of ships, he could control the western end of the lake, making the British throttle hold at Amherstburg useless. By controlling the lake there, Perry had cut the British supply lines. No supplies were reaching the garrison or naval brigade at Amherstburg. Men were going hungry and moral was sagging.

Finally, on the morning of September 10, 1813, Barclay and the British fleet sailed out of Amherstburg to attack Perry at Put-In-Bay. But that was what Perry had been waiting for. He sailed out to meet them in his green ships, built to fight only one battle, this one.

Using unorthodox tactics and with the blessing of the wind behind him, Perry did something no man in history had ever done: he broke a British line of fire and won the battle. Not only did he win, but he captured the entire fleet! What were his tactics? In those days, most battleships had their cannons mounted on the side. The ships would sail past one another, and blast away broadside to broadside. Perry had two sister brigs, the *Lawrence* and the *Niagara,* and a slew of smaller ships and sloops. The British had long-range cannons, while Perry had twice as many short-range connonades.

Rather than sail side by side with the British as Barclay expected him to do, he sailed right at them! The *Lawrence* led the way with the *Niagara* right behind. The *Lawrence* was shelled without mercy with many casualties and much damage as they closed the distance. This unnerved the British enough, but then Perry did something really strange.

As the *Lawrence* was nearly upon the British, nothing much more than a sinking, dying hulk, Perry pulled down his battle standard, boarded his gig and rowed a short distance back to the *Niagara.* He changed ships in the middle of a battle! As the British finally blasted the *Lawrence* out of their way, there they were, face to face with the *Niagara,* fresh, undamaged and blasting from both broadsides. Behind her was the rest of the American fleet. The two principle British brigs, the *Detroit* and the *Queen Charlotte,* both suffered immediate damage and quickly attempted to change their positions, but in the smoke and the confusion they collided and entangled their rigging. Helpless, defenseless and directly under the American guns, they surrendered. The rest of the British fleet tried to scatter and flee back to Amherstburg but the American ships rounded them up and the victory was complete.

That night Perry penned the now famous communiqué to his superior, General William Henry Harrison: "We have met the enemy and they are ours." What followed was a list of ships that had been captured.

With the fleet gone, the garrison at Amherstburg was now in danger. Harrison had an entire army just across the river that outnumbered the British by a significant amount even when you counted their contingent of Indian warriors under the command of Chief Tecumseh. The decision was made to abandon the fort and burn it and the navy yard.

Barclay's career was now over. When he eventually reached England he faced court-martial charges for his handling of the Lake Erie campaign. Perry, while a hero, never went on to greater glory and died at a young age from an infectious disease. The stage was clear for the next two prominent players whose lives and careers would hinge on Amherstburg.

140

As the British retreated up the peninsula, along with them went Tecumseh and his contingent of warriors. It was early October by now. It was cold, rainy, and the British were under-supplied and low on moral. Tecumseh wanted no part of retreat, he wanted to fight William Henry Harrison for personal reasons.

Chief Tecumseh was originally from the Indiana Territory. He had tried to form a defensive confederacy of the Shawnee tribes to halt the advance of the white man. The governor of the territory had cheated the Shawnee people out of a great deal of their land. When Tecumseh tried to raise a war party to retake the land, the governor led troops against the Shawnee stronghold at Tippecanoe, and in Tecumseh's absence, killed the chief's family including his brother who was the high shaman of the tribe. Tecumseh had no choice but to flee to British-controlled Fort Malden with the remains of his great Indian army, and that's where he was when the War of 1812 broke out. That governor so hated by Tecumseh was none other than William Henry Harrison.

As Tecumseh retreated with the British he knew it was William Henry Harrison leading the American troops, and Harrison knew it was Tecumseh leading the Indian contingent.

Finally, the British made a stand along the marshy banks of the Thames River near what is now Chatham. They were tired, cold and very hungry, not having eaten in two days. As the Americans advanced, the British fired one volley, then broke ranks and ran up the road towards Moravian Town. All that is except the Indian contingent, now outnumbered four to one.

Harrison knew he was facing Tecumseh and he wanted nothing more than to finish the job he'd started in Indiana. Tecumseh knew he was facing Harrison and would not consider retreat in any form. The battle raged on for well over an hour, Tecumseh and his braves stopping the American advance cold in its tracks. Near the end of the second hour, Tecumseh fell, mortally wounded. Without their leader the Indian warriors retreated into the marsh and were gone. But the Americans had suffered heavy casualties. Continuing their advance against the retreating British was out of the question.

The British re-grouped at Moravian Town and reinforcements arrived. What had been a complete rout was turned around and in the weeks that followed, the British held their position on the peninsula. Tecumseh's stand is credited with not only stopping the American advance, but buying precious time for the British to re-group. Some say his action prevented the entire Ontario peninsula from becoming a U.S. state.

But because of the events of the summer and fall of 1813, the British high command had to rethink their strategy. They had been winning the war in the east, but now there were Americans occupying Canadian soil and their stranglehold on the lakes was gone. They desperately tried to secure complete control of the Niagara River to control all shipping from that point, but the various battles back and forth across that rocky terrain were indecisive.

Within a year the war was over. The King of England had to grant certain guarantees to the Americans, and never again would the British control the bounty of the Great Lakes as they had before. British army engineers began planning an inland water route that would connect Lake Huron to Lake Ontario—a protected waterway deep within their boundaries that they could readily defend. Today we call that waterway the Trent-Severn.

Tecumseh was honored as a hero but he was one of the last barriers that had contained the western settlement of American pioneers. William Henry Harrison capitalized on his war record and his victory over Tecumseh, and was later elected President of the United States. So much history, so many lives, all hinged around a small piece of land where the Detroit River meets Lake Erie.

ken miller

Harbor Barcelona, New York
Location Harbor Entrance: L42°20.7′N, Lo79°35.84′W
Dockage Monroe's Marina, The Daniel Reid Memorial Park
Limited

Places to Stay On your boat

Places to Eat The Barcelona Harbor House, Jack's, Portage Inn, Calarco's,
Larry's Cantina

Barcelona, New York, is located on the eastern shore of Lake Erie. This is by no means a source of bright lights night life—at least in the conventional sense, but more on that later.

Barcelona is a quiet reclusive harbor without a business district. But there are two very good restaurants catering to the boating crowd. Just up from the docks is the Barcelona Harbor House, a fine dining establishment that specializes in steaks and seafood, but has a complete menu to choose from. Their view of Lake Erie adds even more to the dining experience. Just across the street is Jack's, which is more of a hash-slingin' diner from the good old days, and serves up an excellent breakfast.

These are your choices. If you want more than this, the village of Westfield is just a few minutes away by car. There you will find more restaurants and a nice business district to sweep with your credit card.

Now, about the night life and bright lights of Barcelona: The night life here buzzes and flits towards any light you may have left on. The bright light is a piece of history and sadly, it is dark now. Up on the hill is the most unusual lighthouse in the Great Lakes. It's a private residence now, but from the road you can still get great photos of the extraordinary lantern room. The burner was designed to burn natural gas! This is the only lighthouse ever designed to burn natural gas. In fact the gas was free, piped in from a nearby creek bed. This lighthouse burned between 1828 and 1850 without costing the taxpayers a dime and it was the first Federal building of any kind to be lit with natural gas.

If you don't believe me or want a good look at this light before coming here, get a copy of Bill Penrose's book, *A Travelers Guide to 100 Eastern Great Lakes Lighthouses*.

Harbor Cedar Point, Ohio
Location Sandusky Pier Light: L41°30.0'N, Lo82°40.5'W
Dockage Cedar Point Marina 419-627-2334

Places to Stay The Hotel Breakers, Sand Castle Suites Hotel,
Camper Village

Places to Eat The Bay Harbor Inn, The Boathouse, The Hofbrau,
The Silver Dollar Cafe, Aunt Em's Kitchen

Cedar Point is perhaps the most fun destination on the Great Lakes. That's because it is one of the nation's premier amusement parks. It has earned the title of "Americas Roller Coast" due to the sheer numbers of roller coasters in the park.

Whether you come by land yacht or boat, I strongly encourage you to stay on premises within the park. There was a time when you could come here and really do the entire park in a day, and drive a respectable distance both ways to do so. Now, the park has grown and offers such an expanded range of activities that you need at least two days or so to see it all.

I won't go into detail as to the rides in this section as they often change. Some are retired and torn down to make room for something newer and more exciting. But I will tell you that I have visited other amusement parks in my time and there is just something very special about riding coasters, giant Ferris wheels and strolling down shady Frontier Trail while enjoying the cool breezes of Lake Erie. You will enjoy everything here from wild animal shows, stage shows, and craftsmen at work to giant-screen movies and some of the best rides you will ever find.

Here's a tip: Many of the rides are water rides such as giant logs rafting down waterfalls. During the heat of the day you can stand in line for an hour or two waiting for the really popular rides. But in the last two hours that the park is open, these lines thin out because who wants to ride home in the car all soaking wet? If you stay on the premises you have a short walk back to your room or boat and dry clothes. One evening, my sons and I rode the biggest ride of the year six times in a row and never had to wait in line. We were drenched, but the boat was waiting for us right there in the marina!

Some Amusing History
by Bruce Jenvey

What is now Cedar Point Amusement Park has been the place to go for relaxation and entertainment for well over a hundred years. It all began way back in 1870 when a local businessman responded to the public interest and built a bath house on the bathing beach at Cedar Point, so named for the trees that once lined the peninsula. Before long it was quite the place to spend a warm afternoon. It was affordable too. You could rent bathing attire for as little as ten cents for the entire day!

In the early 1880s the park's very first ride was erected—a water trapeze that would hurl riders into Lake Erie. It was so successful that it was soon followed by other more advanced aquatic swings and a water toboggan as well. Cedar Point was now considered a "resort".

In 1888 another park milestone was constructed. The Grand Pavilion housed an auditorium, bowling alleys and a dining room. A bandstand soon followed along with a dance floor and a beer garden. Of course where there's beer, bands and bowling, you have to have docks. And the docks attracted boats and the boats were filled with tourists. Cedar Point was poised for it's next major milestone.

In 1892 the park's first roller coaster was built. It was called the Switchback Railway and it thrilled guests by dragging them up to the dizzying height of 25 feet and then hurtling them back to the ground at speeds approaching ten miles and hour. But it started something.

In the next few years the park witnessed tremendous growth. In 1905 the Hotel Breakers was built on one of the finest beaches in the Great Lakes where it still stands today. The Cinema was also a big hit that year, showing *The Great Train Robbery* all summer long. It was the first motion picture with a plot. In 1906 an improved electrical plant allowed the opening of the park's first midway boasting one million lights to dazzle and enchant.

Cedar Point was now a full-fledged amusement park and the rest is history. The rides have gotten bigger, faster and more thrilling. The attractions have grown, and there has always been a flow of top-flight entertainers. But there is one thing that hasn't changed in 124 years—Cedar Point is a great destination just for the fun of it!

Harbor Cleveland, Ohio
Location West Pierhead Lighthouse: L41°30.54′N, Lo81°43.8′W
Dockage Channel Park Marina, Riverfront Yacht Services, Edgewater Marina, Edgewater Yacht Club, Lakeside Yacht Club, Forest City Yacht Club, East 55th Street Marina

Places to Stay Various National Chains

Places to Eat The Watermark Restaurant, Longhorn Steakhouse, Landry's Seafood Restaurant, Max & Erma's, Howl at the Moon Saloon, Rock Bottom Brewery

 Believe it or not, Cleveland, Ohio, is one of the Great Lakes' fastest developing destinations. I say developing because it's already fully grown, it's just revitalizing its best features.

When you talk about boating in Cleveland you're talking about the Flats. The Flats is that area on either side of the Cuyahoga River from the lakefront, and then some distance inland. Geologically this was once a massive and wild river that carved a great gorge out of the bluffs along the banks. As the river settled down to the meandering size it is today, it left a great flat expanse of dry river bottom in the shadows of towering bluffs. These are the Flats.

Historically, this has been the heart of Cleveland. This was the first industrial center in the city and later, the heart of its docks and warehouse district. But something strange has been happening for the past few years. While freighters still frequent the river, the Flats themselves have been renovated, overhauled, cleared and rebuilt into the city's leading entertainment district. This is party town deluxe. There are no less than fifty dining and drinking establishments along the banks and almost all have dockage for revelers to pull up, tie up and tie one on. The air is a constant reverberation of rock music, colored lights and shouting party animals. Inside the bars, it's even worse!

I have been told that a trip to Cleveland is now incomplete without an evening in the Flats. Enthusiastically, they are right. There is no place like this anywhere else on earth.

But as long as you're in town, don't forget to hit that big museum not too far from the river—The Rock and Roll Hall of Fame. It's worth the trip too!

Harbor Conneaut, Ohio
Location Pierhead Lighthouse: L41°58.7'N, Lo80°33.5'W
Dockage Port Conneaut Marina & Yacht Club,
Lagoon Marina, Lake Erie Boat Club, Conneaut Boat Club

Places to Stay Bridgeview B&B 216-593-6767, Bussia B&B 216-593-5976,
Campbell Braemer B&B 216-599-7362, Liberty Inn Homestead
B&B 216-593-6000

Places to Eat Gulley's Galley, The Golden Anchor, Tony's Dining Room on
Park Avenue, Lyons Den Diner & Deli, Rainbow Cafe

Conneaut is one of the Great Lakes' oldest commercial ports. Located on Ohio's northeast shore, there are really two entrances to the harbor: One for you, and one for the freighters.

Even though the pleasure craft and commercial craft "bunk separately," this is still a fine harbor for the freighter-watcher in your crew. Just follow Broad Street from the marina, turn east on Park and south on Ford. This will bring you to Seaway Port Look-Out, a great place to relax and watch commerce in action. Don't forget your camera or your binoculars.

I said this was one of the oldest ports in the Great Lakes. That means you're bound to find history where ever you go. Start at the Railroad Museum and see the trains that carried the goods to and from the harbor. The museum itself is built into the old railroad station that dates back to 1900, and on the grounds you'll see various rail cars and locomotives from Conneaut's past.

Next, visit the historic Harwood Block of offices and stores. Its metal-trimmed exterior is unique and of course it's protected on the National Registry of Historic Places. Nearby is Conneaut's historic City Hall, dating back to 1876.

Other historic structures include the Carnegie Library and two remarkable octagonal houses. There's even an octagonal barn! Also, the area has three original covered bridges.

Harbor Dunkirk, New York
Location Point Gratiot Lighthouse: L42°29′38″N, Lo79°21′15″W
Dockage Chadwick Bay Marina, Dunkirk Yacht Club, Stefan's Recreational Marina

Places to Stay Four Points Hotel 716-366-8350, Rodeway Inn 716-366-2200, Comfort Inn 716-672-4450, Don's Motel 716-366-4646, The Vinyards Motel & Restaurant 716-366-4400

Places to Eat Sheraton Four Points Hotel, Crow's Nest, Dockside Cafe & Bar, Dimetri's on the Lake, Katerina's, Cafe Expresso

Dunkirk is along the Lake Erie shore approximately half-way between Erie, Pennsylvania, and Buffalo, New York. At the very entrance to the harbor you are greeted by one of the prettiest lighthouses in the Lakes. The Point Gratiot lighthouse is a truly Victorian structure and is far more ornate than other more utilitarian structures built in this same time period. It has in place a third-order Fresnel lens bigger than most you will find in other harbors. The keeper's quarters is the attached brick home that gives this beacon its architectural identity. You can go inside too! This is now the Veterans Memorial Museum and houses artifacts not only commemorating the area's war veterans, but the local maritime history as well. Around the grounds are anchors and lifeboats too large to display inside.

Another museum of note is the Dunkirk Historical Museum next to Washington Park in the downtown district which has several rooms displaying relics from the Civil War forward. Also see the railroad display at the County Fairgrounds. Here you'll see a real live antique steam locomotive and several associated rail cars. They are the products of the famed Alco-Brooks company and were manufactured right here in Dunkirk.

Downtown Dunkirk is lined with well-kept storefronts reflecting different stages in the growth and the development of the community. The shops you will find there today offer everything from basic needs to fun and enchanting things designed to tickle the fancy.

Lake Erie

Harbor Erie, Pennsylvania
Location Green Buoy "1": L42°09.9'N, Lo80°03.1'W
Dockage Erie Public Dock 814-870-1250, McAllister's Marine 814-452-3201, Lund Boat Works 814-455-1782, Bayshore Marina 814-459-9696, Gem City Marina 814-459-8184, Erie Angler Marina 814-452-2222

Places to Stay Contact: Erie Chamber of Commerce 814-454-7191

Places to Eat Various in Downtown District

Most people don't even realize that Pennsylvania has a port on the Great Lakes. Well they do, and it's called Erie just like the lake it's on, and it is a unique mixture of old and new.

The harbor is formed by the natural sand bar called Presque Isle and is a very busy commercial port that supports a city of significant size. You'll find lots of places to stay and many eateries to sample, but in the midst of all this modern shipping and receiving, is some very important history.

Let's start with that tall, old-fashioned square-rigger tied up at the docks near Dobbins Point. That's the *Niagara*, a real live survivor of Commodore Perry's fleet that defeated the British in the Battle of Lake Erie during the War of 1812. This is not a replica, this is the real thing! Yes, some timbers have been replaced over the past two centuries, but for the most part these are the decks Perry walked on that fateful day.

Perry built his entire fleet, including the *Niagara*, here on Presque Isle in a place called Misery Bay. You can go out on Presque Isle. It's now a state park, and besides beautiful sunsets and sandy beaches, you can see first hand the small bay where Perry changed the course of history. There's also a very historic lighthouse on the peninsula.

There are several other museums and historic sites on the mainland including the Dickson Tavern, a major checkpoint during the days of the Underground Railroad, and the Anthony Wayne Blockhouse where the famous Revolutionary War hero was detained until his untimely death.

149

Harbor Fairport Harbor, Ohio
Location Fairport Rear Range Light: L41°46.05′N, Lo81°16.88′W
Dockage HTP Rack & Marina, Grand River Marina, Rutherford's Landing & Cruise Line

Places to Stay Contact: Town Hall 216-352-3620

Places to Eat Brennan's Fish House, Pickle Bill's Grand River Dock & Grill, The Mango Bay Trading Company, The Harborview Restaurant

Fairport Harbor is one of Ohio's classic small towns along the eastern end of their Lake Erie shore. This is an old community settled by English colonists by the right of a pre-revolutionary grant by King George III.

Today this is a quiet community with the harbor located close to all town facilities. However, there are three points of interest that set this town apart.

First of all, if you're a sailor, this is the home of Tartan Yachts. The legendary "tough boats" of the world are built right here. *GLC*'s Ken Miller currently cruises all over the Great Lakes in a Tartan 34. His is about thirty years old and passed its last insurance inspection with flying colors.

Out at the end of the breakwater is the Grand River Lighthouse. This is the "new" lighthouse, having been built in 1925. It's still a classic structure and you can walk right out to it. It replaced the "old" Grand River Lighthouse (1871) up on the hill, which is now the Fairport Harbor Marine Museum. The lighthouse and its grounds are open to the public and present a fine display of both nautical and household artifacts. There is also the pilot house from the ore carrier *Frontenac* at the back of the museum, allowing you to find out first hand what steering one of these babies is like!

Special note: This is the original pilothouse. Part way through the ship's career, this pilothouse was removed and another newer, nicer one put in its place. That pilothouse is now on display at the Marine Museum in Two Harbors, Minnesota. A fitting end as the *Frontenac* spent her career hauling iron ore between these very ports.

Harbor Fort Erie, Ontario
Location Marina Entry: L42°57.2'N, Lo78°56.2'W
Dockage Niagara Parks Commission Marina,
Erie Basin Marina-AUD Club,

Places to Stay Buffalo Yacht Club Haven Motel 905-871-2171, Gateway Motel
905-871-4438, Super 8 Motel 905-871-8500, Lakeview Inn
Motel 905-871-6806

Places to Eat Artemis Restaurant, Barrel Pizza & Spaghetti House, King Wah
Garden & Tavern, Jack's Restaurant, Ming Teh Restaurant

Fort Erie, Ontario, lies directly across the Niagara River from
Buffalo, New York, at the entrance to the Niagara River and just off
Lake Erie.

Today it is a prosperous community with entertainment for everyone.
You can take a picnic lunch out to the garden-like setting of the Fort Erie
race track and spend a day watching the thoroughbreds run. Or you can
go up to Bridgeburg Station on the town's north edge and enjoy modern
shopping in a revitalized and restored neighborhood. There are a number
of great museums including the Fort Erie Historical Museum, the Fort Erie
Railroad Museum and the Mildred M. Mahoney Doll's House Gallery.

The Doll House Gallery has over $1.5 million of dolls and collectibles
on display, but its location is famous too, for very different reasons. This
museum is located in Bertie Hall and in the basement you can still see the
tunnels used to smuggle runaway slaves from the United States during
the days of the Underground Railroad.

But the biggest piece of history in Fort Erie is the fort, a British stronghold along the Niagara River during the War of 1812. In the summer of
1814 the fort was captured by the Americans and used as a launching site
for a major advance down the banks towards Lake Ontario. The British
stopped the advance and the Americans retreated to Fort Erie with plans
to pull back across the river to Buffalo. But before they could regroup, the
British laid siege to the fort, trapping the Americans inside. The siege lasted over a month and a half and ended with the British pulling back
towards Niagara Falls and the Americans escaping to Buffalo. But when
the casualties were all counted, this was the bloodiest, most costly siege of
the entire war. The fort is open for tourists from mid-May to mid-
September every year.

The Siege of Fort Erie
by Bruce Jenvey

There were a lot of reasons the United States and the British Empire went to war in 1812. Without a doubt, one of the underlying causes was the struggle for control of the Great Lakes region. The Northwest Territory, as it was then known, was a wealth of resources and riches. There were animal pelts, fish, lumber and fertile soil as well as minerals and metals. The Great Lakes themselves provided a natural waterborne highway on which to take this bounty to the world's markets. It was everything a world-dominating empire needed to extend its influence. Unfortunately it was also everything a young emerging nation needed to ensure its future. Conflict was inevitable.

There were no connecting roads or highways in the region. At best there were a handful of wilderness trails that were, for the most part, uncharted and in many cases unsafe for those of European heritage. The lakes themselves became the highways, and it followed that "he who controls the lakes, controls the Northwest Territory." And that was the driving force behind the strategies employed by both sides in this theater during the course of the war.

Just like opposing Little League teams stacking hand-over-hand on the handle of a bat to decide who bats first, the control of the Great Lakes was decided by who had control farther and farther down the waterway. It started in the straits with British control of the fort on Mackinac Island, and with that, control over who and what could leave Lakes Michigan and (by portage) Superior. But then the Americans took control of Fort Wayne at Detroit. In response the British built a large naval yard and fleet at Amherstberg. In September of 1813 Perry defeated the British in the Battle of Lake Erie, taking control of the lake and forcing the British to burn Fort Malden, the navy yard and retreat up the Ontario peninsula.

The next logical vantage point to control the traffic on the lakes was the Niagara River. But just one ride along the Niagara Parkway will tell you why the struggle and the war dragged on. The Niagara River, while scenically beautiful, is a general's nightmare. Sheer stone cliffs stand guard over narrow gorges filled with white-water rapids and deadly whirlpools. There are few footholds for attacker or defender along its unforgiving length, yet this is where the two opposing armies decided to play King on the Mountain.

There had been bloody skirmishes and short-lived invasions back and forth across the river since the very beginning of the war. It was often difficult for even the generals to determine who was in control of the waterway on a day-to-day basis. But it reached a climax in the late summer of 1814 at the very gates of Fort Erie.

In early July of that year the Americans stationed at Buffalo crossed the river and took Fort Erie by surprise. The fort fell to the Americans easily, as it was defended only by militia forces since the British regulars had been pulled back to York (Toronto). Then in a final attempt to control the river's entire length the American commanders pointed their forces north towards the falls and Lake Ontario at the far end of river.

British forces under Lieutenant General Sir Gordon Drummond were dispatched from York to stop the American advance. On July 26th, in what became known as the Battle of Lundy's Lane, the two sides struggled to a draw in one of the bloodiest battles of the entire war. It is said that the sounds of cannon and musket fire completely drowned out the deafening roar of the nearby falls.

Fearing their supply lines might be cut, the Americans fell back to Fort Erie. The intention was to cross the river and take up a defensive position at Buffalo. But several of the executive officers had been severely wounded and Fort Erie became the holding ground out of necessity.

Drummond laid siege to the fort and pounded it regularly with cannon and mortar fire. Throughout August and into September the bloody standoff continued. At one point the British captured one of the fort's bastions, but this victory was short-lived and ended with the explosion of the bastion's powder magazine. The British suffered tremendous losses compared to the Americans.

The British pulled back into the woods and began the process of setting up a new line of siege guns grouped into three batteries. If they were ever put into operation these new guns would probably spell the end of the American occupation of the fort. The American commanders decided on a raid of the batteries before their completion and secretly began to clear a wide path through the surrounding woods in that direction.

Work was paced to keep ahead of British construction, and on September 16th at 3:30 P.M., in the middle of a torrential downpour, sixteen hundred American regulars burst out of the woods and completely surprised the British. They overran two of the three batteries and spiked the guns before they were stopped. Losses were heavy on both sides but the British threat had been removed.

Discouraged, facing worsening elements and an army in declining health, Drummond abandoned the siege and simply marched away. Eventually the Americans regrouped enough to withdraw to Buffalo, and before the war's end a British contingent did reoccupy the fort.

The fort is restored and open to the public during the summer season. Costumed interpreters recreate life in the fort as it was during the American occupation and retell the story of the greatest siege of the War of 1812. Not far from the very same bastions that were the prize for which so many struggled, a solemn monument quietly stands in memory of those who fell in the conflict.

ken miller

Harbor Geneva-on-the-Lake, Ohio
Location East Breakwater Light: L41°51.6'N, Lo80°58.5'W
Dockage Geneva Marina

Places to Stay CharLma B&B 216-466-3646, The Otto Court B&B 216-466-8668, Poolside Motel 216-466-8770, Pera's Motel Apartments 216-466-8675

Places to Eat Capo's Pizza, Times Square Restaurant & Patio, Mary's Kitchen, Angel Mia's Italian Restaurant, Chan's China Express Restaurant, The Old Firehouse Winery & Restaurant

Geneva-on-the-Lake is probably one of Lake Erie's best kept secrets. Located between Ashtabula and Fairport Harbor, this community is recognized as the state's first resort and even has a brand new marina facility. What it seems to be lacking is a burning desire to become Ohio's biggest resort. This is a peaceful, friendly and very relaxing place—and they intend to keep it that way.

This village is a short walk from the marina and is centered around a concentration of business and eateries called The Strip. Yes, there is nightlife here. Depending on which establishment you choose, you can sip a few adult beverages while listening to old time rock 'n roll, cutting edge rock, or the ever-popular kareoke machine. There are some wonderful small eateries in town too.

Geneva State Park is on the water and offers picnic grounds as well as a brand new bathing beach. Nearby is Erieview Park that even has a small amusement park on the premises complete with bumper cars, a carousel, a fun house and kiddy rides.

In town, you can play mini-golf at a place called Mini-Golf. This is the oldest continuously operated miniature golf course in the U.S. There's a big wooden bear near the entrance so you can't miss it.

Also be sure to visit the Jennie Munger Gregory Museum on Lake Road. It's open only on summer weekends and wonderfully re-creates life in this community over 150 years ago.

I encourage you to take the extra time here to explore the local wineries. There are several to choose from—or choose them all! This is part of Ohio's fruit belt, and local grapes often make the best local wines.

Harbor Huron, Ohio
Location The Huron Light: L41°24.2'N, Lo82°32.6'W
Dockage Huron Boat Basin, Huron Yacht Club, Harbor North, Huron River Marine, Holiday Harbor Marina, Huron Lagoons Marina

Places to Stay Captain Montague's B&B 419-433-4756, Buster Brown Shoe House 419-433-3685, Clarion Inn 419-433-8000, Sawmill Creek Resort Hotel 419-433-3800, Gull Motel 419-433-4855, Smith's Cottage House B&B 419-627-8552, Parkway Motel 419-433-3094

Places to Eat East Of Chicago Pizza Company, JP's Downunder

Huron, Ohio, is the southern-most port on the Great Lakes. Located a short distance east of Sandusky, this is a community with a long history that reaches back to the American Revolution.

During that period of time, many farmers in the eastern colonies were burned out of their property by British troops. So many, in fact, that after the war Congress reserved a large section of land in the lower Great Lakes, called The Firelands. This land was to be given, farm by farm and town by town, to those who had lost everything in support of the Revolution. The very first town to be settled in The Firelands was Huron, dating back to 1790.

In the early years Huron prospered with commercial fishing, lumber, and shipbuilding. But as in most Great Lakes ports these enterprises faded in time. For some time Huron was a quiet place that slowly built its tourist trade. Today there is still a reasonable amount of freighter traffic in the harbor to enjoy but the true attractions of the community are its parks and its people.

Right on the river at the boat basin is just one of several beautiful parks, this one complete with an amphitheater and a summer concert schedule that caters to all kinds of musical tastes.

Also visit the section of town called "the old plat" bounded by the lake, Ohio and Center Streets, to see some magnificent, perfectly preserved old homes. These are all private residences but the owners don't mind your taking pictures from the sidewalk.

There are also a number of historic B&Bs in town, including one previously owned by the original Buster Brown of shoe fame.

Harbor Kelleys Island, Ohio
Location Breakwater at Seaway Marina: L41°35.4'N, Lo82°42.3'W
Dockage Seaway Marina, Casino Bar, The Anchor Inn, Kelley's Cove, The Sea Trader, Craft's Lakeview Lane

Places to Stay The Kelley Mansion 419-746-2273, The Sweet Valley Inn B&B 419-746-2750, The Island Charm Guest House 419-746-2615, Zettler's 419-746-2315

Places to Eat Fresch's Island House, The Village Pump, Bag The Moon Saloon, Caddy Shack Bar & Restaurant, The Casino Bar

Kelleys Island is a charming island community that is much more laid-back and quiet than its nearby party cousin, Put-in-Bay. Near the center of the village are a number of very good eateries serving up everything from burgers and fries (the Caddy Shack) to fine steaks (Fresch's Island House). Also don't miss the best brandy alexanders and onion rings on Lake Erie at the Village Pump. Tell proprietor Gary Finger that *GLC* sent you!

Sights to see around the island include the Kelly Mansion, now a bed and breakfast, built by Confederate prisoners during the war between the states; the Native American pictographs at Inscription Rock between downtown and Seaway Marina; and the glacial grooves on the Island's north side. During the last ice age, retreating glaciers scored deep grooves in the island's limestone core. Recent excavation has now exposed the island's entire geologic history.

The local Historical Society is in the process of building a museum in the heart of the village near the old stone church. This project was the recipient of the 1996 Kaplan Award.

The best way to see the island is by golf cart. You can rent one just about anywhere in the village and enjoy peaceful, scenic motoring along the island's shady roads.

Harbor Leamington, Ontario
Location Wharf Light: L42°01'25"N, Lo82°36'11"W
Dockage The Leamington Municipal Marina

Places to Stay Contact: The Town of Leamington 519-326-5761

Places to Eat Thirteen Russell Steakhouse, Diana's, Gallery Restaurant, Gingerbread House, Rick's on Erie, Super Submarine, Toronto Submarine, Wong's Dining Lounge

Leamington is located long the Canadian shore of western Lake Erie. Recently the entire marina and waterfront area has undergone a major renovation and is now one of the premier harbors along this coast.

While the facilities are wonderful and you could easily spend several days right in the marina, Leamington is a quaint town to visit. Right up the main street is the locally famous Tomato Hut. It's a small room-sized building on the sidewalk that is literally a giant tomato! Why is it there? It's the local tourist information center operated by the Leamington Chamber of Commerce. Why is it a tomato? Leamington is one of Ontario's chief agricultural areas and the principal crop is—tomatoes! The fact that the Heinz people opened a major plant here around the turn of the century was also a factor.

In the immediate area you should visit Point Pelee, a Canadian National Park preserving the natural eco-system of the marsh and wet lands on this peninsula. There are several interpretive centers in the park as well as helpful rangers and organized nature walks. There are several bathing beaches as well.

If you're into diving, the Pelee Passage has been called the Bermuda Triangle of the Great Lakes. Strong currents and sudden storms have sent an undue number of ships to the shallow bottom of this waterway. Many of those wrecks have now been located and identified by an organization called ErieQuest Marine Heritage. This organization has helped push for legislation to preserve the bottom as an underwater diving park.

Harbor Lorain, Ohio
Location West End of Main Breakwater Light: L41°28.8'N, Lo82°11.7'W
Dockage Spitzer's Marina, Lakeside Marina, Lorain Port Authority,
Gene's Marine Sales

Places to Stay Spitzer Plaza 1-800-446-7452, Lake Motel 440-245-6195

Places to Eat Broadway Cafe & Lounge, Campbell's Buffet, The Castle Feast
Restaurant

Lorain, Ohio, is one of the Lakes' older industrial ports. For many years this was a port well-known for shipbuilding and the steel trade. It's a port that has survived boom, bust and even the wrath of God. And still they are here, back with a booming tourist trade.

The lighthouse that greets you at the harbor entrance is very special. It's not one of the more picturesque or even the more famous of it's kind. But there is probably no other lighthouse so loved by its people. Back in 1917 they lobbied Congress heavily to have it built. There was a war on then but the people of Lorain were proud as anything to get the lighthouse. They named it the Jewel of the Port. Many years later the lighthouse was decommissioned and the Coast Guard wanted to tear it down. But the people fought, petitioned, organized and still, all hope was lost. But then a series of Great Lakes fall storms postponed the demolition until spring. By then the people had won their case and to this day the Jewel of the Port still greets nautical visitors.

Lorain also has a wonderful downtown district with a very interesting mix of architecture. One of the worst tornadoes in Ohio history virtually destroyed downtown in 1924. Of special interest is the fully restored Palace Theater. This is the world's largest one-story movie house complete with a very elegant ¾-ton crystal chandelier as a centerpiece. Why is it one story? When a tornado devastated the town, most of those who died, died in the old movie theater when the balcony collapsed. When it was rebuilt they designed it to accommodate the same number of people—but no balcony.

The Finger of God...

by Bruce Jenvey

A tornado is nature's most violent storm. As residents of the Great Lakes we are not strangers to their sudden attacks and swift destruction. Still, there is occasionally a storm of such incredible strength, that creates such devastation, such loss, that it reminds us of our own mortality and puts our values into perspective. These storms are called F-5s by professionals, the top of the force scale, the biggest a tornado can be—often called the Finger of God. Such a tornado struck Lorain on Saturday evening, June 28, 1924. Seventy-three years later it is still the most powerful storm in Ohio history.

It had been a hot and miserable summer day along the Ohio shoreline. The dark clouds and the muggy winds were enough to warn any midwesterner that heavy weather was coming. Saturday afternoon shoppers hurried their errands so they could be home and dry before the storm hit. Escaping the heat were a good number of determined swimmers at Lakeview Park on the city's west end. Intermittent showers throughout the afternoon chased them into the bathhouse until the rain passed, but then the swimmers ventured back out onto the steamy beach. Another large group of people opted to spend the afternoon and early evening in the State Theater on Broadway. Within those thick brick walls, they would not even hear the storm passing.

By 5 P.M. Lorain was as dark as night and the rain was coming down in buckets. While Broadway itself was deserted, the street was lined with parked cars. The shops and restaurants were filled with last minute shoppers seeking refuge from the rain.

At 5:14 P.M. one of the most powerful funnel clouds in recorded history came in off Lake Erie at Lakeview Park. The bathhouse where the swimmers had taken refuge was first to go. It was torn from its foundation, killing several inside and injuring many more. The cars in the adjacent parking lot were either thrown down the bluff to the beach or carried into downtown Lorain.

The residential section around 5th and 6th Streets was hit next. Homes and churches were completely leveled. In the words of John McGarvey of the Black River Historical Society, "My mother's house on 6th Street was the only house standing on its foundation, though the roof was gone. Carpenters came and put a roof on that very evening so that everyone from the neighborhood would have a place to stay that night."

Lorain's main drag, Broadway, was hit the worst. Those who took shelter in the stores watched as automobiles, horses and people, along with other unidentifiable debris, blew past.

In the State Theater the roof began to give way and the walls trembled. As panicked theater goers dashed for the exits, the roof collapsed bringing both levels of the balcony and part of the walls with it. Most who died in the storm died here.

But the State Theater was not alone in its fate. The tornado ripped down Broadway tearing walls off brick storefronts and completely razing others.

The twister leaped over the Black River, plowed through the working-class neighborhoods of the east end and devastated the shipyards that were one of the community's financial mainstays.

At 5:19 P.M. it left the Lorain city limits. It was only five minutes in duration, but five minutes is a very long time for a storm of this magnitude to remain within an area the size of Lorain, Ohio (1924 population was approximately 40,000.) There were 78 killed, around 1,200 injured and financial damages estimated at $35,000,000,00 (1924 dollars!).

There was no communication with the outside world except for one ham radio operator in town who managed to get his set on the air. His distress call was picked up by another ham in nearby Cleveland who alerted local authorities. Within minutes a relief effort was launched that brought sadly needed medical supplies as well as doctors and nurses to Lorain yet that night by tug boat, for the roads were all out. A make-shift hospital and morgue were set up at what was left of Central High School, and the National Guard and Red Cross were summoned. When Henry Baker, national director of Red Cross relief out of Washington, D.C., arrived in Lorain, he declared "It is the most complete devastation I have ever seen."

So as you visit Lorain and spend a few hours in Lakeview Park, try to imagine that day in 1924 when the giant funnel came ashore. When you walk past the historic buildings on Broadway, notice how many were built after 1924, and pay special attention to those that survived that day. And then pay close attention to the sky for while this may be the worst tornado in Ohio history, records are bound to be broken someday.

Harbor   Port Clinton, Ohio
Location   Breakwall Light: L41°31.1'N, Lo82°56.2'W
Dockage   Brand's Marina, Chaffee's Marina, Drawbridge Marina, Jackknife Marina, Lakefront Marina, Portage River Marina, Riverside Marina, Westdock Dockage

Places to Stay   The Island House 419-734-2166, The Inn at Spiess Harbor 1-800-999-ERIE, Scenic Rock Ledge Inn & Cottages 419-734-3265, Beachfront Motel & Resort 1-800-732-6684

Places to Eat   Victory Dining Room, Madison Street Cafe, Phil's Restaurant

Port Clinton is located on the southwestern shore of Lake Erie, just a short ways west of Sandusky and the Cedar Point Amusement Park. It's actually a quiet community in which to rest and relax from more hectic destinations, but there are a few sights to see.

The first and the most obvious is the Whistling Bridge. This art deco draw bridge across the river was built during the 1930s as a public works project. It was one of the first bridges anywhere to use a welded steel plate instead of traditional decking for the road surface. Consequently, as you drive a car across the bridge, it distinctly whistles! I am also told that local law enforcement officers have been alerted to speeders crossing the bridge by the pitch of the whistling.

Also in town, you can catch the speedy Jet Express boats to South Bass Island and the popular destination of Put-In-Bay.

Besides exploring this old village, the best thing to do while here is to take the Bay Area Trolley Tours (419-734-9530). They put you on a cute trolley-type bus and for the next three hours give you a narrated tour of the area's most famous historic sites including Johnson's Island which served as a prisoner-of-war camp for Confederates during the Civil War.

Lake Erie

Harbor   Port Colborne, Ontario
Location   Tallest Red Light at Breakwater: L42°51.9'N, Lo79°15.4'W
Dockage   Sugarloaf Marina, Marlon Marina

Places to Stay   Ingelside B&B 905-835-5062, The Port Motel 905-835-5202,
Seaway Motel, 905-834-9854, Sherkston Shores 1-800-263-8121

Places to Eat   The Upper Deck, The Roselawn Center, Showboat Festival
Theater, Joe's Place, Jacar Cafe, The Windjammer Tavern, The
Harbourfront Inn, Sauve's Bar & Grill, Tie Pink

Port Colborne lies on the Canadian shore of northeast Lake Erie
and is the southern terminus for the famed Welland Canal. For
those of you new to the Great Lakes, the Welland Canal is the high-
tech shipping lane that connects Lakes Erie and Ontario—and then on out
to sea. The Welland bypasses Niagara Falls and is obviously a much safer
(though slower) route.

If you're into freighter watching, this is the place to be! Fountainview
Park offers a great vantage point as it is adjacent to Lock #8 on the system.
There are beautifully manicured lawns and gardens with shaded picnic
areas from where you can watch the largest lock in the St. Lawrence
Seaway in action. Ships come in and in minutes are raised or lowered to
match the water level of Lake Erie or the rest of the canal system. This is
great fun for everyone.

Other sights to see include Arts Place—note, no apostrophe. There is
no one here named Art. Instead, Art is the subject or the content as it were.
This is one of Canada's finest galleries where local professional artisans
showcase and sell their work. Art is on display in virtually every medium
you can imagine from paintings and sculpture to jewelry and glasswork.

You can also visit the historic downtown district of Port Colborne.
Historic West Street is filled with shops and eateries in buildings dating
back well into the 1800s. The Street is closed twice a year for Canal Days,
and International Week, two of the biggest festivals in Ontario.

There are many more things to enjoy in Port Colborne including live
theater and fine dining in the European tradition.

Harbor Port Dover, Ontario
Location Port Dover Lighthouse: L42°46.8'N, Lo80°12.1'W
Dockage The Government Dock, Mathews Marine, Port Dover Yacht Club, Bridge Marine Services, Port Dover Harbour Marina

Places to Stay The Crabapple Creek B&B 519-583-2509, Peggy Jane's B&B, The Bed & Breakfast by the Lake 519-583-1010, The Port of Call B&B 519-583-1642, Erie Beach Hotel 519-583-1391

Places to Eat Cove Room, The Terrace Lounge, Memories Bar & Grill, Cairn's Corner, Frank's for the Memories, The Arbor

Chances are, if you're an American you've never heard of Port Dover, Ontario. If you're a Canadian you already know that this is one of the most popular resort communities along the Lake Erie shore. This is a place of sugar-sand beaches, quaint shopping and shaded walkways. It's one of Canada's best kept secrets and here am I, blowing the lid off things!

The first thing you should do after arriving in Port Dover (after calling into customs), is to catch the Port Dover Rover. This is nothing more than a tractor dressed up like a fishing tug that pulls a train of cars with bench seats. But what a ride! First off, Port Dover is full of hills and the Rover can really smooth those out for you. Also, the driver gives you a constant narration, pointing out all the sights to see along the route. During lunch hours, the Rover modifies its usual route to pass through some of the community's more historic neighborhoods. The Rover regularly stops in the marina and at many other spots around the city. Look for the framed signs with the orange flags, or you can just flag it down when you see it. The ride is free but your donation helps defray the cost of this service.

Among the things to see in Port Dover is the Lighthouse Festival Theater. This is a professional theater group that performs in a wonderfully maintained, acoustically perfect turn-of-the-century theater complete with tin ceilings. It's easy to find. Just look for the old clock tower in town. The theater is on the second floor of the old firehouse, above the Board of Trade (Chamber of Commerce). The building is just as fascinating. The clock tower dates back to 1906 and is still hand-tended today. Every Sunday morning two volunteers climb the tower, oil the mechanism and wind the clock. After nearly a hundred years of continuous operation it does tend to lose two or three minutes a week.

Harbor Port Maitland/Dunnville, Ontario
Location Grand River Front Range Light: L42°51'10.7"N, Lo79°34'47.3"W
Dockage Port Maitland Marina, Port Maitland Sailing Club, Dunnville Boat Club, Riverside Marina, Betamik Harbour, The Grand Island Bar-B-Q (Yes, for dockage)

Places to Stay Betamik Harbour Loft 905-774-2827, Grand Old Cellar B&B 905-774-5965

Places to Eat Arrow's Roadhouse, Bob's Place, Godfather Pizza, Yo Ho's Restaurant, Lorna's, Buckwheat's, Knowle's Restaurant

Located in northeast Lake Erie along the Canadian shore, Port Maitland is a mere shadow of the harbor it once was. Today you will find little here other than transient boating facilities. However, just a few miles up the Grand River you'll find the town of Dunnville, a thriving provincial town with a lot to see and do. In between the two you'll find five miles of protected marsh and wetlands on either side of the river. Altogether a quiet harbor, an ecologically rich marshland and a thriving town, this is one of the more interesting destinations you will enjoy along this shore.

If the peace and quiet and the communing with nature grow old, take a shopping trip in town and eat at any of the casual eateries you'll find along the way. Or just spend an afternoon window shopping on the main drag.

An excellent time to visit the area is in early July, in time for the Mudcat Festival. There are boat races on the river, parades in town, a fishing derby and a golf tournament. On the Saturday night of the festival the entire town turns out for the biggest fireworks display in the area.

Also of special note: The river entrance here is marked by the Mohawk Island Light. Now in disrepair, a local group of preservationists is desperately trying to save this example of the famed Imperial Towers lighthouse group. There were only six built and few are still standing today.

Harbor Port Stanley, Ontario
Location West Breakwater Light: L42°39′28″, Lo81°12′49″
Dockage Kettle Creek Marina, Stan's Marina, Kangio Yacht Club, Port Stanley Sailing Club, Barry's Bend Marina, Harbour Club Marina

Places to Stay Mitchell House 519-782-4707, Kettle Creek Inn 519-782-3388, The Windjammer 519-782-4173

Places to Eat Bookee's Pizza, Godfather Pizza, Wharf Restaurant & Bar, GT's Portside, San Saba Cafe

Port Stanley is a small commercial port on the north central shore of Lake Erie at the mouth of Kettle Creek. This is an old town. The navigational light at the end of the pier dates back to 1844. They still have a very active fishing fleet with a line of steel tugs tied up along the sea wall and a very rustic looking collection of net sheds along the harbor shore. Nets are wound on giant wooden frames while drying and awaiting repair. This gives the town a very quaint New England appearance and at the same time lets you see the inner-workings of the last of the fishing trade.

The village itself is surprisingly small considering the amount of commercial traffic you see. Many of the storefronts are over 100 years old and not redone in false Victorian gingerbread decor. They are the way they have been for all these years. Nothing fancy, purely functional. There are a number of interesting shops to discover, but this is not a port where shopping is high on the "to do" list.

What is? How about a ride on the *Kettle Creek Queen* excursion boat. It's styled after an old side-wheeler, but underneath the decks it's safe and modern. It'll take you anywhere there is a sight to see throughout the area. You can also ride the train. The Port Stanley Terminal Railroad is located in, of all places, the old train station. This railroad and its cars have been lovingly restored by avid rail buffs and now take you on a simply wonderful excursion ride. Leave your bags on the boat, it's a round-trip.

Then there are always the beaches. Port Stanley has two and they are both long, wide and sandy!

166

Harbor Put-in-Bay, Ohio
Location Perry's Monument: L41°39.8'N, Lo82°48.7'W
Dockage Municipal Marina 419-285-2068, Ohio State Park Docks,
Boardwalk Boarders 419-285-6183, The Crew's Nest 419-285-
3625, Ladd's Marina 419-285-2571

Places to Stay Contact: Put-in-Bay Chamber 419-285-2832

Places to Eat Beer Barrel Saloon, Round House Bar, Chicken Patio, Frosty's,
The Cresent Tavern, The Boat House, The Village Bakery &
Sandwich Shoppe

Put-in-Bay is really the name of the town located on South Bass
Island in western Lake Erie. Of course, you can get here by boat,
but you can also get here by car or bicycle if you catch the ferry
from Sandusky or Catawba Island, Ohio.

This is the original party town in lake Erie. It's a very busy port that is
home to various boating regattas and rendezvous over the summer. All
the action centers around De Rivera Park in the heart of the harbor. While
one side of the park is bordered by the Municipal Marina, the other three
sides are a carnival of shops, snack shops and bars. Places that you won't
want to miss include the Beer Barrel Saloon which has the longest bar in
the world. Also, the Round House Bar is a well-known drinking establishment with a history over a hundred years strong. One more place I'll
mention is Frosty's. Supposedly named for the temperature of the beer
you can find there, it's their pizza that makes the mouths of sailors water!
"Don't miss!"

However, if you take the time to rent a golf cart, you can see the "other
Put-In-Bay." This is an island steeped in history. It was the base used by
Commodore Perry before and after the famous Battle of Lake Erie during
the War of 1812. The tall monument in the harbor commemorates this battle and if you take the elevator to the top, a recorded narration will re-tell
the heroic story and point out all the sights. Don't miss the local historical
society's museum just off the main drag near the Bear Barrel Saloon, nor
the two sets of caves near the island's center.

Harbor Rondeau Bay, Ontario
Location Erieau Light: L42°15.4′N, Lo81°54.4′W
Dockage Erieau Marina, Erieau Yacht Club, Rondeau Bay Marina

Places to Stay Rondeau Bay Lodge, Johnston's Motel

Places to Eat Lester's on the Bay, Eau Bouy Galley Restaurant, Slip-In Restaurant and Lounge, Molly & O.J.'s Restaurant

Rondeau Bay is a quite cottage community along the north shore of Lake Erie. A large natural sandbar forms the shallow well-protected bay with its only entrance on the west end, anchored by a settlement (not quite a town) called Erieau. This is a quiet place to fish or day-sail. There are shade trees and pathways to enjoy. The only night life here buzzes, croaks and is occasionally swatted.

But while you're relaxing along the shady shoreline you may notice one thing this community is really quite famous for: All those small sailboats racing about the bay.

They're called Larks and are a one-design, racing-day sailor made famous by a man known as Pop Weir. One day, an American tourist came into Pop's boat-building shop with the 1880 plans for a Dutch sailboat called the Lark. "Can you build this?" he asked, and the rest is history. Pop and his brother Al built quite a few of the boats. They were sixteen-feet long, six-feet wide, and only drafted a foot and a half on a swing keel. Yet they carried an amazing 210 square feet of sail.!

Needless to say, these boat were very fast. At one regatta in Toronto, a Lark performed at speeds estimated at 30 miles per hour. Not bad for a wooden boat. Unfortunately the craft was constantly being disqualified in many competitions because it was "just too darn fast."

Pop and Al Weir died in the mid-1960s and everyone thought that would be the end of the Larks. But local craftsmen have preserved the jigs and often rebuild old Larks they find abandoned in backyards around the bay. It is still said that if you want a real challenge, take a gutsy Canadian, put him in one of these white-knuckle wonders and just try and catch him! Somewhere, Pop Weir is smiling...

Harbor Sandusky, Ohio
Location Sandusky Bay Buoy "G1": L41°30.4'N, Lo82°39.8'W
Dockage Battery Park Marina, Dock Of The Bay Marina, Deep Water Marina, Cedar Point Marina, Sandusky Yacht Club, Sandusky Sailing Club

Places to Stay Contact: The Sandusky/Erie County Visitors Bureau 419-625-2984

Places to Eat Damon's, Angry Trout Fish & Steakhouse, Daly's Irish Pub, Timothy's Casual Dining, Neat Sweets

Sandusky, Ohio, is on the southern shores of Lake Erie near the very famous amusement park, Cedar Point. The town was originally settled in 1812 by farmers and shopkeepers who were burned out by the great forest fires in the east. The town was laid out by Masons. In fact all the streets are perfectly square except two which run at what appear to be odd angles to the rest. In the center of town is a wonderful park with a floral clock and other perfectly maintained flower beds. But when viewed from the air, the street pattern and park combine to create the familiar symbol of the secret society of Free Masons.

Almost immediately the town was fortified against the British during the War of 1812. In fact Battery Park Marina was originally the eastern fortification of the town. Some of the cannons are still there today, but the British have kept their noses out of here for quite some time now.

In town, you'll find old storefronts and interesting shops. Of special interest, do not miss the Merry-Go-Round Museum, a collection of wooden horses and giant swans set to the background of calliope music. Also be sure to visit the historic State Theater. Now perfectly restored, the facility is home to film and live stage presentations. There are several marine museums in town, each with its own unique collection as this community has a seafaring history like no other.

If you tire of museums, parks, floral clocks and storefronts, Cedar Point Amusement Park with more roller coasters than any other park is just across the bay.

Harbor Scudder, Ontario
Location Outer Wharf Light: L41°48′51″N, Lo82°39′35″W
Dockage Scudder Marina 519-724-2377

Places to Stay Contact: Pelee Island Public Relations, Pelee Island, Ontario N0R 1M0

Places to Eat Various small eateries

If you've been looking for a place to be alone, to escape the rat race, or just a little peace and quiet, Scudder on Pelee Island should fit the bill. Pelee Island is the northern-most of the Erie islands in the western end of the lake. This is Canadian soil and is really only accessible by private boat or the ferry out of Leamington that visits the port on the island's north shore.

Scudder itself is little more than a small collection of stores and municipal buildings. You can spend a nice afternoon here, but the real fun of this destination is to explore the rest of this rural island.

On the most northern point of the island, you will find the old Pelee Passage Lighthouse, or rather what's left of it as it is in ruins with no plans for restoration. The rest of the island is farmland and countryside, with the ruins of an old winery slowly being covered by advancing plant life.

There is no night life here, no excitement, no city lights—and they like it that way.

Harbor Toledo, Ohio
Location Toledo Harbor Light: L41°45.6'N, Lo83°19.5'W
Dockage The New Harrison Marina, Pier 75 Marina

Places to Stay Contact: The Greater Toledo Convention & Visitors Bureau
800-243-4667

Places to Eat Tony Packo's, Fritz & Alfedo's Restaurant, Andre's, Aztec Grille
Steakhouse, Garden Cafe, American Plaza Cafe, Murphy's
Place, The Spaghetti Warehouse, Old Navy Bistro, The Bagel
Place, My Brother's Place, Manos Greek Restaurant

When you think of exotic cruising destinations, you usually don't
think of Toledo, Ohio. But if you've been passing by this port on
your way around the Lakes, you've been missing a lot!

Toledo has a wonderfully restored waterfront park and several very
nice museums. These include the Toledo Museum of Art, The Firefighters
Museum and the *S.S. Willis B. Boyer*, a retired coal-fired lake carrier turned
museum. Also, don't miss Murphy's Lighthouses. This is a nautical gift
shop that features hand-crafted lighthouse lamps and models, all created
by Murphy himself. You will find his work here and in the homes of the
rich and famous including Katherine Hepburn.

There are many eateries to try, but of special note is Tony Packo's. This
is the hot dog eatery made famous by Max Klinger of TV's M*A*S*H*. On
the wall you will find petrified hot dog buns autographed by some of the
worlds most famous hot dog eaters! (They tend to be Hollywood stars
too.)

Toledo has two points of historical note: This was the site of the war of
1835, a short-lived border skirmish between the militias of Ohio and
Michigan. Shots were fired but the only casualty was a pig. Ohio got the
Toledo corridor and Michigan was given the Upper Peninsula as compensa-
tion. There is also a most historic lighthouse in the harbor that for many
years was rumored to be haunted—but the phantom in the lantern room
turned out to be just a mannequin placed there by the Coast Guard to
deter vandals.

Harbor Vermilion, Ohio
Location East Breakwater Light L41°25.7'N, Lo82°21.9'W
Dockage Vermilion Port Authority Docks, Romp's Waterport, Vermilion
Yacht Club, Vermilion Boat Club, Moe's, Valley Harbor Marina

Places to Stay Contact: Vermilion Chamber 440-967-4477

Places to Eat McGarvey's, Chez Francois, Nemo's Subs & Pizza,
Old Prague Restaurant

Vermilion is located on the southern shore of Lake Erie just west of Cleveland at the mouth of the Vermilion River. This is a wonderful Ohio small town with a lot going for it.

Right out at the harbor's edge is the Inland Seas Maritime Museum. This was originally the home of Commodore Fred Wakefield and his family, but was donated to the local historical society in 1953. Inside, the house is packed with relics of Vermilion's nautical past. You see, Vermilion was once home to no fewer than 50 lake captains. There are certainly many more artifacts to see than there is room to display them. On the grounds you can also see a replica of Vermilion's first navigational light, which has been commissioned by the Coast Guard and is listed on the charts as a privately maintained aid to navigation. You'll also find the pilothouse from the old freighter *Canopus*. If you've ever wondered what it was like to stand behind the wheel of one of these giant lake boats, or maybe pore over the chart table, here's your chance.

This should put you in the frame of mind to go house hunting. Not to buy but to admire. Remember, this town was once home to 50 lake captains who made good money and built homes to reflect their status. The homes are all private residences today but they are beautifully maintained and make wonderful photographs.

Vermilion also has an historic downtown business district that has been preserved and restored for your shopping pleasure. There are many quaint shops to explore ranging from The Teddy Bear's Garden to Brummer's Homemade Chocolates. This is a small town you can really relax in and enjoy!

Harbor Chatham, Ontario
Location Thames River Entrance Buoy: L42°20.6′N, Lo82°28.7′W
Dockage West End Docks, Civic Center Docks, Southside Docks, Northside Docks (all along the river front)

Places to Stay Best Western Wheels Motor Inn 1-800-265-5257

Places to Eat 104 Wellington, Dimitar's and Dimitar's Diner, The Bistro-on-the-Half-Shell, Thames Bistro Seven Seas, Hillary's, Hillary's Too, Rossini's Restaurant

Chatham, Ontario, is located a ways inland from Lake St. Clair, up the Thames River. This is a modern, cosmopolitan, small city filled with trendy restaurants, bistros and boutiques. Put these establishments into perfectly maintained historic storefronts and you have a good feel for what awaits you.

The most popular place to stay is the Best Western Wheels Motor Inn. This is an entirely indoor resort with plenty to do for the kids, dad, and there's even a complete beauty and health spa for mom.

One of the most popular things to do in town is the self-guided historic walking tour. The buildings are fantastic and the names associated with their creation are interlinked with Canadian and American history. Want an example? Right next door to historic City Hall is the Kent Club, a fantastic old structure that dates back to 1880. Inside is a plaque that honors William Chrysler, the town's founder and first citizen. He's very famous here but not as famous as his great grandson is in the States. The great grandson was named Walter and stamped the family name on a large number of automobiles in Detroit (yes, that Chrysler!)

The Chatham Railroad Museum and the old courthouse and jail building are other stops on the walking tour. But as long as you're about, stop by Tecumseh Park along the river bank. This is just one of the beautifully landscaped parks, but remember who it honors: Chief Tecumseh of the Shawnee who fought with the British during the War of 1812. It was Tecumseh who stopped the American advance up the Ontario peninsula in the Battle of the Thames while his British allies retreated. Outnumbered four to one, Tecumseh fought until he was mortally wounded. This park is allegedly the spot where the great Shawnee leader died.

Harbor Clinton River, Michigan
Location Red & White Buoy Near River Entrance: L42°35'65"N,
Lo82°44'75"W
Dockage

Belle Maer Harbor 810-465-4534, Markley Marine 810-469-6000,
Sun Dog Marine 810-468-5400, Burr Yacht Charters 810-463-8629
Places to Stay

Contact: Boat Town Chamber 810-468-3989
Places to Eat

Crew's Inn, Breakers, Gar Wood's, Shannon's Steak House,
Terry's Terrace, Hadley's Oar House

The Clinton River entrance along the western shore of Lake St. Clair is one of America's boating capitals. There are more boats here per square mile than anywhere else on earth! Also known locally as Boat Town, it's a strip along the north and south side of the river lined with restaurants and the favorite watering holes for generations of boaters.

There's not much for the cruiser to do here other than eat, drink and boat watch, but boat watching is one of the favorite pastimes. You will see virtually every kind of boat, make and model on parade here as they work their way up and down the river between the many marinas and the lake.

Of special interest to boat watchers will be the *Pride of Michigan* on the south side of the river across from the Crow's Nest Restaurant. The *Pride* is a retired navy mine sweeper, now a training vessel currently under the command of the local unit of the U.S. Naval Sea Cadets. This teenage crew runs the ship and takes it on extended training missions across the lakes. LCDR Luke Clyburn, captain of the vessel, has been taking kids across the Lakes for over twenty years now. Currently they are involved in a multi-year mission to gather data to find the lost ship *Griffin*. The *Griffin* was the very first sailing vessel on the Great Lakes and belonged to the famed explorer LaSalle. It disappeared without a trace on its maiden voyage in 1679.

You can't miss the *Pride*. She looks like a small destroyer without the guns, and bears hull number YP673.

Lake St. Clair

Harbor Detroit, Michigan
Location North End of the Detroit River (you can't miss it)
Dockage St. Aubin's Park Marina L42°19.9'N, Lo83°01.3'W,
Erma Henderson Marina, Detroit Yacht Club

Places to Stay Contact: Detroit Visitors & Convention Bureau 313-202-1800

Places to Eat Summit Restaurant, Greek Town (various), The Caucus Club,
Dunleavy'z River Place, The Soup Kitchen

Detroit is a massive metropolitan city experiencing a renaissance along it's waterfront. For boaters the best place to stay is the St. Albin's Park Marina. It's clean, modern and yes, secured. It's a short walk to the Renaissance Center where the Marriott hotel's preferred dockage for land yachters is located. From here you can catch the People Mover, an elevated monorail system to other major points in the city.

If I may suggest, Hart Plaza with its many ethnic festivals and annual fireworks display is right next door to the Marriott. The People Mover will take you to Greek Town, an enclave of Greek restaurants and eclectic shops you won't find anywhere else. This is where you will find Trapper's Alley, an old converted warehouse now filled with eateries and stores.

You can also ride to the Theater District where the beautifully restored Fox Theater is home to national stage acts and classic films. The Fox was one of the last grand movie palaces built before the Great Depression. After years of abandonment it was purchased and brought back to life by Mike Ilitch, the well-known businessman behind Little Caesar's Pizza. The Ilitch family will also entertain you with the Detroit Red Wings hockey team that plays in Joe Louis Arena on the waterfront, and the Detroit Tigers baseball team that currently plays in the classic old Tiger Stadium at the corner of Michigan and Trumble, but will soon move to a new stadium near the Theater District. This will be a double stadium complex, and will also house the Detroit Lions football team.

There is much more to Detroit, of course. Besides museums and restaurants, there's always freighter watching. On a per-tonnage basis, the Detroit River is the busiest waterway in the world. You can literally watch the world sail by.

Hi Ho, Trolley!
By Bruce Jenvey

In Detroit in the golden days of yesteryear, trolley cars were the principal means of public transportation. Their surface tracks and suspended electrical feed lines covered much of the city's main routes. They could take the early-century commuter pretty well wherever he needed to go.

This included routes all the way up Woodward Avenue through what is now the Cultural Center and right past the current School Center Building. Back in the early 1930s this building was the home of WXYZ radio. It was in these studios along Woodward Avenue that several famous radio shows of the era originated.

"Sergeant Preston of The Yukon," "The Green Hornet" and "The Lone Ranger" were among the most famous programs to call Detroit home. And as was the tradition in those days, they were broadcast live. In the specific case of "The Lone Ranger," the broadcast itself was live but the opening sound sequence was pre-recorded on a transcription disk and played back while the actors took their places around the microphone. It included the orchestra pounding out the familiar "William Tell Overture," Silver's thundering hoof beats, and the announcer beckoning us back to those thrilling days of yesteryear.

But times change, shows are eventually replaced and in the case of radio, can even be supplanted by a more advanced medium. People forget. And then one day it can all come racing back from the past, and quite accidentally, as in this incident told to me by my good friend (and subscriber) Jim Zinser.

In the late 1960s the old studios of WXYZ belonged to WDET and Wayne State University. Right next door was the transmitter site for WGPR television where Jim was then employed. During renovations they came across a closet containing some long forgotten articles nearly forty years old. Among these was a box of old transcription disks. Of course the young engineers couldn't wait to hear what they had found and started plopping these records down on their modern turntables and pumping the audio through their state-of-the-art sound systems.

Sure enough, up from one disk came the familiar strains of the "William Tell Overture" and the announcer's beckoning voice. But there, right in with Silver's thundering hoof beats, was the sound of distant bells!

It took the engineers some time to isolate and identify the sound. Finally an older member of the staff who had grown up in the city recognized it as the distinctive bell of the Woodward trolley. Apparently recording devices of the 1930s were far more sensitive and accurate than even the WXYZ engineers had known, and far more sensitive than the playback equipment of the day. Undetected for hundreds of broadcasts, these trolley bells had been riding right along with the Lone Ranger and Tonto, and had kept their secret for nearly forty years.

ken miller

Lake St. Clair

Harbor   St. Clair, Michigan
Location   Pine River Drawbridge: L42°49.3'N, Lo82°29.3'W
Dockage   Charles F. Moore Municipal Boat Harbor

Places to Stay   The St. Clair Inn 810-329-2222, The Murphy Inn 810-329-7118

Places to Eat   The Saint Clair Inn, The Murphy Inn, Voyageur Restaurant, Rachelle's, London's Ice Cream

St. Clair, Michigan, is very historic town located on the St. Clair River between Lake Huron and Lake St. Clair. A drawbridge that crosses the entrance to the marina opens on the hour and the half-hour. If you are patient enough to wait, you will discover a truly wonderful town with friendly people and a very gracious setting.

The marina is on the south side of the Pine River and the town is on the north side. It's a short walk across the drawbridge or there is a courtesy van that will take you anywhere you want to go. By all means visit the downtown district. There are shops and stores along the river-front highway, some are even in an open air mall! There's everything from eclectic book shops to Captain Jim's Gallery where all nautical art can be found. Right across the street is a wonderful shady park right on the bank of the river where the freighters pass by up close and personal.

There are also some wonderful buildings in town and a great museum on south 4th street in the old Baptist Church. Historically, this town was settled by the Hopkins Family. One of the Hopkins made a fortune in the California gold rush (he sold picks and shovels to prospectors but never mined for gold himself). He died young and left his fortune to his brother and his family, settling this town. Many of the historic churches were built with donated gold-rush money.

Also of interest is the site of the famous Langell Brothers Shipyard where some of the most famous steamers to tame the lakes were built. It was located where the marina is now. Just south of town is the site of the old Hotel Oakland, a luxury resort hotel that rivaled the Grand Hotel on Mackinac Island. It went bankrupt, burned and was then demolished, all by the 1920s.

The Oakland Hotel

by Bruce Jenvey

Not far south of the AKZO Salt plant in St. Clair, Michigan, you come to two very important structures along the St. Clair River bank. One is the St. Clair Post of the Michigan State Police. Next to it is a bait and tackle shop known as the Angler Rod & Sports. They have both taken up residence on the former site of the famed Oakland Hotel. To replace one of the "grandest of the grand," this must be one important tackle shop and a most impressive police post. But we're getting ahead of ourselves. We'd better start by rolling back the clock over one hundred years.

In brief, local millwright and pipe joiner Samuel Hopkins was fortunate enough to have an extremely wealthy brother who lived a shorter life than Samuel. The brother, Mark Hopkins, had made his fortune first in the gold rush and then on the transcontinental railroad. When he died in 1879 he left his entire estate worth more than twenty million dollars to his brother and his brother's children. Samuel's son, also named Mark, took over most of the family finances and soon put this vast fortune to work improving the lives and the livelihoods of the local residents.

Amongst several business investments the family made was the construction of the luxurious Oakland Hotel on the site of a small mineral spring. In the late Victorian era mineral springs were generally believed to be the magic cure for any ailment. Of course, mineral springs tended to be in remote areas, and extended stays were the standard course of treatment. This meant that such cures were really only accessible to the wealthy.

So the doctors prescribed a month in the magic waters and the rich Victorian industrialists would pack up their families, leave the polluted air of the coal-burning factories and the stress of their six-day work weeks, and head for the mineral springs. Hotels near these health-giving waters tended to be more than just comfortable, they were downright elegant, opulent, and the most luxurious facilities you could imagine.

Taking a month in the clean country air, basking in the sun, and playing croquet on the manicured lawn tended to have very positive effects on the health of the guests. But should you ask anyone, it was without a doubt the magic in the minerals in the water! The Oakland Hotel was no exception.

This grand resort was among the most luxurious in the Great Lakes.

She was 235 feet long, four stories high and constructed entirely of wood. Huge covered verandahs stretched out from the first and third floors, and the entire structure was nestled into the hillside on the banks of the river. Below, the Oakland's private docks awaited those wealthy guests who arrived by luxury steamer. If you preferred rail travel, the hotel's own rail terminal sat on the southern edge of the property.

Guests were pampered in private suites that rivaled the *Titanic*, complete with marble fireplace mantles and Brussels carpets. There were approximately 115 such rooms ranging in price from $3 to $5 per day, the same price charged by the Grand Hotel on Mackinac Island in the same era.

The Oakland was a complete resort with grass tennis courts, a riding stable, a gymnasium, a two-hundred-acre woods with hiking trails and picnic grounds, fishing facilities and several other more mundane pastimes including a private bowling alley and billiard parlor. The Oakland had something for everyone.

But times and people change. Eventually telephone lines were installed so busy industrialists could stay in touch with their factories. The Interurban Railroad extended its line making commuting to and from the hotel a possibility for those too busy to just "pack up and go." Then came the automobile so that guests could come and go as they wished, or as they needed.

Then the strangest thing happened. The magic waters seemed to lose some of their magic. A month at the resort no longer seemed to have the positive effect it once did. Occupancy dropped. Soon the hotel was only open during the height of the season. In 1915 it partially burned and didn't have the strength to recover.

In the late 1920s the Oakland was demolished and removed from the river bank in the name of progress. The land was sold off for private residences, of which there are plenty in the area. But the heart of the hotel, the center of the resort, is now occupied by the two aforementioned establishments. Someone should call the police...

Harbor Wallaceburg, Ontario
Location On the Sydenham River, off the Chenal Ecarte
Dockage All along the seawall throughout the village, look for the white pilings with red caps.

Places to Stay Oak's Inn 519-627-1433

Places to Eat Acorn Dinner Theater, Leftfield Lounge

Wallaceburg is a sleepy provincial Canadian town just a short distance northeast of Detroit. You can get there by boat through a series of rivers, or by car by catching the ferry in Algonac, Michigan.

The village is built on both sides of the Sydenham River, making this a town of drawbridges and waterfront parks. Boaters can tie up wherever they see the white poles with the red tops. There is always a harbormaster's office close at hand as well as a Canada Customs phone. The parks are beautifully landscaped and meticulously groomed and maintained. It's a lovely summer afternoon to sit in the shade and watch the bridge tenders in action.

There are two big celebrations in town every year. The WAMBO is the gathering of antique boat and motor buffs from all over the central lakes. You'll see perfectly restored vessels from nearly a century ago (or less) that run and shine like the day they were first launched. You'll also get a chance to share the secrets and the passions of those who rebuild these classic crafts.

The other big celebration is the annual (mid-July) Pow Wow at the nearby Walpole Island First Nation, or Indian reservation. This is a weekend of colorful pageantry and spirited competition among those of native decent. The public is welcome.

Iron Men and Wooden Ships
The Story of the Langell Shipyard

by Bruce Jenvey

One of the most famous industries ever to call St. Clair home is now a foot-note in history. Gone, and to many people forgotten. But if you're staying in the marina, this piece of history is close at hand. You just have to look around or below for a possible trace or a glimpse into the past. If you still can't see it, I encourage you to visit the St. Clair Historical Commission Museum located in the old Baptist Church on South Fourth Street. They can give you more than a glimpse; they can show you maps and photographs of the famed Langell Brothers Shipyard. In preparing this story, we were most fortunate to have the help of the Museum which allowed us access to a narrative written by William Langell in 1934. History this good needs to be repeated!

Captain Simon Langell was born in Nova Scotia in 1835, the son of French Huguenot refugees who fled France during the revolution. When Simon was only eight years old his father moved the family to Newport, Michigan, a small town on the St. Clair River better known today as Marine City.

Simon struggled to educate himself and eventually secured a teacher's certificate. But the shipyards called louder than the classrooms and Simon Langell began building boats. First for others, and then for himself farther north in St. Clair.

In 1878 Captain Langell moved his shipyard from the shallow waters of the St. Clair River bank just south of the Pine River to property just inside the first bend of the Pine River on the south bank, a site today occupied by the public boat harbor and the adjacent private boating facility. The marina's horseshoe pit stands approximately where the bow end of some of the Great Lakes' finest schooners and steamers took shape.

Ship building in those days was a rugged business. Huge wooden beams were roughed-in by hand-ax and cut to size with hand-operated whip saws. Holes for structural supports were augured into the wood by hand. Who built these ships? Half of the Langell Brothers yard crew were French-Canadians from Montreal and Quebec who had built ships for the very demanding British. The other half were Scottish immigrants who had also built ships for the British. These two groups rivaled each other as to who could build the toughest, the fastest... you get the idea. Some of the finest ships ever built came out of this yard, and commerce on the Great Lakes was the true benefactor of their labor. These were definitely, as William Langell himself said, "Iron men building wooden ships."

Some of the more famous ships to leave these ways included the *Fontana* and the *Kaliyuga*. In their days each was rated the best wooden ship on the water. The *Kaliyuga* was also the largest ship the Langells ever built at 1941 tons. The entire town turned out for her christening in 1887. But shipping in those days before radio and weather radar was a dangerous profession. The *Kaliyuga* was lost with all hands in the teeth of a Lake Huron gale in 1905.

The steamer *Langell Boys* also deserves mention here because of the name she bore and because she was built for use by the Langells themselves. She met her end, as so many wooden steamers did, by fire. A blaze started in the engine compartment and overtook the ship on Saginaw Bay. While there was no loss of life, the *Langell Boys* burned to the waterline and sank before anyone could help her.

I once heard an old man near the Soo telling stories to young boys about the early days of shipping on the Lakes, and the vast number of steamers lost to fire. "When you start building fires inside wooden boats and then toss 'em about on the likes of these Great Lakes, well—you're bound to singe the carpet now and then."

By the turn of the century, steel boats were the preferred construction method and the iron men who built the wooden ships faded into history.

ken miller

Lake Ontario

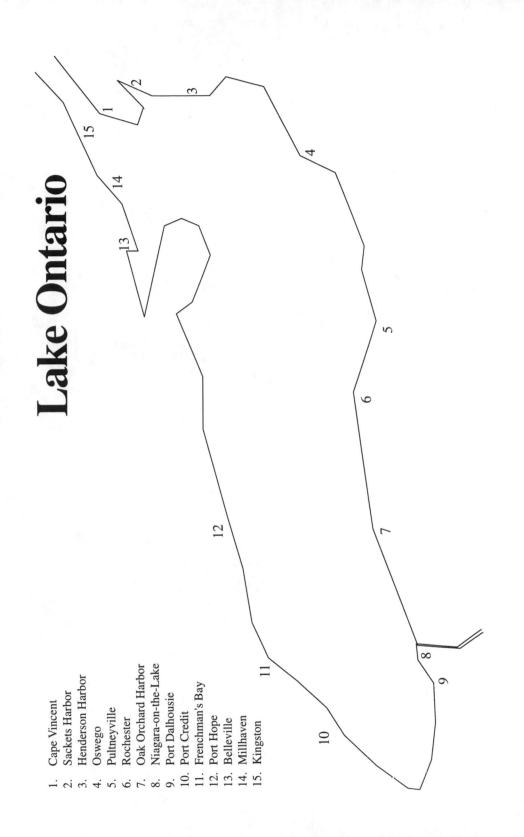

1. Cape Vincent
2. Sackets Harbor
3. Henderson Harbor
4. Oswego
5. Pultneyville
6. Rochester
7. Oak Orchard Harbor
8. Niagara-on-the-Lake
9. Port Dalhousie
10. Port Credit
11. Frenchman's Bay
12. Port Hope
13. Belleville
14. Millhaven
15. Kingston

Harbor Belleville, Ontario
Location The Norris-Whitney Bridge: L44°08.9'N, Lo77°23.3'W
Dockage Meyer's Pier, The Government Wharf, Morch Marine

Places to Stay Best Western 613-969-1112, Comfort Inn 613-966-7703,
Ramada Inn 613-968-3411, Quality Inn 613-962-9211,
The Avalon Motel 613-966-6622,
Clarion Inn & Suites 613-962-4531

Places to Eat Gatsby's Lounge, Angus Buffet House, Kelsey's, The Lobster
Trap, Bailey's, Danny's Diner, The Royal Garden Buffet

Belleville, Ontario, is perhaps one of the nicest destinations you will find. First of all this is a good-sized city, not a small out-of-the-way hamlet. It's also a very old city, founded just after the American Revolution by a band of British Loyalists and Mohawk Indians forced across the border by intolerance in the newly independent colonies. They vowed to build a community based on acceptance and tolerance. Over two hundred years later, it's still here.

But first things first. Belleville is on the beautiful Bay of Quinte near the southern entrance to the Trent-Severn Waterway. The bay is really a twisting, turning series of rivers and waterways that eventually open onto Lake Ontario. Along the way they form some of the most wonderful beaches and parks in this part of the Lakes.

Belleville has an excellent selection of eateries and shoreside accommodations. While you're enjoying these modern amenities, take time to explore the historic downtown district's eclectic collection of shops. There are many wonderful old buildings to see here including City Hall, originally built as the Market Building and used as an indoor farmers' market. Eventually this function was moved outdoor along the east end of the building, and the municipal offices were allowed to expand.

Don't miss the Glanmore Historic Site, a perfectly restored Victorian mansion filled with antiques and relics of daily life from the era. An afternoon here can do much to provide an understanding of what life was like.

One more attraction you have to see is Reid's Dairy. This headquarters facility for Ontario's principal dairy producer has evolved into a dairy theme park complete with a fairy-tale castle. The Dairy Princess lives in the tower and you can visit her ten stories above the ground. And no, the Princess does not believe in elevators.

Harbor Cape Vincent, New York
Location West End of Breakwater Light: L44°07'54"N, Lo76°20'06"W
Dockage Cape Vincent Village Dock, Anchor Marina,
The Department of Fisheries

Places to Stay Buccaneer B&B 315-654-2975, Point St. Basin B&B 315-654-2982, Sunny Morn B&B 315-654-2477, Riverside Cottages 315-654-2001, Sleepy Hollow Motel 315-654-2944, Roxy's Motel 315-654-2456, Tibbetts Point Lighthouse Hostel

Places to Eat Captain Jack's, Cape Restaurant & Lounge, Aubrey's Inn

Cape Vincent, New York, is at the most eastern end of Lake Ontario where the lake becomes the St. Lawrence River. This is a sleepy settlement where there are only two things to get excited about: Sport fishing, any time you can get to go, and the annual French Festival. Actually there's more, but after fishing and the festival, who cares?

So why is there a French Festival here? Many of the town's early residents were French nationals loyal to Napoleon. After the battle of Waterloo, many were forced to flee France and they settled here. In fact on the site of the town library once stood a stately house built to be the exile home of Napoleon himself! But he could never escape his island prison and years after his death, the house in Cape Vincent was sold. Eventually it burned and the library took its place.

There were other famous residents here, though. Among them was General Delos Sacket of the U.S. Army. This particular General Sacket served in the Mexican and Civil Wars. You can visit his house today, where for years after his retirement he was known to entertain his old army buddies—guys like General McClellan and General Sheridan just to name a few.

The rest of the historic walking tour of town is just as impressive and will take you past the local historical museum which itself is part of the display, having served as a soldiers barracks during the War of 1812. You'll also see the New York Fisheries and Wildlife Building. This ivy covered structure was the first limestone industrial building in town. Today it houses a public aquarium, among other things.

Just west of town is historic Tibbetts Point Lighthouse, now a youth hostel.

Harbor Frenchman's Bay, Ontario
Location Red & White Mid Channel Buoy: L43°47.2'N, Lo79°05.0'W
Dockage Frenchman's Bay Yacht Club, The East Shore Marina, Swan's
Marine, Port Pickering Marina, Moore Haven Wharf

Places to Stay Contact: The Town of Pickering 905-420-4625

Places to Eat Massey's Restaurant, Square Boy Pizza & Subs,
Regalis Restaurant, The Old Liverpool House

You won't find Frenchman's Bay on many maps. It's really the old name still attached to the recreational harbor in the Toronto suburb called Pickering. It's an interesting history that has allowed this name to remain.

Originally it was a natural harbor used as a settlement and as a transient facility by French voyageurs. As the English moved into the area and started their own settlement called York just to the west of here, they left the French alone. At first it was a very successful settlement that the French civilians would fight to keep. Also, the English feared the local Indians who had a wonderful relationship with the French. York grew and Frenchman's Bay kept its autonomy.

Eventually York grew so big as to virtually swallow the French settlement, but it never incorporated the real estate. This was about the time of the big name change. A small town to the east gave up a local Indian name it had been using and called itself Port Hope. York, now under a civilian government, took up this name and called itself Toronto. Eventually Pickering absorbed Frenchman's Bay, but still today the harbor area is called by the old name.

The bay is in the sprawling metropolis of Toronto. There are wonderful beaches and fantastic parks to enjoy along the waterfront, but you are just minutes from the GO train station and a short commute into the heart of Toronto.

Harbor Henderson Harbor, New York
Location Green Buoy "1": L43°54.7'N, Lo76°11.8'W
Dockage West View Marina, Henchen's Marina & Fishing Camp, Captain's Cove Motel Marina, Henderson Harbor Yacht Club, Ron Ditch & Son's Fishing Camp, Cornell's Marina, Harbor Marina, Harbor's End, Lake Ontario Mariners

Places to Stay The Gill House Inn 315-938-5013, Dobson House 315-938-5901, The West View Lodge 315-938-5722,

Places to Eat The Gill House Inn, Verrilli's

Henderson Harbor in located in a quiet bay along the eastern U.S. shore of Lake Ontario. If there's a fisherman in your crew, his eyes just lit up! Henderson Harbor is one of the best known sport fishing harbors in the eastern lakes. It is also home of the famous "Rod & Reel" television show created by the well-known angler Bill Saiff. Many episodes of the show have been shot right here in this harbor.

If sport fishing doesn't get to you, how about sailboat racing? The Henderson Harbor Yacht Club revived one-design racing in this area just after World War II. The well-protected waters of the wide bay proved to be a tremendously popular race course too. In fact the Olympic trials were held here in 1976.

How about historic buildings? Henderson Harbor and the surrounding countryside is loaded with them, and the local chamber would be pleased to provide you with a map and directions. This area is old, very old. This was a very active community at the time of the War of 1812, and continued to grow and prosper after that. (Be sure to read the associated story, "The Cable".) Of special note on the tour is the old Mark Hopkins Hotel. This was once the palatial country home of a railroad magnate. It was later run as an inn, hence the name. But today it has been taken over by the local chamber and is in the process of becoming a center for the local performing arts. An outdoor concert series on the grounds is already a major attraction. Remember, you are just around the corner from historic Sacketts Harbor. These two have a related history.

"Just Clean Up the Table When You're Done, Georgie..."
by Bruce Jenvey

Since it's beginnings, Rochester, New York, has been a city of innovation and the American Spirit. There are lots of things you have and enjoy today that somehow can be traced back to their earliest roots, right here. Want some examples?

It was 1853 when two friends named John and Henry decided to open a small optical shop together. The growing community needed one, and it looked like a promising business opportunity. This could have been a rather inconspicuous moment in time other than the fact that I'm talking about John Jacob Bausch and Henry Lomb—yes, the very men whose names still grace the Fortune 500 company's world headquarters here in Rochester. The optical business was just the beginning for them.

It was even earlier than that when a young man named Jesse Hatch developed something most all of us once had—baby shoes. The very first ones! And at the same time, a young woman developed an undergarment for ladies that has carried her name throughout history—Amelia Bloomer.

In 1849 two Rochesterites changed the way the world would write. Absalom Bishop and Thayer Codding threw away their quills and straight pens and introduced the modern fountain pen to the world.

If you're hungry, feast on this: In 1895 the very first commercially produced marshmallows came from Rochester, and just two years later in nearby LeRoy, a very silly thing called Jell-O was invented.

But wait, there's more! In 1906 a small firm called the Haloid Company opened its doors in a loft above a Rochester shoe factory. After a slow but steady business with many failures along the way, they hit on an idea in 1959 that would make it easier to reproduce important documents. Two years later the Haloid Company changed its name to Xerox.

But there's one more I have to share with you. In the late 1880s, a young bank clerk spent his evenings experimenting with photographic equipment in his mother's kitchen. Back then, photography was for professionals only and the whole process was messy and quite involved. What this poor woman must have gone through, trying to prepare meals and preserve food around her son's chemicals and experiments. But this bank clerk saw the possibility that anyone could become a photographer, and that personal moments could be preserved. In 1888 he did it and brought to the marketplace his first camera for the common man. This must have made Mrs. Eastman very proud. Oh, did I forget to mention? The bank clerk was George Eastman and somewhere on that table between the roast beef and the applesauce, the Eastman Kodak Company was born. It's still here in Rochester today but the facilities are a bit nicer.

Is this creative period in Rochester's history over? Think about this: Patents continue to be granted to Rochester-area residents at a rate three times higher than anywhere else in the United States. Makes you kinda wonder what's on the kitchen table right now, doesn't it?

ken miller

Harbor Kingston, Ontario
Location Carruther's Point Light: L44°12.5'N, Lo76°32.9'W
Dockage Portsmouth Olympic Harbour Park, Kingston Yacht Club,
The Kingston Marina, Confederation Basin

Places to Stay Rosemont B&B 613-531-8844, Conway's Inn 613-546-4285,
First Canada Inns 613-541-1111, Hochelaga Inn 613-549-5534,
Hotel Belvedere 613-548-1565

Places to Eat The Harbor, The Copper Penny, The Pilot House, Chez Piggy,
Buffet Uncle Tong, Dan Aykroyd's Ghetto House Cafe

Kingston is a major Canadian city located at the far eastern end of Lake Ontario at the mouth of the St. Lawrence River. Really, Kingston is in the center of things.

Some of the most beautiful scenery in the Great Lakes region is found in the famed Thousand Islands. While I have never counted them they form an impressive barrier between the end of the lake and the beginning of the river. They are rustic and oh, so magnificent! You can see them without the need of your own boat by buying a ticket on the many cruise boats that give guided tours of the area.

From here the Rideau Canal locks its way north to Ottawa, this nation's capital. The canal was very important to the British after the War of 1812. They had found out that even an upstart nation could disrupt their shipping on the open lakes. The Rideau Canal, in conjunction with the Trent-Severn Waterway and the Ottawa River, gave the British a navigable waterway that didn't flow along the American border.

There is all kinds of history here with no less than a dozen museums to visit. Each one is truly top-flight too. But just for highlights: Visit the Bellvue House, the private home of Sir John A. MacDonald. He was this area's most famous resident and eventually served as Canada's first prime minister. Also on this same theme, visit the Old City Hall building in the heart of downtown. If it looks a little fancy for a city hall, you're right. It was originally built to be Canada's first Parliament Building until a last minute compromise took the capital to Ottawa.

Also visit Fort Henry. In its day this was the largest fort/military installation in North America. Because it never saw battle it is perfectly preserved and open to the public.

Harbor Millhaven, Ontario
Location Millhaven Creek Buoy: Approximately L44°11.5'N, Lo76°44.4'W
Dockage The Government Ferry Dock (do not tie up in area reserved for the ferry!)

Places to Stay The Millhaven Inn 613-352-7822

Places to Eat Millhaven Grocery

I was the one who labeled Millhaven as conveniently located in the middle of nowhere. And it's true. Here at Millhaven you can tie up at the government dock as long as you don't use the area reserved for the ferry boat. You can buy food at the Millhaven grocery store. They have it carryout or eat-in which means there is a small dinette attached to the grocery. Then there is the magnificent Millhaven Inn. This is an old stagecoach house that dates back prior to 1800. No one knows for sure exactly how old it really is but it has been an anchor in the countryside for travelers for over two-hundred years now. Today its a very popular Bed & Breakfast.

And that's the town. That's it, that's all, that's what you get here. Yes, there's beautiful countryside in the Bay of Quinte area and yes, they aren't far from other civilization. In fact you can travel down the Loyalists Parkway to some of Ontario's finest parks for a day in the sand. Or visit the nearby town of Bath for antiques or just browsing. You can take the ferry to Amherst Island and watch the craftsmen at work or enjoy the summer concert series. And that's just for starters.

When you think about it, Millhaven really is conveniently located in the middle of nowhere.

Harbor Niagara-on-the-Lake, Ontario
Location Fort Mississauga Light: L43°25.5'N, Lo79°04.6'W
Dockage Niagara-on-the-Lake Sailing Club 905-468-3966, Williams
Marine 716-745-7000, Youngstown Yacht Club 716-745-7230

Places to Stay The Olde Angel Inn, The Pillar & Post Inn, The Prince of Wales
Hotel, The Colonel Butler Inn

Places to Eat The Olde Angel Inn, George III, The Luis House Restaurant,
The Prince Of Wales Hotel, The Buttery Theatre Restaurant,
Bella's

This is one of my favorite destinations on the Great Lakes. It's a perfectly preserved Victorian village where shopkeepers sweep their sidewalks and bells ring as the doors open and close.

It is also at the mouth of the Niagara River just a few minutes drive from the famous falls and whirlpool rapids. The way to the falls is one of the most beautiful drives you will find in any season you decide to go. If you prefer, there is also a paved walkway for bikes and rollerbladers to follow, and much of the river bank is under the control of Parks Canada. All along the way you will see magnificent gorges carved from the layered stone and lined with trees and flowers. You'll pass through Queenston Heights, the site of one of the most famous battles of the War of 1812

It was also the War of 1812 that gave Niagara-on-the-Lake it's most famous resident. In the heart of the town on Regent Street is a small eatery and B&B called The Olde Angel Inn. During the American invasion a young British officer was captured and executed here by the American army. The ghost of Captain Swayze has often been known to haunt the old inn creating mayhem by rearranging place settings and messing about with the silverware. On several occasions he has been seen in the basement storage room where he was allegedly shot.

Of course there is more to do in this charming village. I would be in great error if I didn't at least mention the annual Shaw Festival, a season's worth of professionally presented stage plays that date back to the time of George Bernard Shaw. For a season's schedule, contact the local Chamber of Commerce at 905-468-4263.

The Olde Angel Inn

by Bruce Jenvey

Hidden away on Regent Street between Johnson and Queen is The Olde Angel Inn. It's possible to miss this old public house, being off the beaten path and surrounded by so much to see and do, but I strongly suggest you make time to find it and explore one of the village's most infamous structures.

The use of the word infamous is perhaps uncalled for, but if I have your attention, it worked. The Angel Inn is an experience you won't long forget and I dare say any trip to Niagara-on-the-Lake would be incomplete without at least taking a brew in Upper Canada's oldest existing Inn. Let me tempt you further.

The Angel Inn was originally built some time before the War of 1812. No one knows for sure and those who claim to know have conflicting dates. It's old, very old. During the American invasion in 1813, the Angel Inn was one of the structures burned but not completely destroyed. It was rebuilt (as was virtually the whole town) in 1816 and maintains its original foundations and appearance even to this day.

But the Angel Inn is its own witness to its past. Just one glance about the ceilings and rafters in the north dining room tells the story of 1813 with the charred timbers and supports still quite evident. Along one beam you can see where a musket once hung, its outline having shielded that section of the beam from the flames. Want more?

The Inn is still an active public house or pub in every British sense of the word. Stepping through these doors can not only take you back a few years but transport you a few thousand miles as well. It's delightful!

It's also one of the best restaurants in town with a full service menu for lunch and dinner. Go ahead and bring your kids, this is a pub, not a bar. There's something on the menu for everyone and everyone will like what they find. This place is old world charm at its best with fascinating antiques and curiosities to admire while you eat. Still want more?

What would an inn be without rooms? There aren't very many, and you usually have to make a reservation well in advance to have the honor of staying here, but it's worth it. The rooms are cozy, colonial and haunted. Yes, I did say haunted.

In fact, the entire Inn is haunted by at least two spirits, the least famous of which is a cat. Over the years more than one guest has remarked to the management that during the night a cat entered the room and made itself comfortable on the foot of the guest's bed. Apparently the cat knows it is choosing the room of a cat lover for no one who has ever seen the cat has had any desire to chase it from the room. But in the morning the cat is gone. And when the guests inquire as to the whereabouts of the creature, they find out there hasn't been a cat inside the Angel Inn in years—but apparently there was one once.

The other ghost of the Angel Inn is far better known. During the war of 1812, Captain Swayze was a British officer stationed at Fort George. During the invasion of 1813 he was caught by the Americans in the Angel Inn. Here, the story differs depending on who tells it, but there is bound to be some truth in all versions.

Some say the Captain was brutally beaten and tortured by the Americans near the fireplace in the main room not far from where the musket-shaped image remains on the rafter. Some say it was this very musket that killed him. Some say it happened right there in the dining room, while others say he was taken to the basement and killed there. Some say it wasn't Captain Swayze at all but another young officer whose name has slipped from the history books, but generally he is at least known as "The Captain." The details of who, where and how hardly seem to matter for the spirit seems to roam freely about the interior of the entire Inn.

He has been seen only once, by recent accounts, by a barmaid who had gone to the basement for supplies. There among the kegs and the well-stocked shelves, she saw the white phosphorescent figure of a man standing against the wall. He was there only a moment or two and then he was gone.

But Captain Swayze makes his presence known in other ways. There have been repeated accounts by the previous management of windows in the guest rooms opening themselves in the middle of the night. It seems the good captain likes fresh air!

He is also a mover and a shaker, in that he is often credited with moving objects from their usual placement, or one of his favorite tricks, shaking the silverware bins which not only makes a tremendous racket but creates a great degree of disorder the staff must correct.

Just a couple of years ago the Inn changed owners. Peter and Diane Ling from Toronto became the new keepers with Peter moving in alone during the cleaning and moving process. One afternoon he was interviewed by a local newspaperman who asked about his knowledge concerning the famous ghost. While aware of the legends, Peter admitted that he had had no contact.

The next morning Peter was awakened by a tremendous racket downstairs in the main room. A heavy horseshoe he had brought with him from Toronto and left on the fireplace mantle had been flung some twenty feet across the room, striking the front door. The horseshoe seemed to be pointed directly at the door so Peter opened it to find the morning paper with the headline staring him directly in the face, "New Inn Owner Wants To Meet The Ghost." He considered himself introduced.

Over the decades countless mediums have visited the Inn. While many will tell you that every such investigation deals in "possibilities," and often have dissenting opinions, every psychic who has ever set foot here has agreed: Someone not alive is doing very well at the Angel Inn.

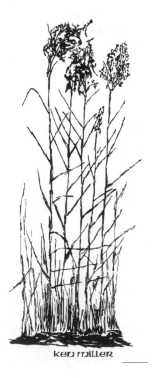

ken miller

Harbor Oak Orchard Harbor, New York
Location Main Breakwater Light: L43°22.5'N, Lo78°11.36'W
Dockage Orleans County Marine Park, Four C's Marina, Oak Point Marina, The Captain's Cove Resort

Places to Stay Contact: Orleans County Tourism 716-589-3187

Places to Eat The Barbary Coast, The Black North, The Breeze Inn Cafe, Veronica's Tea Room, Brown's Berry Patch, Tillman's Village Inn

 Oak Orchard Harbor is what upstate New York is all about. Here you will find a very well-protected harbor carved out of a very rustic existence. There is really no town to speak of, so I hope you didn't plan to finish your Christmas shopping here. But you will find a large number of bait and tackle shops dotting the countryside.

That's because sport fishing is the primary industry around here. And here, this is big business. The waters of central Lake Ontario are cold and clear and loaded with prize-winning fish. The rivers and streams that converge on this area carry a bounty of sport fish to be reeled in. Whatever you want, you can probably find it here. Is it any wonder than that the primary employment around the area relates to the tourism/fishing industry? You can charter a captain, a boat and a captain, or just a guide. The guide can take you out on your boat, or merely show you the best land-based fishing in the area. What stream where, yields what kind of fish, when? The guides know!

There are a number of very good restaurants here and there around the local countryside. They tend to be at intersections rather than in organized communities. Just pick one off the list above and ask a local how to get there. They all know where they are. And all the eateries are winners.

One more thing to see while you're here is the Cobblestone Society Museum (716-589-9013). This is a collection of genuine cobblestone houses and buildings from the area's past. You see, many years ago, the farmers were quite prosperous here. A wooden frame house would no longer reflect their status and position in the county. That's when they started building them from cobblestone with ornate decorations and patterns. You can see some of these beautiful structures right here, in one place, today.

Harbor Oswego. New York
Location West Pierhead Lighthouse: L43°28.4'N, Lo76°31.0'W
Dockage Oswego Marina 315-342-0436, Wright's Landing 315-343-8430

Places to Stay The Best Western's Captain's Quarters 315-342-4040,
The Oswego Inn 315-342-6200

Places to Eat The Ritz Diner, Cam's New York Pizzeria, Canale's Restorante,
The Office Tavern & Restuarant, Vona's, The Char Pit,
Lombardo's Bridie Manor, The Captain's Lounge Restaurant

 You have three ways to get to Oswego: by land yacht, by boat by crossing open Lake Ontario, or by canal! Yes, the Old Oswego Ship Canal begins in the harbor and progresses through a series of locks inland to where it joins the Erie Canal and leads you to Lake Erie at Buffalo.

No matter how you get there, you will find Oswego a wonderful place to relax and enjoy the friendly atmosphere. However, there are a few things to put on your "Don't miss" list besides their infamous haunted lighthouse.

First, visit the Oswego Maritime Foundation in the harbor. This non-profit organization is in the process of building their own replica of a nineteenth century Lakes schooner named the *O.M.F. Ontario*. When finished, she will serve as a classroom for students of all ages and will teach history, ecology, biology and sailing during regularly scheduled outings. Stop in and see how they're doing.

Another "Don't miss" is Fort Ontario at the mouth of the river. A fort of some kind has stood on this site since the mid-1700s. First built by the British, it has been destroyed and rebuilt a number of times by the French, the British and the Americans. The current incarnation of the fort dates back to 1840 and has served as a military training ground during the Civil War, as a major gathering point for the famed Underground Railroad, and it has even housed refugees from the Nazi concentration camps of WWII.

Every July, Harborfest is a major celebration of history at the fort and is complete with a Civil War encampment and an open attack by British tall ships. The Civil War guys usually win and the captured square-riggers are tied up to the pier for your inspection.

The Haunting of the Oswego Light

by Bruce Jenvey

Oswego Harbor gives us an attraction worth noting—a haunted lighthouse. The very lighthouse that you round at the end of the breakwater when you enter the harbor is host to a number of bizarre happenings linked to a ghostly presence.

The light was built in 1934, modern enough to discount it on your list of possible haunted houses, but all that changed one night in 1942.

An early winter storm that year had raged for days, stranding the lighthouse keeper alone at this post with dwindling supplies. In a courageous effort reminiscent of the old Life Saving Service days, eight Coast Guardsmen from the local station set out in a long boat to relieve the keeper.

They succeeded in reaching the lighthouse and put a fresh keeper and supplies in the station. But when they turned their boat back towards shore, an unexpected swell smashed their craft against the lighthouse crib. Six of the eight drowned and therein lies the tragedy that seems to have triggered the ghostly visitations.

From that night on, the peace and serenity of the lighthouse was often disrupted by the sounds of strange voices and footsteps in the stairwells. Frequently, malfunctioning lights are found to be caused by unscrewed bulbs. And most unsettling of all, from shore, lights are sometimes seen illuminating every window in the structure—even those sealed over with steel plating! To the relief of many, this light was automated in 1968.

ken miller

Harbor Port Credit, Ontario
Location Breakwater Entrance: L43°33.72'N, Lo79°33.37'W
Dockage The New Port Credit Municipal Marina, Lakefront Promenade Marina, Port Credit Yacht Club, Port Credit Harbour Marina, Bristol Marina, LTD

Places to Stay The Ports Hotel 905-274-7390

Places to Eat Auntie Alba's Eatery, VanGo, Lainey's Cafe, Halina's Deli, Gray's Lakehouse Restaurant, Country Fish & Chips, The Suisse Marmite Restaurant & Tavern, J.J.'s Cafe, The Aielli Restorante

Port Credit is just 11 miles west of Toronto on the northern shore of Lake Ontario. It was founded in 1834 and was a well-known, rough-and-tumble trading port for only the saltiest of Great Lakes sailors. Those days are gone now. Even though Port Credit officially became part of the city of Mississauga (a large suburb of Toronto) in 1968, it has never lost its small town or small port feel.

I'm a firm believer that if you're new in town, the first stop you should make is the local tourist information center. The people of Port Credit wanted to make theirs easy to find so they put it in the lighthouse. You pass it coming in by boat, or if you find the harbor by car, you can't pass it by without notice. Here you'll find all sorts of local knowledge.

The town today is a large collection of interesting shops and eateries with landscaped walkways and shaded benches. But then this has always been a place to shop. In the days of the voyageurs, this was a major trading post with the local native tribes. Sometimes they didn't bring enough furs with them to buy all the products they wanted. Since the trading post was so well established, it was not uncommon for the merchants to extend credit to the shoppers. Eventually this place became known as the "River of Credit." When it officially became a town, an established port, the original name stayed on. If you have the right kind of plastic, that tradition is still honored by merchants today.

Harbor Port Dalhousie, Ontario
Location Eastern Breakwall Light: L43°12.5'N, Lo79°15.8'W
Dockage Port Dalhousie Pier Marina, Dalhousie Yacht Club, Albert's Marina, City of St. Catharines Docks

Places to Stay Contact: City of St. Catharines Economic Development 905-688-5601

Places to Eat Albert's on the Water, Murphy's Restaurant & Peg Leg Tavern, The Lakeside Hotel, Port Mansion Restaurant & Dinner Theater, Da Pizza Joint, Taco/Tequila Taqueria

Port Dalhousie is an historic village on the southern shores of Lake Ontario. Once, it was the northern entrance to the Welland Canal that connects Lakes Ontario and Erie. But as ships grew and larger more modern facilities were needed, the canal's course changed over time, now exiting at Port Weller some two and one-half miles to the east.

This village is now a neighborhood in much larger St. Catharines, Ontario, but manages to maintain much of its independent charm. There are perfectly maintained storefronts to explore and a wide range of shops and eateries to patronize. On the top of your "Don't miss" list of prime eateries include Murphy's Peg Leg Tavern, Marie's Seafood and Albert's on the Water, When it comes to wonderfully preserved architecture, save time to stroll around the old city hall in the heart of the village.

But one of the biggest pastimes here is rowing—you know, with the long pointy boats and the guys who all row in unison. You can join a team, join the club or just be a spectator, but competitive rowing is serious business around here. It began in the mid to late 1800s and by 1880 the Canadian Association of Amateur Oarsmen was founded here. In 1903 the new Welland Canal was opened leaving a long stretch of well-protected, abandoned canal literally at the C.A.A.O.'s disposal. What is now called Martindale Pond is the permanent venue for several rowing competitions including the prestigious Henley Regatta. With grandstands and controlled water levels, it is considered to be the finest facility of its kind in the world.

Lake Ontario

Harbor Port Hope, Ontario
Location West Breakwater Light: L43°56.4'N, Lo78°17.5'W
Dockage Port Hope Yacht Club, Port Hope Municipal Marina

Places to Stay The Brimar B&B 905-885-9396, The Uppertowne Inn B&B 905-885-5694, The Carlyle Inn 905-885-8686, The Hillcrest Inn 175 Dorset Street West

Places to Eat The Carlyle Inn, The Beamish House, The Owl & The Pussycat Tea Room, Ye Olde English Fish & Chips, The Dover Seafood House, Slurp's, Shubert's

Port Hope, Ontario, is a perfectly preserved Victorian town on the Canadian shore of Lake Ontario. Located just minutes east of Toronto (by car) at the mouth of the Ganaraska River, this is a community that definitely marches to an olde world drum.

Wonderfully restored storefronts are home to a huge selection of antique shops, art galleries, clothing boutiques and antique jewelry stores. You'll get your exercise here too as the town is built into a series of high bluffs on either bank of the Ganaraska River. And as long as you're walking, take the self-guided historical tour past the grand old churches and homes of the town. You can get a map for the tour from the tourist information center in the heart of downtown. I greatly encourage you to see these old buildings. This is perhaps the finest collection of such structures anywhere in the Great Lakes.

Amongst all these antiques and British culture, who would expect to find a tremendous sport-fishing industry? You will here! Trout and salmon hunters from all over the Lakes know of the record-setting catches that come out of the Ganaraska. And there's one more thing that you need to know comes out of the river—weird boats! Yes, every April the local chamber sponsors the "Float Your Fanny Down The Ganny River Race." The term "race" is used kindly. It's more of a survival thing as people take to the river in about anything that sort of floats. Prizes are awarded for creative presentation as well as simple completion of the course. It's great fun and must be seen to be believed.

Also, Port Hope is the final resting place of Galermo Antonio Farini, The Great Farini of Victorian circus fame. Turn the page to read about his unique link with this provincial city.

204

"Don't Do It, Bill!"

by Bruce Jenvey

On January 17, 1929, the town of Port Hope laid to rest Galermo Antonio Farini—The Great Farini. He was 92 at his passing, and he left behind a legacy of show-stopping courage and international fame.

In the late 1800s The Great Farini made headlines for his command performances as one of the world's most daring high-wire acts. He entertained and thrilled millions worldwide with his amazing balance and expertise on the tightrope. His most famous performances would have to be his repeated crossings of Niagara Falls. Yes, he strung a rope across the most powerful cataract on earth and amazed the crowd as he carried objects, even grown men, from one side of the gorge to the other. And he did so on several occasions! He was perhaps the most famous, most talented tightrope artist of all time.

So why was Galermo Antonio Farini buried in Port Hope, Ontario? Because he was born there. In fact he started his career there, except in those days, he was known simply as William Leonard Hunt.

On a cold October day in 1859, twenty-one-year-old Bill Hunt slipped into his rubber shoes and prepared for his first public performance. He had strung a rope from the top of one building in downtown Port Hope, across the Ganaraska River, to a building on the far shore. And he was going to walk across it.

The town thought him mad. What had driven him to think he could do this? Was it the visit of P.T. Barnum's circus just seven years ago? Whatever it was, the townsfolk shouted at poor Bill to give it up, to climb down. Surely he'd wind up splattered on Walton Street.

But Bill Hunt ignored the chants, the jeers and the pleading shouts from the crowd and climbed out on the tightrope. What happened next held the crowd spellbound, the first of many crowds he would hypnotize. He walked across the rope not once but several times. He performed stunts. He even paused halfway across and hung by his feet above the surging river. The crowd was in awe, and all shouts of discouragement ceased.

It may have been young Bill Hunt who climbed out on to the tightrope that day, but there was no doubt in anyone's mind that it was The Great Farini who climbed down.

Harbor Pultneyville, New York
Location Flashing Buoys at River's Entrance: L43°17.2′N, Lo77°11.0′W
Dockage Pultneyville Marina, Pultneyville Yacht Club, Huges Marina

Places to Stay Captain Throop House B&B 315-589-8595, Hermitage B&B 315-589-2174

Places to Eat None in the village, visit nearby Williamson

Historically, the town of Pultneyville was attacked and captured by the British navy during the War of 1812. The town really put up no struggle and was therefore spared the agony of being burned to the ground as was the common practice by both sides during this conflict. However, there were a few cannonballs lobbed into town and one of the older residences on historic Washington Street still has one lodged in the floorboards. The current owners are forbidden to remove it, as it is protected by the local historical society and is a condition of the deed.

Pultneyville is a very old New England-style settlement with legends and superstitions enough for any reclusive hamlet. We included this destination in our October 1995 issue of *Great Lakes Cruiser* magazine because of the high incidence of supernatural happenings in town.

The Captain Throop House is a popular bed and breakfast despite the fact that the ghost of the good captain himself is regularly known to drag heavy furniture about in the attic while guests are trying to sleep in the rooms below. On one occasion Captain Throop even invaded the dreams of a small boy who awoke the next morning with tales of an old man working in the yard with windmills. It seems Captain Throop once experimented with a windmill-driven propeller system for ships.

The Craig mansion is also one of the locally known haunts. Here, a Mrs. Stell who once visited the house predicted in a letter to the owners that she would be a frequent visitor after her death. That was many years ago and all the poltergeist activity has made it hard to keep workmen on the job.

Harbor Rochester, New York
Location Rochester Harbor Light: L43°15.8'N, Lo77°35.9'W
Dockage Rochester Yacht Club, Pelican Marina, Voyager Boat Sales, Riverview Yacht Basin

Places to Stay Contact: Great Rochester Visitors Association 1-800-677-1102

Places to Eat Schooner's Riverside Pub, The Anchor Inn, Chesterfield's Neighborhood Restaurant, Pelican's Nest, Driftwood Inn, Charlotte Tavern, Doc's, Tony's Bootlegger, Portside Cafe

Rochester is a major city on the southern shores of Lake Ontario. Inside the breakwalls of the ship canal is one of the most historic lighthouses on the Lakes. The tower itself dates back to 1822, and the building and grounds now serve as a museum. But that's not the only "old thing" that's "new again" in Rochester.

Ontario Beach Park was once one of the premier bathing beaches in upstate New York. In recent years the famous bathhouse and the 1904 Dentzel Carousel have been completely restored to their turn-of-the-century perfection. A modern boardwalk along the beach has been added with several gazebos for rest and comfort while you admire the Lake Ontario shoreline.

In the center of town the High Falls are now a major attraction in what used to be the warehouse district. Now, many modern shops and eateries populate the old buildings in the district called Brown's Race. Also don't miss the *Sam Patch*. This is a tour boat modeled after an antique canal-boat design, and gives narrated excursions of the river. Remember that Lake Ontario connects here, through Rochester, to the Erie Barge Canal system allowing you access to Lake Erie and the Finger Lakes Region.

Rochester is a town of famous names and inventors. Of particular note is the Eastman Kodak Company. The mansion of their founder, George Eastman, is open for tours. Be sure to read the associated story, "Just Clean Up the Table When You're Done, Georgie."

The Cable

by Bruce Jenvey

It was June 1814, late in the War of 1812. The British navy had slowly gained control of most of the lower lakes including Lake Ontario and were bringing great pressure to bear on Sackets Harbor, the largest most fortified American outpost on the Great Lakes that also served as our principal shipyard and naval base. Commodore Chauncey was in the process of building the battleship *Superior* in the yard, a vessel that could change the balance of power in Lake Ontario. With the hull completed and the spars taking shape, great lengths of rope were needed to stay the rigging. The cable, as it was called, was in Oswego—and between Oswego and Sackets Harbor was the British navy.

But those upstart American colonists would not be thwarted. The vast amount of cable was moved up the coast by ship to Sandy Point, as far as safety would allow. It was then unloaded and a rag-tag band of sailors and soldiers shouldered the great length of cable and proceeded to snake it up the country roads through farms and villages all the way to Sackets Harbor. But the soldiers and sailors were too few and the cable was too heavy. Near the village of Henderson, the progress of the cable began to slow and the future of the much needed *Superior* fell into question.

The word went out across the countryside that volunteers were needed. Men, women, children, farm hands and shopkeepers alike fell into line along with the navy and the army and kept the cable moving to Commodore Chauncey. How much cable finally made it to Sackets Harbor? Enough to build a battleship!

ken miller

Harbor Sackets Harbor, New York
Location Horse Island Light: L43°56.6'N, Lo76°08.8'W
Dockage Navy Point Marina, Grunerts Marina, Sackets Harbor Town Dock, Liberty Yachts

Places to Stay Ontario Place Hotel 315-646-8000, Madison Barracks 315-646-1234

Places to Eat Ian's Eatery, Harbor Master Inn, 1812 Steak and Seafood Company, The Old Stone Row, The Barracks Inn

Sacketts Harbor is one of the most historic sites on all the Great Lakes. During the War of 1812, this was the principle naval base and shipyard for the American forces. A large garrison of soldiers and marines were also stationed at the fort. Two important battles were fought here, the second in the spring of 1813 proving to be the more decisive and costly to both sides.

Today, preservation has won out over renovation, and much of Sacketts Harbor looks as it did during "the second war for independence." But there are a few differences inside. The shops along the harbor road are now occupied by boutiques and entertainment establishments. There is really quite a night life here with a comedy club, live entertainment and fine eateries. However, it's the history lover in your crew who will be in heaven here. To fully enjoy all the history, stop by the Visitors Information Center in the center of town. For a $2 donation, you can get a book called *Harbor Walk*, which is a detailed guide to the fort, the many museums, the military cemetery and the Madison Barracks among other sites.

Two interesting footnotes: In the cemetery you will find the grave of General Zebulon Pike, who died at the Battle of York. Before the war he was an explorer who discovered Pike's Peak. Also, the barracks burned in 1879 and were rebuilt and maintained as a military base only because of the insistence of an officer who had served here as a lieutenant fresh out of West Point. Of course he had since attained the rank of general— General Grant to be exact—and at the time of the fire he was President of the United States. They rebuilt the barracks.

The Battles of Sackets Harbor
by Bruce Jenvey

While everyone refers to The Battle of Sackets Harbor during the War of 1812, it is important to remember that there were two. And it was the first one that set the stage for a long line of historical events including the second battle, the big one, the one everyone remembers.

The first Battle of Sackets Harbor took place in July of 1812, just one month into the war and was probably nothing more than a trial balloon on behalf of the British navy. A handful of British and Canadian ships approached the harbor but cannon fire from the brig *Oneida* and the meager land-based fortifications there at the time scattered the ships and sent them sailing back to Kingston. The Americans celebrated a great victory while the king's forces took notice that the upstart Americans were darn serious about this little war.

Meanwhile in Washington the powers that were decided that Sackets Harbor must be a gem the British dearly wanted otherwise they wouldn't have attacked it so. This meant it had to be fortified, and so it was done. By the spring of 1813 Sackets Harbor was a massive military installation with thousands of troops, several small forts all walled and linked together into a fierce fortification, and a navy yard where sizable warships were built, serviced and stationed.

As soon as the ice broke on Lake Ontario it was decided that this sizable force needed to prove its worth and was sent off to attack the British installation at York (now, Toronto). Why York? York was at the opposite end of the lake. This would be a wonderful way to prove domination of the waters. York was also the regional capital and a victory here would make excellent press. At the same time, fortifications at York were still under construction so it would be a lot easier to storm the beaches here than at heavily fortified Kingston. In late April 1813 York was attacked, looted and much of it burned.

In retaliation just one month later, in late May 1813, the British mounted an attack on Sackets Harbor from Kingston. Why Sackets Harbor? It was so built up that it was now the principal American base in the Great Lakes. A British victory here would not only devastate the Americans militarily, but it would also drain their morale and put an end to "this silly war." It was also home base to the force that had attacked York. But most important, if Sackets Harbor were to fall to the British, the back door to the former colonies would be wide open. This second front would split the American forces and spread them too thin to be effective; the war would be as good as won. And this was the perfect time to attack as far as the British were concerned. Captain Chauncey, General Dearborn and much of the fleet and the garrison were off attacking Fort George at what is now Niagara-on-the-Lake at the end of the Niagara River. They left a scant 400 regulars behind to defend the fortress. In essence, "the cat was away..."

On May 28, 1813, the British Commander, Sir James Yoe, led a well-equipped fleet across the lake towards Sackets Harbor. There were gun ships and schooners towing strings of large flat bottomed barges lined with red-coated soldiers. And these weren't just any soldiers. These were combat-hardened veterans representing some of the Empire's most distinguished units. The task force was spotted by the lookout aboard the American dispatch ship, *Lady of the Lake*, the fastest craft on Lake Ontario. The British intentions were obvious so the *Lady of the Lake* tightened sail and sped towards Sackets Harbor. As she rounded the point she started firing her single cannon as a warning and set the American forces in motion.

Chauncey had suspected the British might attack while the fleet was away and had left a contingency plan in effect. Lt. Colonel Backus, who was left in command of the base and its contingent of 400 American regulars (the Light Dragoons), followed his orders. He immediately contacted General Brown just over in Brownville to take command of the forces, and then he sent out the call for the militias. But as in the Battle of Lake Erie, the wind was about to play a major role in the outcome.

The British strategy was simple. They had planned to land their 750 crack troops on Horse Island. The island is connected to the mainland by a narrow sandy isthmus. Since this was back in the days when the British liked to wear red coats and march in a straight line, this seemed like a wonderful advantage. They could safely land their troops on the protected side of the island, fall into formation and then march across the sand to victory while the ships maneuvered close enough to the harbor to shell the fortifications and give support to the infantry.

But the wind did not agree. Yoe had planned to land his troops by early morning on the 28th, but by late afternoon they were virtually becalmed and still ten miles away. This gave Brown plenty of time to plan his defense. The call to arms had more than doubled the size of his force and he deployed them in three defensive lines in the woods and the rocks that stretched between the Horse Island isthmus and the walls of Fort

Tompkins. (The British were terribly predictable and the Americans had already learned the advantages of hiding behind rocks and trees when they fired).

The first line was a mixture of regular troops and militia. Militia troops were notoriously unseasoned and it was hoped that the mixture of regulars in their midst would help them hold the line in the face of fire. The second line was all militia and the third line consisted exclusively of Backus's Dragoons. The plan was that each line could fall back, if necessary, into the next line and eventually back into the fort, all the time under the protection of the fort's cannon fire.

The British finally arrived late in the afternoon of the 28th and proceeded to position their ships for a cannon barrage on Sackets Harbor. Their cannons roared but the calm winds prevented them (according to Yoe) from getting into effective range and their shots were wasted. Wasted, that is, from their standpoint. It turned out to be a help to the Americans! The British cannons were so loud they were heard as far away as Lewis and Oneida Counties. Those farmers who hadn't heard the original call to arms did hear this and immediately grabbed their rifles and headed for the harbor.

The British troops went ashore on Horse Island by torchlight around midnight that evening. In the morning they formed their straight ranks and prepared to march down the isthmus to face the American force that had, overnight, swelled to 1,000 muskets strong.

The battle was underway and the hardened British troops quickly scattered the first line of American defense soon after the Americans had fired their first volley. The second line held briefly before collapsing onto the third line but here, the battle changed its tempo. Confronted by Backus's Dragoons supported by the deadly grape shot coming from the cannons in the fort, the British were forced to fall back.

For the next two hours the bloody process repeated itself. The British would regroup and march down on the Americans who would fire at will, their muskets being directed through the smoke by those bright red coats. The British would once again be forced to fall back. But with each attack, the British would progress a little farther until on their last advance the forward units actually reached a barracks on the outskirts of the fort.

At this point the battle seemed lost to the Americans, and here the Americans suffered their biggest loss. A young navy officer out on Navy Point set fire to over half-a-million dollars of goods and supplies so that they wouldn't fall into the hands of the British. Gone were the supplies captured in York just one month before as well as the entire set of sails for the *General Pike*, the new American gun ship still under construction on the point. Several ships were also damaged in the blaze.

But the battle was not lost. While the British had indeed reached the edges of the fort and the dragoons had indeed retreated inside, it was the last gasp for the redcoats. Under heavy fire and with significant losses, they found themselves alone on a battlefield with limited cover from the fort and "no obtainable objective within sight" as it was later worded. They were forced to withdraw all the way back to Horse Island. A contingent of the militia had been rallied and now threatened to cut off the British from their barges. They escaped back to their ships under fire, forced to leave their dead and wounded behind. Then the wind that was insufficient to maneuver their ships' guns into effective range, filled their sails and took them back to Kingston.

It was a stunning victory for the Americans. Their casualties totaled a little over 100 men while the British troops, the best the king could send, had lost a full third of their 750-man force. Back in Kingston the British had a lot of explaining to do while the Americans rebuilt and restocked the fortifications at Sackets Harbor, an outpost they would actively maintain for the next 150 years.

The Trent-Severn Waterway

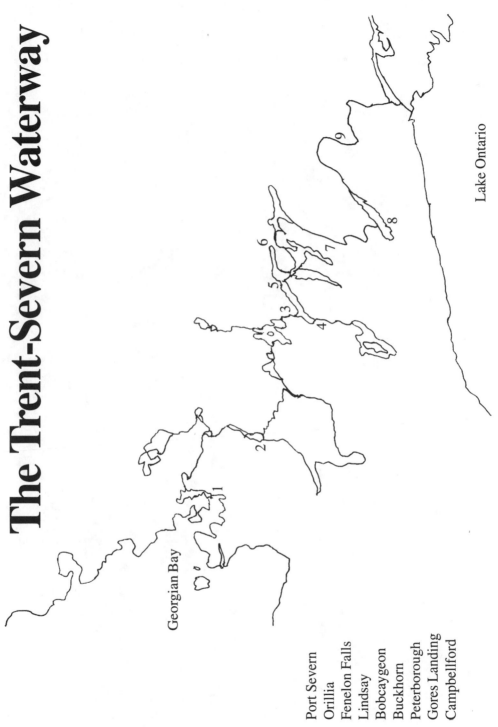

Georgian Bay

Lake Ontario

1. Port Severn
2. Orillia
3. Fenelon Falls
4. Lindsay
5. Bobcaygeon
6. Buckhorn
7. Peterborough
8. Gores Landing
9. Campbellford

Harbor Bobcaygeon, Ontario
Location On the TSW in the Center of the Kawartha Lakes
Dockage Travis Lodge & Marina, Gordon Yacht Harbor, Centre Point Landing

Places to Stay The Bobcaygeon Inn 705-738-5433, The Princess Motel 705-738-5058, The Riverside Lodge 705-738-2193, Courtleigh Place B&B 705-738-4969, Lighthouse Point B&B 705-738-4366, La Grande Shaque 705-738-4416

Places to Eat The Harbour Bar & Restaurant, Just For The Halibut, The Bobcaygeon Tea Room & Coffee Shop

Bobcaygeon is in the very heart of the Trent-Severn Waterway. In fact it has the honor of being the very first lock in the system. Built by British army engineers in 1833, this lock was not fully operational until 1835. It seems the army engineers had not accounted for the draft of the vessel in their plans and the very first boat that attempted to lock down, hit bottom and listed to one side before the lock chamber was drained. Hmmm.

Today the locks function flawlessly under the direction of Parks Canada, and the town of Bobcaygeon is a thriving hamlet along the banks. There are many shops and parks to enjoy but without a doubt, be sure to visit Kawartha Settler's Village on the north edge of town. This is eight acres of locally historic buildings brought together as an outdoor museum and craft exposition. The Henderson House is actually home to several of the village's artists and craftsmen.

One more historical footnote: Bobcaygeon was the site of the great buffalo experiment of the late 1800s. A local farmer crossed buffalo and cattle in hopes of achieving a bovine better suited to face the harsh Canadian winters. Unfortunately these "cattalo" were most unmanageable and eventually had to be moved to Big Island in Pigeon Lake where they could do no damage. However, the cattle-half of these hybrid beasts resented being alone, and the buffalo-half were excellent swimmers. So they paid the town a surprise—and very expensive—visit. The last trace of this experiment still hangs on the wall of the municipal office: the stuffed head of Bonaparte, the prize "cattalo" bull.

Harbor Buckhorn, Ontario
Location At the Junction of Buckhorn Lake and Lower Buckhorn Lake in the TSW
Dockage Buckhorn Yacht Harbor Ltd., Reach Harbor, Sunrise Resort

Places to Stay Westwind Inn 705-657-8095, Sunrise Resort 705-657-8713, Shady Point Resort 705-657-1021, Buckhorn Narrows Resort 705-657-8802, Oak Bay Resort 705-657-8872

Places to Eat Mainstreet Landing Restaurant, Westwind Inn

Buckhorn is a small settlement in the heart of the Kawartha Lakes district of the Trent-Severn Waterway. If you come this way looking for pristine scenery, rustic cottages and the colorful, rocky shores of the Canadian Shield, you've come to the right place!

I have always felt that the Kawartha Lakes is the most beautiful section of the famed waterway. It's a chain of inter-connecting lakes filled with crystal-clear water where rocks in varying shades of purple jut forth from the bottom. Many of these giant slabs of polished rock bear trees and other hearty foliage, seemingly untouched by the human existence. This is something that has to be experienced to be understood.

Buckhorn exists here in these surroundings and seems to disrupt Mother Nature as little as possible. There is a small settlement near the lock, which is not much more than a couple shops and a restaurant or two. Here you'll find the local library, the general store and the Main Street Landing. This, along with the Cody Inn, are the only eateries in the village. Fortunately they are both excellent.

Other places of interest are the Westwind Inn, a truly luxurious rustic resort in the pines and on the lakeshore. Like the facilities, the food here is exquisite. Right next door is the locally famous Gallery on the Lake. This is an art gallery and studio dedicated to the promotion of local artists. Unfortunately the Gallery has recently met with hard financial times and is presently closed. There are plans to reorganize and reopen it in the future.

Harbor Campbellford, Ontario
Location On Lower Reaches of Trent River, TSW
Dockage Old Mill Park Municipal Docks, Campbellford River Inn Dock, Turner's Marina

Places to Stay Linda's B&B 705-653-3536, A Touch of Taste B&B 705-653-0156, Linden House B&B 705-653-4406, Whippletree B&B 705-653-1434, Sundyl House B&B 705-924-3392

Places to Eat Country Kitchen Restaurant, Front Street Bar & Grill, Riverview Restaurant, The Players Lounge, Hydra Restaurant

Campbellford is a charming Canadian small town on the banks of the southern reaches of the Trent-Severn Waterway. If you are taking the Waterway from Lake Ontario to Lake Huron, this is a practical first night's stop. You will have 12 locks behind you and a beautiful town to explore.

The town has an interesting history behind it's name. It was settled by two brothers, Robert and David Campbell. They were given rights to the land by a land grant in recognition of their service to England during the Napoleonic Wars. The first business they established here was a ferry service across the Trent River. It was referred to as Campbell's Ford, and later shortened by some official cartographer to its current name.

Today this is a cheery town filled with old storefronts and some of the most interesting shops and establishments you will ever see. How about several museums including one called the Indian Motorcycle Museum dedicated to all things that go "potato, potato, potato." Then there's the Empire Cheese factory, makers of some of the finest cheeses in Ontario. For dessert, stop off at the World's Finest Chocolate Factory. That's the name, and one taste will make a believer out of you. Just outside of town is the Cow Patch. This shop carries all things bovine from dolls and mailboxes to coffee mugs and wind chimes, all sporting a cow theme. If you love cows, this one's for moo! (Sorry).

But in all seriousness, this is a wonderful town that's proud of its past and its heritage. You can get a map to a walking tour of historic homes from the Chamber of Commerce located in the Old Mill Park Marina.

Harbor Fenelon Falls, Ontario
Location At Lock 34 on the TSW, West of the Kawartha Lakes
Dockage The Long Beach Boat Livery, King's Marina

Places to Stay The Rhubarb Patch B&B 705-887-9586, The Olde Rectory 705-887-9796, The Gazebo Inn 705-887-6800, The Fenelon Inn 705-887-9000, The Olde Country House B&B 705-887-5576,

Places to Eat The House Around the Corner, The Dockside Grill, Jackie's Fish & Chips, The New Fallsview Restaurant, The Chatter Box Inn, Taggert's Landing

 Fenelon Falls is located at lock 34 in the Trent-Severn Waterway between Sturgeon and Cameron Lakes. This is in the heart of the Waterway at the western end of the Kawartha Lakes, and only one lock west of the Waterway's high-water mark at Bobcaygeon.

This is as provincial as rural Canada gets. I have to admit, this is one of my favorite stops along the TSW. There is just something about the sharp limestone cliffs that frame the narrow twisted waterway as you enter the town. Then all at once you can hear the roar of the falls at the same time that you are greeted by impeccably maintained parks and gardens lining the banks in the village area. A flower bed spells out the town's name, making no mistake as to where you are.

The lock is in the middle of town, with tie-ups just above or below (tie-up above and avoid walking the steps). There is a wonderful collection of shops and stores to explore. The storefronts on the main street are perfectly preserved Victorian structures, looking like one continuous row of shops. As the tourist trade has grown in this town, businesses have branched out and are now found in restored homes that were once strictly residential neighborhoods. Of particular interest, visit the fantastic jewelry store, Stokes on Trent (you can't miss it), and the craft and collectable store, The Livery Stable (which was once just that), directly across from the lock.

Another highlight of your stay here will be the Maryboro Lodge, which is now a museum run by the local historical museum. This community has a long history of lumber, ice farming and steam trains. These people always find new ways to bring this history to life. Let them tell you about the mysterious locomotive at the bottom of the lake!

Harbor Gore's Landing, Ontario
Location On the Southern Shore of Rice Lake in the Trent-Severn, just
South of Peterborough
Dockage Coxie's Cove 905-342-2138

Places to Stay The Victoria Inn 905-342-3261

Places to Eat The Victoria Inn year 'round, The Chill & Grill seasonal

Gore's Landing has my vote as the most interesting, undiscovered destination in the region. You'll find this little blip of a settlement on the south shores of Rice Lake in the Trent-Severn Waterway. It's just minutes from Peterborough and oddly, just minutes outside of Toronto.

This was an enclave of writers and artists around the turn of the century. The most famous of these was Gerald Hayward who made his name painting highly detailed miniatures of the era's renowned and wealthy. He built a magnificent home on the lakeshore that he used as a summer cottage—a grand, Victorian mansion called The Willows. Now it is better known as the Victoria Inn, and is the only shoreside accommodation in the village. It's also the only full-service eatery too. But it is magnificent! There are several private suites and the food is top drawer. Hayward left his mark here, literally. It seems he liked to drink. And when he drank he carved—often on whatever was closest at hand. On the beams on the wall next to the fireplace in the living room, there is a wonderful rendition of a moose he carved there over a hundred years ago.

Gore's Landing is very unique in another aspect. The town's oldest building predates the town by several years. How? The Bennett Tavern was originally at Bennett's Landing. But when the wooden road was directed to the new settlement of Gore's Landing and Gore's ferry began getting all the business, Bennett's Landing suffered. That winter, Bennett loaded everything he owned into his tavern and hooked it to a team of mules. He then dragged it, lock, stock and barrel, across the ice to it's new location, where it stands today, in Gore's Landing. If you can't beat 'em...

Harbor Lindsay, Ontario
Location At the Southern End of Sturgeon Lakes, the Kawartha Lakes, in the TSW
Dockage Rivera Park, McDonnell Park

Places to Stay Days Inn 705-324-3213, Lindsay Inn 705-324-0314, 910 Motel 705-324-6744, Be Our Guest B&B 705-324-2277

Places to Eat Pizza Twins, The Grand, The Cambridge Restaurant, Carmel's Family Restaurant, Olympia Restaurant, Bonfire Chicken & Ribs Restaurant, The Casablanca Tea & Coffee Company

Lindsay, Ontario, is located in the heart of the Trent-Severn Waterway at the extreme southern end of Sturgeon Lake in the Kawartha Lakes district. It's not easy to find by water and most would consider this a car trip that happens to have some water involved. Unfortunately many boaters traveling through the TSW pass by this town because it is so far off the shortest route through the lakes. But here's what they are missing:

This is a very provincial large town/small city in the heart of Ontario. You could shop through the business district for a day or two and still not see all there is. Antiques are big here, as the surrounding countryside is full of old farms and homesteads that date back nearly two hundred years. You may have to reload the credit cards twice to take it all in.

If you just want to enjoy the scenery, take the *Skylark VIII* tour boat through town and the surrounding area. This is a modern, enclosed tour-bus-on-a-hull with live narration. If you'd rather take a nice stroll, don't miss the Victoria Recreation Transportation Corridor. It's a very fancy name for a rail-trail. A rail-trail is a nature trail developed from an abandoned railway bed. In Canada, inventive minds realized these old easements would eventually grow over and be lost forever. The land is otherwise useless. (Who needs a very long, narrow lot?) Trails like this are now being developed all over Ontario, and are a wonderful example of recycled amenities.

One more "Don't miss!" is the Kawartha Summer Theatre. This is top-notch summer-stock theater presented in the fantastic background of the completely restored Academy Theatre.

Harbor Orillia, Ontario
Location Along the North Shore of Lake Simcoe in the TSW
Dockage Port of Orillia Marina, Blue Beacon Marina, Couchiching Marina, Orchard Point Marina, Crate's Marine

Places to Stay Lakeside Inn 705-325-2514, The Orillia Highwayman Inn 705-326-7343, Betty & Tony's B&B 1-800-308-2579, The Vacancy Referral Service 705-326-4424

Places to Eat Sweet Dreams, Ossawippi Express Dining Cars, The Zoo, Gian Carlo, Frankie's Restaurant, Brewery Bay Food Company

Orillia is a small provincial city on the north shore of Lake Simcoe on the Trent-Severn Waterway. This is an old community but one that is proud of its past and has preserved it carefully.

There are many old Victorian buildings in town including several churches with great spires that punctuate Orillia's skyline. But the most striking memory I have of Orillia is how new everything looked. Even buildings a century-and-a-half old, churches, houses, storefronts and apartment blocks, were perfectly maintained and in use every day. I walked up the great hill from the marina into the heart of the business district and could find no sign of urban decay, financial ruin or neglect. Everything was neat and tidy in a very provincial way that made exploring this town a joy.

The shops and stores in the business district are about as varied as anyone could expect. We visited everything from drug stores and stationery shops to specialty boutiques and antique collectibles. When you tire of shopping, try your luck at the local casino. Shuttle busses and shuttle boats will whisk you away to the edge of town for an evening of Vegas-style excitement.

Orillia has two favorite sons. Stephen Leacock was perhaps this nation's most beloved humorist. He authored several books and essays I have always found very amusing. His stories deal with daily Canadian life, and he is revered here much as Mark Twain is in the States. The Steven Leacock museum in Orillia is well worth your time and effort.

Orillia's other favorite son is a folk singer who did some recording in the 1970s. He sang songs about sundown and the *Edmund Fitzgerald*. He's a very talented man by the name of Gordon Lightfoot.

Harbor Peterborough, Ontario
Location On the South Shore of Little Lake on the TSW
Dockage Peterborough Marina

Places to Stay Peterborough Holiday Inn 705-743-1144, Ramada Inn 1-800-854-7854, King Bethune House 705-743-4101, Blue Willow B&B 705-742-0433, The Sherwood House 705-742-8944, The Elizabeth Davidson House B&B 705-749-6960, many more!

Places to Eat Eaton's Steamboat Landing, Hi Tops, Jeff Purvey's, Hot Belley Moma's, Miss Susannah's

Peterborough, Ontario, is the largest city on Canada's famed Trent-Severn Waterway, and is complete with a wide selection of restaurants and a very busy business district. The fact that it is almost exactly mid-way through the system also adds to its popularity. Here, on the shores of Little Lake, you can launch trailered boats, charter sightseeing cruises, board the famed *Kawartha Voyageur* cruise ship or simply sit on the banks and watch the water flow.

There is much to do and see here. By all means visit the Peterborough Lift Lock on the edge of town. This is the world's largest non-reinforced concrete structure and is nearly 100 years old. This is not your typical flood-style lock as you might envision. Two gigantic "bathtubs" are filled with water and perhaps twenty boats. Then the entire tub is lifted hydraulically, much like a mechanic's hoist, some 65 feet in the air to the next level of the system. This gives you breathtaking views of the Ontario farmland around you. It also is quite unsettling to realize that there is no water under you for some six-and-a-half stories! Be sure to visit the Interpretive Centre next to the lock that explains its history and the super-human effort it took to build this technological wonder.

Also in Peterborough, visit the new Canoe Museum. It sounds rather dry but it makes for a truly wonderful afternoon of seeing every type of canoe from around the world, from locally-made fishing canoes to Polynesian war canoes.

I encourage you to learn more about Peterborough and the rest of the Trent-Severn by contacting the Friends of The Trent-Severn Waterway at 1-800-663-BOAT.

Harbor Port Severn, Ontario
Location Mouth of the Severn River at Georgian Bay
Dockage Severn Boat Haven, Driftwood Cove, Severn Marine, Double A Marina

Places to Stay Driftwood Cove Cottages 705-538-2502, Rawley Lodge 705-538-2272, Severn Lodge 705-756-8313, The Inn at Christie's Mill 705-538-2354, Sunnylea Resort 705-538-2527

Places to Eat Bee Jay's Pizza & Grill, Rawley Lodge, Elk's Bakery & Pizza, The Principal's Schoolhouse, The Inn at Christie's Mill

Port Severn is the northern terminus of the Trent-Severn Waterway. It sits in a sheltered rocky cove of southern Georgian Bay and is often the very first lock of a TSW vacation.

Because it is often the very first locking experience for many boaters, it is also recognized as a great source of entertainment for boaters and land yachters alike. It seems people get a great deal of satisfaction seeing others fumble through the baffling process of elevating their boat about six feet. Not to worry, by the time they reach Bobcaygeon they will be locking through like pros.

To accommodate the attraction provided by the neophyte lockers (locally referred to as "Harvey Wallbangers"), Parks Canada and the City of Port Severn have provided a number of strategically located picnic sites so that you won't miss a "bump" or a "smack" of the locking action while passing the potato salad. Of course the sites are well equipped and exquisitely maintained in the Parks Canada tradition.

In town you will find a small collection of shops and a number of nice eateries. Of special note is the Rawley Lodge and The Principal's Schoolhouse.

Within reasonable travel from here is the Big Chute Marine Railway. Rather than build a lock by blasting through a boulder the size of an apartment building, the Waterway built a railroad lift that comes down into the water, then hefts your boat (and several others) up over the boulder and into the river on the other side. This is something to see!

The Day Dave Bombed Detroit
by Bruce Jenvey

Passengers aboard the Trent-Severn's cruise ship, the *Kawartha Voyageur,* are interesting people. While I am just in my forties and most of the passengers on this trip were senior citizens, I have to tell you we enjoyed their company immensely. We met retired school teachers and corporate executives alike, and heard some very fascinating and entertaining stories from them all.

One man in particular, Dave, shared a story with us over dinner one night that I will never forget. Dave celebrated his seventy-fifth birthday on board, but during World War II he was a young lad in the Royal Air Force. Dave taught air force navigation. Specifically, he taught bomber crews how to find their targets and how to get home again.

Very early in the war Dave was transferred from England to an Ontario base near Lake Huron, as the skies were safer for instruction there. One day the Americans who had just entered the war called up and asked the boys of the R.A.F. if they would make a mock bombing run on Detroit so they could practice scrambling their air defenses. Dave planned a course that took them east from the Port Huron area, zigzagged across the Ontario peninsula, and entered Lake Erie. Then they made their attack run on Detroit from the south-southeast. To them, this was good practice and an exercise of standard difficulty.

Unfortunately the Americans had expected the bombers to come straight down the St. Clair River and hit the city head-on from the northeast. This meant that when the R.A.F. got to Detroit, they were very much alone. No one (of the military persuasion) had seen them coming. And worst of all, no one would see them go. There is no glory in a stunning victory if there are no witnesses and no way to leave your mark.

But necessity is the mother of invention and lo and behold, each bomber carried a fresh-from-England supply of toilet paper. Now for those of you who don't know, British toilet paper is not high on their list of popular exports and there is a reason for this. The toilet paper the R.A.F. boys could buy locally in Canada was much preferred, and very reasonable. However, the rules state that you must first use what the Crown provides, so they used it.

The bomb racks in all the planes were quickly stuffed with every last roll of British toilet paper that could be found. The planes circled about and harmlessly dumped their loads on unprotected Detroit. There was toilet paper everywhere! There were shocked citizens on the ground. There were angry American voices on every channel of the radio.

To this day, to our knowledge, this is the only time an entire city has ever been T-Ped! Leave it to the rascals of the R.A.F.

ken miller.

The Erie Canal System

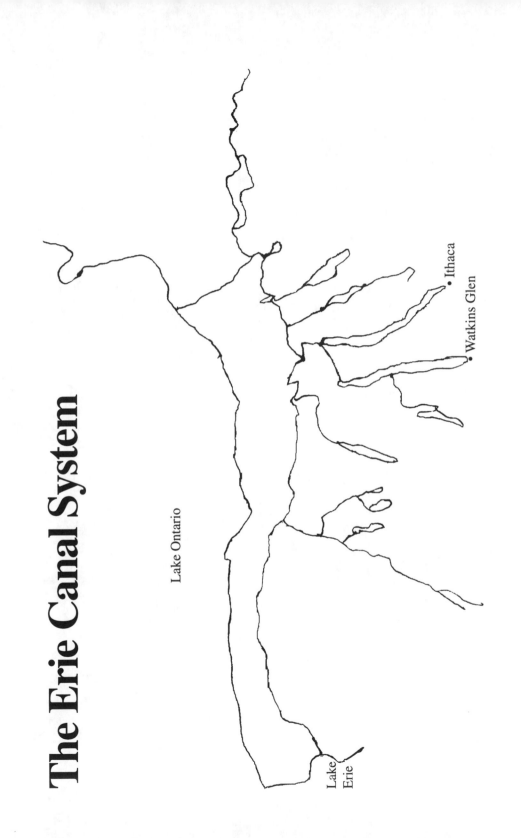

Lake Ontario

Lake Erie

Ithaca

Watkins Glen

Harbor Ithaca, New York
Location Cayuga Lake, Ithaca Front Light: L42°28.13'N, Lo76°30.95'W
Dockage Treman State Marina Park, Johnson Boat Yard & Marina, Ithaca Boating Center

Places to Stay Contact: Ithaca Convention & Visitors Bureau 1-800-28-ITHACA

Places to Eat Oldport Harbor, The Station Restaurant, The M/V Manhattan, Kelley's Dockside Cafe, Max's Night Club, Ithaca Commons

Ithaca, New York, is located at the extreme southern end of Cayuga Lake in the picturesque Finger Lakes region. You can get here by boat through the Erie Canal System or trailer to your heart's content.

This is a very old community with much to see and do. My first choice would be to enjoy the scenery from the decks of the *Manhattan*, a replica sternwheeler that makes regularly scheduled excursions out on the lake. There's even a dinner cruise. I suggest this first because if you come by car you'll miss it, and if you come by boat you'll be too busy playing skipper to relax and enjoy the high bluffs that frame these deep blue waters.

Also on nature's hit parade is nearby Ithaca Falls. This 150-foot-high cataract has created a mile-long gorge with yet another six falls, cascades and rapids to view. You'll find the falls and the starting point of the gorge walk on Lake Street at the Falls Creek Crossing.

Within a healthy walking distance along the lake shore is Cornell University, one of the Ivy League's most picturesque campuses. There are many places the public can visit such as the Cornell Plantations, which feature a botanical garden and an arboretum.

Shopping in Ithaca is also a unique experience. Ithaca Commons is one of the most popular shopaholic stops, and is an outdoor pedestrian mall. Here you can find everything from shops and eateries to just a good place to people watch.

Harbor Watkins Glen, New York
Location Seneca Lake Breakwall: L43°23.1′N, Lo76°52.3′W
Dockage Village Marina, Glen Harbor Marina, Ervay's Marina, Reynold's Marina Service

Places to Stay Contact: Schuyler County Chamber 607-535-4300

Places to Eat Castle Grisch Winery & Restaurant, The Town House Restaurant, Paradiso's Restaurant, Bianco's Daughters Restaurant, Savard's Family Restaurant, 4th Street Deli & Grocery, Tobe's Coffee & Doughnut Shop and Bakery

Watkins Glen is along the southern shore of Seneca Lake in the Finger Lakes of New York State. *GLC* covers this part of the Great Lakes region because it is in the Great Lakes drainage basin and it is easily accessible via the Erie Canal. You can come in off Lake Ontario or Lake Erie and eventually get here.

While the name of this place may conjure up psychedelic images from demonstrations past, what you will find here today is a charming community surrounded by unique natural beauty.

The town itself provides all services a cruising boater or land yachter could want. There are also many shops to explore in the business district ranging from teddy bear collectibles to antiques and crafts. You will also find these businesses in some of the most picturesque upstate New York architecture you have ever seen.

But the real beauty here is the Glen, as in Watkins Glen. The Glen is the Glen Gorge and is just part of Watkins Glen State Park. You could spend several days here exploring the natural beauty of things. The Glen is a heavily wooded river gorge with no less than 19 waterfalls, many mysterious caverns, charming grottos and several natural amphitheaters. The scenery is breathtaking no matter when you visit. And the park has organized excursions to help you hit all the highlights during your time here, no matter in which season you visit. In summertime there is a nightly laser show in the Grove that highlights the Glen's 45-million-year history. In the fall there are organized color tours of the Glen. Of course in the spring there is the great Ducks In The Glen Race. Ducks of the rubber and plastic variety race through the Glen in an annual rite of spring.

Destinations That Move

I have done my best to give you some of the most interesting destinations to explore in the Great Lakes. But what do you do when most of the fun is getting there? What do you do when the destination moves? I have found three destinations for you to discover that do not require a boat—or even a car! And they may be the best destinations on the Lakes.

1. The *Kawartha Voyageur*. This is a cruise ship that travels the Trent-Severn Waterway and Rideau Canal. Actually, it's kind of like a double-decker bus with a rustic attitude. There is no floor show or glitz. There is no dressing-up for dinner. Meals are served family-style and feature home cooking right off the Ontario farm. This is casual, laid-back—it's almost a cushy camping trip. The boat has a large protected common area and a delightful upper sundeck. Chris and I spent several days aboard and it was the best vacation we've ever had! Tell Captain Marc Ackert that Jenvey said he'd let you drive the boat. He won't but it'll sure get a rise out of him! The *Kawartha Voyageur* is handicap accessible. For more information call Ontario Waterway Cruises at 1-800-561-5767.

2. The Traverse Tall Ship Company. Here's a company that runs a couple of replica nineteenth-century lake schooners out of Traverse City. They have day, evening and dinner cruises in the local waters, or you can do like *GLC*'s Cynthia Johnson did and spend a week aboard the tall ship *Manitou* cruising the North Channel. You may have signed on as a passenger, but you are welcome to lend your hand and hoist sails, weigh anchor and trim the sheets. It's great fun and a chance to see the famed North Channel from an antique point of view. Call the Traverse Tall Ship Company at 616-941-2000.

3. The *Badger*. This is the only car ferry in operation on the Great Lakes, crossing from Ludington to Manitowac several times a day. You can take your car along if you like but pedestrians are welcome aboard the spacious ship that provides a party-like atmosphere. Once there was a day when dozens of ships like this crossed between various ports on the Lakes. Now your only chance to enjoy this unique experience is aboard the *Badger*. Call 1-800-841-4243.